This book was donated to the

*Independence Public Library's
Aviation shelf*

*by the Polk County
Oregon Pilot's Association*

D1095199

Tale of a Tiger

Tale of a Tiger

By R.T. SMITH

Copyright © 1986 by Robert T. Smith

All rights reserved. Reproduction or publication
of the contents in any manner without express permission
of the publisher is prohibited.

Library of Congress Catalog Card Number 85-90545

ISBN 0-9618012-0-4

Second printing July 1988
Third printing November 1990

Published by Tiger Originals
Van Nuys, CA

Printed in the United States of America

*For my sons—Brad, Bob,
and Bill, and of course, for
Mom and Dad*

RTS

For some we lov'd, the loveliest and the best
That from his Vintage rolling Time hath prest,
Have drunk their Cup a Round or two before,
And one by one crept silently to Rest.

Omar Khayyam

CONTENTS

MAPS

To; R. T. Smith
one of the best —
C. L. Chennault
Maj. Gen. U.S.A.F. Ret'd

Claire Lee Chennault

Introduction

For many years now I have considered the idea of writing a book about my experiences as a pilot in the American Volunteer Group (AVG), or **Fly-ing Tigers,** as our little band of adventurers was to become more widely known. But I always managed to find a number of reasons for putting if off: not enough time; not many people would be interested; others had already written books on the subject, etc. Add to all that a normal inclination to laziness, and you get the idea; I knew that writing a book was likely to en-tail a lot of hard work, while **not** writing one was easy as could be.

I'm not exactly sure why I decided to go ahead and do it at this late date. It's not that I believe there's a breathless public out there eagerly waiting to devour my words, nor do I expect to reap any significant financial reward from such a project. Perhaps it's because my excuses, except for laziness, are no longer valid. Certainly I now have plenty of time, and I have become more and more aware in recent years that there is still a surprising amount of interest in things having to do with the Flying Tigers, even among later generations. And while some of the many books that have been written about us give a reasonably accurate account from a historical viewpoint, in my opinion these third-person accounts often fail to capture the true picture of events that could be seen only through the eyes of a pilot and described in his own words. But perhaps the greatest incentive of all was that in the pro-cess of writing the book I would once again re-live those hazardous and often desperate months in the company of that wild and wonderful little group of pilots and ground support personnel. Thinking of them, remembering the things we shared and endured, was bound to bring back a flood of vivid memories, both happy and sad. So far as I am concerned, that in itself is reward enough.

Fortunately, I had kept a daily diary throughout the nine months spent in Burma and China during the brief existence of the AVG, so I figured much of the writing had already been done. I could simply write a few introduc-tory chapters, then copy those diary pages, add a few footnotes and photos, and Bingo! A book, just like that. Well, friends, it ain't been all that easy but it *has* been fun, and once I'd sunk my teeth into it I discovered I'm not even as lazy as I used to be.

Of course there is nothing new or unique about publishing a diary. In fact, I'm not even the first among Flying Tigers. Just a couple of years ago my good friend, Charley Bond, used such a format with his book, *"A Flying Tiger's Diary,"* which I heartily recommend. Consequently, some of the same ground is of necessity covered by both of us, but I believe the reader will find that in many respects our stories differ greatly, primarily because we were in different squadrons and dealing with different people and cir-cumstances. Bond flew with the 1st squadron, the *"Adam & Eves"* while I was a member of the *"Hell's Angels,"* or third squadron.

In reading Charley's fine book, I was amazed to discover how little I really knew about the activities and individuals of his squadron despite having rubbed elbows off and on with them for several months. The reason was quite simple; once the AVG swung into combat action the three squadrons were seldom all together for more than very brief periods of time. While one squadron was fighting for its life in Rangoon, another might be enjoying relative inactivity in Kunming, while the third could be moving to still another base of operations in Burma or China. We were moved around like Knights (or pawns, as some would have it) on a gigantic chessboard by our tough and crafty commander, Claire Lee Chennault. Even when a couple of squadrons shared the same base they had separate quarters and operations facilities, and more or less tended to stick together. Thus the closest bonds of friendship developed between members of the same squadron, much as might be the case with members of three different baseball teams within the same league.

And so, just as Bond has revealed many of the experiences that he and his comrades shared as members of the 1st squadron, I decided to do much the same from the perspective of the "Hell's Angels." And who knows, maybe some day someone from the 2nd ("*Panda Bears*") squadron will do likewise, for there are many intrigueing stories yet untold, and all too few who feel inclined, or are left, to tell them.

I decided in the very beginning to make at least one rather unusual departure from the ordinary diary format, however. The actual pages of my diary, unedited, are reproduced here exactly as written in my own hand at the time. I thought that somehow this might make it more personal, and at the same time eliminate the temptation to delete or add comments or thoughts from the safe and sage perspective of hindsight. Within these pages such comments appear clearly as footnotes in printed form, or as what-might otherwise be considered chapters before or between actual diary entries. I have also included a large number of photos. some of which have appeared in prior publications but many that have never before been seen by the public. Several of those that appear here in black and white are pictures that I took with Kodachrome film, and of course are less appealing than they appear in full color. I was most fortunate in this regard; so far as I know, I was the only one in the entire group to get any really good color pictures.

So, having decided upon the make-up of the book, all that remained was to sit down at my typewriter and start banging away.

I'm sure most people agree that every story should have a beginning, a middle, and an end, but right away that ancient axiom presented me with a problem. The middle and the end are easy enough to pinpoint, but trying to decide just where and when this story should begin was not as simple as might appear at first glance. Was it the day when I was ten years old and the wheels of that rickety old biplane lifted from the bumpy cow pasture just outside the little town of Red Cloud, Nebraska, where I lived? Certainly that first airplane ride with a barnstorming pilot, the very essence of daring and adventure in his black leather helmet and goggles and trim mustache, was the start of *something*. Still, that's reaching pretty far into the past, for while it planted the seed that made me determined to become a pilot, the events which I was to experience in 1941-42 were still in the dim and distant future.

Perhaps I should start off with a real bang, that first combat action over Rangoon, Burma, on the 23rd of December, 1941, barely two weeks after the disaster of Pearl Harbor. I could begin by describing how it felt when I got that first glimpse of the enemy, and knew that within a couple of minutes I would get my first taste of war in the air. I was in a flight of seven P-40s patrolling an area just east of Rangoon, with another flight of seven a couple of miles to the north. . All eyes were nervously scanning the skies to the east; the British ground radar, not noted for its reliability of late, had reported a large number of enemy planes approaching from that direction, no doubt from bases in Thailand. Eventually one of us would spot them and then, following the standard reporting procedure and using code words prescribed by our limited training during the preceding weeks, would calmly announce his discovery over the radio. We would hear someone say something like," Red leader from Red four, many Bandits at two o'clock low." Instead, a voice suddenly screamed, *"Hey, Mac! I see the bastards!...off to the right and a little below us, a whole slew of 'em"* And sure enough, there they were, what appeared to be the entire Imperial Japanese Air Force, large specks in the distance, many clusters of them making up two huge formations of twin-engined bombers, with about thirty smaller specks, fighters, above and behind them. All heading in our direction and closing fast.

Suddenly I was aware of the pounding of my heart as my pulse rate doubled, chest heaving as I gulped pure oxygen from a slimy rubber mask at fifteen thousand feet, mouth full of cotton, the sudden and embarrassing urge to go to the bathroom, and another awe-struck voice coming through the headset, irreverently saying what all of us were thinking, *"Jeezus Keerist!"* Sounded like Tom Haywood, but I couldn't be sure, followed immediately by the calm voice of McMillan, our flight leader, saying, *"Okay, knock it off...check your gun switches...here we go!"* just like he'd been doing this sort of thing every day for years. And then, moments later, one after another at regular intervals, our handful of little P-40s peeling off to attack, following Mac's lead as he dove toward the right flank of the first bomber formation and began firing. And now it was my turn, diving and turning to line up my gunsight with plenty of "lead" at a bomber, squeezing the stick-trigger and hearing the crackling sound of my four .30 caliber wing guns and the slower, powerful thudding of the two .50s in the nose, like twin jackhammers ripping up pavement; and the pungent smell of cordite filling the cockpit, a good smell. Now aware that dozens of guns from the bombers were firing back, tracers criss-crossing the sky in every direction, black smoke and flames streaming from the left engine of a bomber up ahead, and all the while that creepy-crawly feeling at the back of the neck, knowing their fighters must surely be about to pounce down on us at any moment, sneaking up in the blind spot to the rear, set for the kill.

3

I have often been asked if I was "scared" that day, which is about like asking if *McDonalds* sells hamburgers. Let me tell you, friends, that anyone who claims he didn't feel any fear under such circumstances either (a) didn't fully understand the gravity of the situation, (b) is lying through his teeth, (c) is full of crap, or (d) all of the above! There is simply nothing quite like such an experience when it comes to getting the old adrenalin pumping while at the same time putting a severe strain on the bladder. No doubt you have heard athletes speak of having "butterflies" in their stomach before a big game. Imagine, then, a flock of buzzards flapping around down there just before the deadliest game of all is about to start, and you get the idea. Fortunately, it lasts for only a few moments in most cases, after which things settle down to a state best described as semi-controlled panic.

Well, that first combat was the beginning of the shooting part of the story, but of course it fails to explain how we happened to be in that forsaken part of the world at that particular time, or how we get there, or why. Too much of a gap between the cow pasture and the macadam runways of Rangoon's Mingaladon aerodrome, as it were. So perhaps it would be best to back up about six months, back to Randolph Field, Texas, a few miles outside San Antonio. Since that is where I first learned of the embryo existence of what was to become known as the American Volunteer Group, I guess that's the logical place for a beginning.

Just a final thought before we get going; while I have been told by many people that my handwriting is quite legible, I am aware that now and then the reader may have to work at it a bit to decipher a particular word or passage appearing in the diary. My sincere hope is that he, or she, will find it worth the effort.

R.T. SMITH

A Matter of TIME

The weary old Wright Cyclone up front ground on with its steady half-muffled roar while beneath us south Texas wilted in the heat and humidity of early summer, 1941. From the rear cockpit of the BT-9 basic trainer I watched the back of my student's head bobbing like that of a puppet, as if to acknowledge a series of rapid-fire commands that I might have issued through the radio-intercom system. But it was only the hot, turbulent air through which we were flying that caused his head to bob sharply with each tooth-jarring bump. I hadn't spoken to him for several minutes, in fact, not since telling him to make a few precise 90-degree turns while maintaining exactly four thousand feet. I might as well have asked him to draw a perfectly straight line without the aid of a ruler, and he was really working his tail off. But then, the life and times of a Flying Cadet in the Army Air Corps had never been easy.

I was thankful that Cadet Gibson was my fourth and final student of the day. It had been a long afternoon, our glass-enclosed cockpits converted to ovens by the "greenhouse" effect. My khaki shirt was soaked with sweat, as was the seat of my pants, and my butt was numb from sitting too long on the thinly-cushioned seat-pack of my parachute. Even worse than the physical discomfort, however, was the persistent feeling of boredom and frustration which I felt in my role as a flight instructor. True, I was a pilot in the Air Corps, which had been my goal ever since I was just a starry-eyed kid, but this kind of flying was a far cry from what I'd had in mind all along. At least I had learned by now that feeling sorry for myself didn't help a bit, so at the moment I simply looked forward to getting back to my quarters for a cool shower and a tall, icy highball.

I looked into the rear view mirror mounted high inside the curved windshield in front of Gibson, saw the nervous sweat glistening on his forehead. His crew-cut hair was mashed down by the bows of his headset, ears encompassed by the big foam-rubber pads containing the tiny speakers connected by an umbilical cord to the radio-jack. He was one of four new students who had been assigned to me only a few days before. I knew little about him other than that he was from Ohio, and at twenty-two only a year my junior. As a Flying Cadet he was something of a military hybrid, somewhere between officer and enlisted man, his ill-defined rank being simply "Mister." He was probably as much in awe of a Sergeant as a Colonel at this point, and to be safe would address either as "Sir." The specter of failure would hover over him constantly for the next few months, and despite his highest hopes and best efforts the silver wings of the Military Aviator and the gold bars of a 2nd Lieutenant would often seem completely beyond reach. I knew; I'd been through the same mill only fifteen months earlier.

5

I took my hand mike from the metal clip next to the radio panel, pressed the button on its side, and said, "Okay, Gibson, give me a few lazy-eights now...and get your head out of your ass! We're not alone up here, remember?" Embarrassed, he nodded and immediately began to look all around, scanning the area for other planes before beginning the series of up and down figure-8s, a standard coordination exercise. Vigilance was something he would have to learn, and fast, until the nearly constant swiveling of his head became habit, eyes searching a three-dimensional world that held the ingredients of disaster; there were dozens of other blue-and-yellow BT-9s in the limited airspace surrounding Randolph Field, flying in every direction. The threat of a mid-air collision was ever-present, and near-misses were commonplace.

I settled back once more and almost immediately my thoughts drifted back to what I considered my unfortunate situation. Why was it that being a flight instructor caused me so much dissatisfaction while most of the others seemed perfectly content? Thousands of fellows my age, I knew very well, would have given their eye-teeth to be in my position.

Certainly there was little to complain about so far as life on the base was concerned. Randolph Field, lying to the northeast of San Antonio, was a beautiful, relatively new and modern installation. Proudly proclaimed *"The West Point of the Air,"* It was headquarters for the Flying Training Command of the Army Air Corps, and temporary home of Cadets while undergoing the second, or Basic, phase of their flight training. And while the Cadets lived a severely regimented existence, with about as much freedom as undergraduates of San Quentin, such was not the case with the officers assigned to the base. Though most of us were mere 2nd Lieutenants, we enjoyed many privileges that made for the good life in a peacetime military organization; comfortable quarters, excellent food, a beautiful Officer's Club, Post Exchange, movie theater, and all available at ridiculously low prices. Even a bachelor 2nd Lieutenant, such as myself, could live well on his $225 monthly paycheck despite still having to make payments on the uniforms and second-hand car he'd bought the moment he was commissioned.

There were a couple of welcome distractions that helped to break up the everyday routine. One of these lasted for a couple of weeks in the fall of 1940 when a troupe of actors and technicians from Warner Brothers studios came to Randolph Field. They stayed in hotels in San Antonio, but spent their days on location at Randolph for much of the filming of the movie *"I WANTED WINGS."* This was the story of Flying Cadet life written in the mid-thirties by Beirne Lay, a book that for me had been both inspirational and informative while still in high school. Now, here I was practically rubbing elbows with stars like Brian Donlevy and Ray Milland, as well as such promising newcomers, of about my age, as William Holden, Wayne Morris, Alan Hale, Jr., and a cute blonde with the peek-a-boo hair-style, Veronica Lake. The Air Corps, of course, was cooperating to the fullest extent, and on one occasion put on a massive formation flight of nearly three hundred

6

planes, all flown by instructors from Randolph, Kelly, and Brooks fields. Later, in the Spring of 1941, the picture was previewed at the base theater at Randolph; it was attended by practically all of the officers on the base, to what can best be described as mixed reviews.

As for working conditions, flight instructors were required to work only half-days, five days a week, so there was plenty of time off to do more or less as we pleased. We flew with each of our four students for nearly an hour each day, teaching and demonstrating the maneuvers and techniques they were required to master. It involved a lot of pleading, cursing, and patience, but in spite of our best efforts only about three out of four would display the necessary aptitude to become proficient military pilots. That unlucky fourth would be "washed out," just as many of his classmates in Primary training had already been dismissed, and a few more would be found wanting during Advanced training. The good part, so far as the instructors were concerned, was that we got a lot of flying time, and of course flying time is the life's blood of any pilot. Strangely, to my way of thinking, most of the others appeared to enjoy being instructors, but I knew from the start that I could never be content in the rear seat of a BT-9, that "underpowered abortion" as it was often referred to, and confined to the limited horizons imposed by the nature of the job itself.

It all went back to my boyhood and those recurring dreams of one day flying those speedy little single-seater pursuit planes that I'd seen pictured in stair-step formation on recruiting posters outside countless Post-offices. *"Be a Flying Cadet — Join the U.S. Army Air Corps,"* the posters had beckoned. And I was eager to do just that long before reaching the minimum age of twenty years and getting the required minimum of two years of college under my belt. At last, in the spring of 1938, I sent in my application and a few weeks later passed the toughest physical exam known to man; luckily, I was one of only three who passed, out of seventeen who took the exam at the time. But Uncle Sam was in no big hurry to welcome me into the flying training program; I was advised that my name had been added to a rather long list of qualified applicants, and that I'd be called in due time. Disappointed, and with nothing better to do, I went back to the University of Nebraska for another year, and it wasn't until the late summer of 1939 that I was ordered to report for flight training as a Flying Cadet at the Primary flight school located in Santa Maria, Calfornia, in September. I arrived there about two weeks after Nazi Germany had invaded Poland, touching off World War II and already beginning to overrun France and the low countries. I was certain that before long the United States would be drawn into the conflict, and like an idiot hoped that it wouldn't all be over before I could complete my training and see some combat action.

The next nine months went by quickly, three months spent in each of the flying training stages required in the making of a military pilot; Primary at Santa Maria, Basic at Randolph, and Advanced at Brooks Field, also near San Antonio. I was lucky. Flying seemed to come naturally, and I was for-

RTS as a flying cadet, primary training—Sept., 1939

BT-9 Basic trainer over Randolph Field, Texas

tunate in having excellent instructors throughout. I even enjoyed the many tedious hours spent in ground-school, absorbing all the knowledge I could in such subjects as Meteorology, Air Navigation, Theory of Flight, Aircraft Engines, Morse Code, etc. I loved it all, and was supremely confident despite the fact that more than a third of those in my class would fail to make it all the way.

It was during my days as a Flying Cadet that I was to undergo a name-change of sorts. While I had always been called Bob by my family and friends, it was not long after my flying training began that my classmates began calling me "R.T." There was a very simple reason for this; there were three Smiths in my class, and the cloth name-tapes sewed on the left breast of our uniform shirts read, "Smith, B.P.", "Smith, F.M.", and "Smith, R.T." That's the way they were called out whenever we had to respond to a roll-call, which was several times a day, and since our initials were constantly on display while our first names were not, our classmates adopted the easy way out. As time went on Bernard P. was often called "Beep," and Frederick M. was occasionally called "Fum." By the same logic it would appear inevitable that I would become "Art," or "Artie," but strangely enough that never happened; it was always just "R.T.", and it has stuck to this day.

My first solo flight was in a Stearman PT-13 biplane just a couple of weeks after arriving at Santa Maria and after seven hours of dual instruction. It was easily the greatest thrill I'd ever experienced, difficult to describe, but a feeling which all pilots know and remember. Things continued to go smoothly, but a cloud appeared on the horizon that was to spell doom to my hopes of ever flying those hot little pursuit planes that I'd dreamed about for so long. It seems that there was a new Air Corps regulation which stated that no pilots over five-feet ten inches in height could hereafter be assigned to a pursuit squadron. Small planes, small pilots, in other words. Since I was nearly six-foot four this meant that I couldn't even come close. That regulation made about as much sense to me as if the musicians union had told Tommy Dorsey he couldn't play trombone because his arms were too long. I knew, of course, that pursuit planes didn't have cockpits as big and comfortable as bombers or other types, but I was bitterly disappointed nonetheless. After reading all that pulpy prose between the covers of *Flying Aces* and *Wings* as a kid, picturing myself as one day becoming a cross between Rickenbacker and von Richtofen, blasting enemy planes from the skies in furious dogfights, suddenly some joker in Washington had, in effect, cut my legs out from under me. Disgusted, I knew there wasn't a thing I could do about it, and as my training progressed could only hope that I might be assigned to an Attack outfit rather than Bombardment or Observation.

As things turned out, I was to be a victim of the times. With graduation near, all of us who had survived were sweating out our next assignments, hoping that the preference we had been allowed to express as to choice of planes to fly and tactical branch would be fulfilled. But it was June of 1940, and the political and military geniuses in Washington had belatedly concluded that the United States might some day become actively embroiled in the war now raging in Europe. Suddenly factories were gearing up for vastly increased production of the materials of war, particulary combat aircraft, both to supply the British and to build up our own scanty inventories of first-line fighting machines. More and more bombers and fighters were rolling off the assembly lines, but still only a fraction of what was to come.

Perhaps even more belatedly came the recognition that unless drastic steps were taken immediately there would soon be a critical shortage of pilots and crew-members and ground personnel to man and maintain what threatened to become a glut of new and ever-more sophisticated equipment. A simple equation was at work here: thousands of new planes meant thousands of new pilots, which in turn meant hundreds of new instructors required to train them. Which is how, just prior to graduation and much to my chagrin, I found my name listed along with about eighty of my classmates—about one third of class 40-C—ordering us to report back to Randolph Field for a brief period of additional training in order to become Basic flight instructors

As you might imagine, I was in a state of shock upon receiving this piece of news, and with a few friends who were destined to share the same fate, tried to drown my sorrows in San Antonio that weekend. A few days later, instead of packing for the long trip to the Philippines and the duty assignment I had requested, I found myself throwing my few belongings into the trunk of the '38 Buick Century coupe I had bought upon hearing the bad news. I drove the few miles back across town to Randolph Field with mixed emotions. I was proud and happy to have survived, and to have won that coveted pair of silver wings and a 2nd Lieutenant's commission, but having to become an instuctor was one hell of a far cry from what I'd had in mind for so long.

Now, a full year later, the disappointment lingered but at least I had become more or less resigned to the situation. San Antonio had its fair share of beautiful girls, many of whom were willing to demonstrate the true spirit of southern hospitality. Many of us had found them to be much more demonstrative now that we were 2nd Lieutenants than when we were mere flying cadets, and life was anything but grim. And, as if we were not getting enough flying time in during the week, we could take a plane for a weekend cross-country trip any time we wanted to, thus improving our navigational skills as well as providing new social opportunities. Now and then we would encounter a former classmate who had been assigned to a tactical outfit, and always they would bemoan the lack of flying time they were accumulating. Due to budget squeezes which severely limited supplies of gasoline, most of them felt lucky to get in ten or fifteen hours of flying per month, less than we were flying in a week. And so, at least in that respect, we instructors could consider ourselves fortunate. That added flying time meant that we were gaining valuable experience and becoming more proficient pilots; instructors, I had reluctantly discovered, still had much to learn while at the same time imparting their so-called wisdom and expertise to their neophyte students.

A glance at my watch showed that it was nearly 5:00 p.m. I tapped the stick lightly to get Gibson's attention, then said into the mike, "Okay, Gibson, let's head for the barn." He nodded, looked back over his tail, and turned back toward Randolph Field. From a distance it appeared as a miniature complex of spanish-styled buildings and tree-lined streets located on a broad plain some eighteen miles northeast of San Antonio. Its broad pasture-like landing fields surrounded the huge square which encompassed the living area. Long rows of hangars and acres of macadam parking areas for the planes bounded two opposing sides of the square. And dominating the entire scene was the tall, stately domed-tower of the administration building, an unmistakable white landmark which was particularly welcome during periods of bad weather and restricted visibility.

We continued slanting down at reduced power. Below us was a patchwork of irregular fields and grazing land, a gently rolling landscape of browns and greens, mottled clumps of mesquite and chapparal, a small stream's course defined by tall cottonwoods and willows. Horses and cattle could be seen moving purposefully toward water tanks beneath whirling windmills, or standing in corrals near dilapidated barns and weathered ranch-houses. A kid of perhaps ten or twelve looked up and waved as Gibson levelled off at five hundred feet, fighting the rough air while angling in at 45 degrees to the downwind leg of the rectangular traffic pattern. It was the rush hour now, with dozens of other BT-9s suddenly converging at the end of the flying day, like so many pigeons racing for their loft. My sweating student needed no reminders now to keep looking around, and a minute or so later had successfully negotiated the traffic pattern and made an acceptable landing.

Gibson taxied onto the wide macadam ramp in front of L flight's hangar and parked between two other planes. He cut the engine and rolled back his canopy, then reached for the Form 1 to log the flight. By the time the prop had stopped turning I was out of my seat and had jumped down from the wing, immediately unbuckling the crotch-straps of my parachute harness. It was a relief to be able to stand up straight again, but the oppressive heat and humidity there on the ramp were about as welcome as a steam bath. I was in no mood to linger for even a brief critique of his flight, so merely indicated to Gibson that it hadn't been entirely miserable and that I'd see him on Monday. He was obviously relieved, and no doubt would rest easier over the coming weekend.

I entered the instructor's ready-room located in a corner of the hangar. It was equipped with a row of large metal lockers, a couple of tables, and a few well-worn chairs. Always the room was littered with grimy, dog-eared aviation magazines. Massive ashtrays made from discarded pistons sawed in half rested on the tables, always brim-full of cigarette butts; there seemed to be an unwritten rule that prohibited anyone from ever emptying them. The place reeked of stale tobacco and sweat.

As I entered the room I could hear the familiar clanging of locker doors, the thud of a parachute being dumped, and the desultory undertone of voices belonging to the half-dozen tired and sweaty instructors who had arrived just ahead of me. A couple of them were former classmates who had shared my fate, but unlike me they seemed to enjoy the assignment. Bev Steadman across the room, and Lou Van Mullem, whose locker was next to mine, had been good friends even while we were still cadets.

Van turned from his locker as I approached, grinning as he noted the sour expression I wore. "Fun day, huh R.T.?" he said.

"Hilarious," I growled in response.

"Come on," he laughed, "you know it beats hell out of working for a living."

"True," I agreed, "but dammit, there's gotta be a better way."

I opened my locker and put my radio headset on the top shelf, then dumped my chute inside without bothering to fold the harness neatly around it in the prescribed manner. Van reached up and took a magazine from the shelf of his locker before slamming the door shut. He held the magazine out toward me. "I'm through with this," he said, "you want it?" It was a copy of *TIME* magazine, with a picture of some navy Admiral beneath the big block letters on its cover. I checked the date up in the corner and saw that it was the current issue. "Yeah, thanks, Van," I nodded, and followed him toward the door. We sauntered out of the hangar and then parted company. Van had married his long-time sweetheart immediately upon being commissioned, and now lived in one of the Spanish-style bungalows in the married officers section nearby.

My destination, the Bachelor Officers Quarters, was only a couple of hundred yards distant. I set out at a leisurely pace, wondering whether or not to make a run into San Antonio later in the evening. The sound of engines in the traffic pattern and on the ramp was diminishing as the last of the birds straggled home to roost. Soon a strange, tentative quiet would settle over the field, lasting only until darkness had arrived and the dozen or so scheduled for night-flying on either Stage cranked up the still-warm old Cyclones once more. Then, until nearly midnight, the calmer air would be filled with the steady drone of engines, interspersed with short, loud bursts of take-off power as touch-and-go landings were practiced on the flood-lighted fields. I was thankful that night-flying for my new students, and thus for me, wasn't scheduled to begin for another three weeks. When the time came, judging from past experience, I knew I could count on some unexpected thrills.

I mounted the broad steps at one of the entrances to the B.O.Q. building where I shared one of the typical bachelor apartments with my close friend and former classmate, Paul J. Greene. Paul was a Texan, which

BT-9 trainers on the ramp at Randolph Field

RTS—as a flight instructor with cadets, Randolph Field, 1941

automatically made him a "character," but he could get away with it better than most; a personable extrovert, he was about six feet tall, athletic build, wavy brown hair, and disgustingly handsome. His most difficult decisions were likely to be concerned with which of a bevy of beautiful girls—his "stable of fillies," as he called them—to make a date with for a given occasion. Most guys, myself included, would have been delighted with any of his rejects.

I continued on up the outside stairway to the second floor. It was somewhat cooler in the shade of the wide, colonnaded balcony that fronted the building's courtyard, with a slight breeze stirring the humid air. From one of the apartments came the voice of Helen O'Connell belting out *Amapola* along with the band of Jimmy Dorsey, as reproduced on the record-player of a neighbor. Like many another young guy at the time, I was madly in love with Helen.

Our quarters consisted of living-room, bedroom, and bath. The rooms were of modest size, comfortably furnished with what the Air Corps considered the necessities, plus whatever personal touches we saw fit to supply. Since Greene and I continued to think of duty at Randolph as a temporary assignment, despite all the evidence to the contrary, we hadn't done a great deal in making the place into something that might rate a page in *House Beautiful*. The government-supplied furnishings consisted of a sofa and a pair of easy-chairs, a small writing desk, and some innocuous lithographs of rural scenes that helped to fill up the wall space. The hardwood floor was covered with a well-worn rug; a large stain of dubious origin was only partially hidden by a small coffee table.

There were twin beds, dressers, and a small refrigerator in the bedroom. A couple of closets were jammed with golf-clubs, cases of bottled goods, uniforms and other incidentals. As for the personal touches, Paul had managed to scrounge a small bar for the corner of the living room, and I had supplied a portable phonograph and a large but temperamental electric fan. We had maid service of sorts once a week, which was all too seldom since neither of us could be considered a devoted housekeeper.

I tossed the copy of *TIME* onto the end of my bed and began to get out of my shoes and sweaty clothes. Greene wasn't back yet from his flying chores over on A-stage, which was on the opposite side of the field and considerably farther from the B.O.Q. area. In short order I was enjoying the cool shower I'd been looking forward to, got dried off and into a fresh pair of jockey shorts, and then moved to the little refrigerator. I dumped the contents of an ice tray into the little ice-bucket and grabbed a bottle of soda. With these and the magazine in hand I returned to the living room and proceeded to the little bar. I poured a generous slug of *I.W. Harper* into a tall glass, added ice and soda, and took a big swallow even before the fizzing had subsided. At this point life was beginning to look more bearable, and there was an entire weekend still ahead.

I switched on the big electric fan that sat on a corner of the desk. Nothing happened, so I twisted the cord at its base until it began to turn and rev up to full speed. One of these days, I thought for the hundredth time, I'm going to fix that damn short in the cord. At last I plopped down on the sofa, hoisted my feet up onto the coffee table, and picked up the copy of *TIME*, dated June 23, 1941. Today was only the 20th, and I wondered once more why it is that magazines insisted on dating each issue a week ahead of actual publication. I never did learn the answer.

Idly, I began to leaf through the magazine, as usual working from back to front. I learned of the Yale crew's victory over Harvard's varsity eight for the 6th year in a row. And that Princeton had defeated Yale by a score of 5 to 3 in baseball. Such news meant absolutely nothing to a Westerner, but then I'd long been convinced that *TIME* regarded anything west of the Susquehanna as still being undeveloped Indian territory.

More interesting items began to appear as I leafed toward the middle: Mention was made of a new book entitled *"Berlin Diary"* by William L. Shirer ($3.00); *Cinemoguls* Louis B. Mayer and Harry M. Warner had been cited by the California Racing Board on charges of doping their horses.

Getting into news of perhaps more lasting importance, I learned that an American ship called the *Robin Moore* had been sunk by a German U-boat, prompting the U.S. government to sieze Nazi assets in the United States and close the 25 German Consulates. Well now, I thought, that should put us a step closer to tangling with the Krauts; it can't be long now!

I read on: *Franklin D. Roosevelt* had a sore throat and had to cancel plans to attend Harvard's commencement exercises. (Poor old Harvard seemed to be on quite a losing streak these days); *John L. Lewis* was reported to have won a big victory when the Southern Coal Operators finally agreed to wipe out a 40c per day pay differential between workers in the northern and southern Appalachian coal fields. Somehow, as I thought about that one, 40c per day didn't sound like much of a victory. But then, I wasn't a coal miner, for which I was extremely thankful.

At last I came to a series of brief articles of international import. One told of how the Germans were massing troops in the East preparatory to attacking Russia. Another revealed that the Netherlands East Indies had informed Japan there would be no increased shipments of rubber, oil, and tin. England, it was reported, was still fighting for her life, while the French were beginning to prosper under the heel of their German conquerors. And in Italy, *Il Duce* was basking in reflected glory like a poor relation.

I turned back to still another page, this one headed *WORLD WAR*, and under the sub-heading *FAR EASTERN THEATER* was an article entitled *"Convoys" to China*. I began to read it, only casually interested at first. But then, as I read further and it began to dawn on me what it was all about, my interest and pulse-rate both started to pick up. Once finished, and now very excited, I went back to the beginning and read the story again, this time more deliberately. It looked like this:

FAR EASTERN THEATER
"Convoys" to China

The U.S. has searched its soul about how to assure U.S. goods on their risky way to Britain, but with no to-do the U.S. is now sending both men and machines to fight in order to assure U.S. goods on their equally risky way to China.

China's only unblockaded supply route for U.S. goods is the Burma Road. Since the Japanese occupation of French Indo-China last January the Road has been within 350 miles of Japanese airfields. The Road is peculiarly vulnerable: it passes over two bridges slung precariously in gorges of the Mekong and Salween Rivers, and as it winds around the shoulders of huge hills it is as easy to see as a yellow ribbon binding a pile of green bundles. That is has not been permanently cut has been due to the halfheartedness and poor aim of Japanese bombers, and to the amazing Chinese capacity for regeneration. Thousands of coolies mend steel bridges with bamboo and rope, fill craters and landslides with little basketfuls of dirt.

The best way to keep U.S. supplies running over the Burma Road is to keep Japanese planes away from it. Chinese anti-aircraft equipment and technique are inadequate. The Chinese fighter Air Force is practically nonexistent. Only solution, therefore: air patrols by U.S. planes flown by U.S. fighter pilots. The Japanese have stationed no more than 300 planes in Indo-China. Chinese experts consider that to keep these away from the Burma Road would require at most 200 pursuit planes in capable hands; at the present rate of Japanese attack, half that many.

Last week half that many—100 Curtiss P-40 planes—had reached Burma. For the past few months tall, bronzed American airmen have been quietly slipping away from east- and west-coast ports, making their way to Asia. Pilots to fly the P-40s and ground crews to maintain them will soon be scattered over southwest China from the Burma border to Chungking. These pilots were not just a crew of barnstormers turned warstormers. They had been, until recently, crack U.S. Army Air Corps pilots. To take on this combat job they had been allowed to resign their Air Corps posts, enlist in the Chinese Air Force on the understanding that their U.S. Army seniorities would not be affected. Another somewhat whimsical technical understanding is that they will not "take the offensive" against the Japanese Air Force, but will merely defend the Road.

When this "convoy" system has been set up, next projected step is an airtransport system, which ought to be far more efficient and far speedier than uncertain Chinese gasoline-, mule- and coolie-propelled transport. Chinese in Washington are desperately trying to obtain priorities for 24 U.S. transport planes, which will operate from Myitkyina, Burma, the railhead north of Mandalay, to a point two-thirds of the way up the Burma Road.

Convoys to China are designed to serve a double purpose: enable Chinese troops to take advantage of their long seasoning and go on the offensive; enable U.S. pilots to get a little seasoning against the day when they may have to go on the defensive.

TIME, June 23, 1941

Copyright 1941 Time Inc.
Reprinted by permission

The full meaning of the story had hit me like an electric shock. I slammed the magazine down on the coffee table, spilling my highball in the process, and leaped up from the sofa. *"Holy jumpin' Jesus!"* I shouted with all the fervor of a reformed sinner at a Holy-roller revival, *"That's gotta be it!"*

"Hey, what in the hell's all the hollering about?"

Startled, I wheeled and saw Paul Greene standing in the doorway, a puzzled look on his face.

"Boy, am I glad you're home," I said, quickly picking up the magazine. "Wait'll you see what I found in here, just read this friggin' article!" I waved the magazine in his face and he pushed it aside with annoyance.

"Paul," I insisted, "seriously, here's the answer to our prayers. You gotta read this!"

"Well, dammit, it's going to have to keep until I can get out of these stinkin' clothes." He moved toward the bedroom, adding, "Build me a drink and I'll be right there."

I retrieved my own glass and moved back to the bar, found another glass for Paul, and poured generously from the big bottle of bonded bourbon. With *I.W. Harper* and *Johnny Walker Red* selling for only two bucks a quart at the Club, there was no reason to hold back. I added the ice and soda, then waited impatiently for him to return. Greene had bitched and moaned almost as much as I had at getting stuck with instructor duty; he, too, had his heart set on flying the hot stuff in a tactical unit. Now, I couldn't wait for his reaction to what I'd just stumbled across within the pages of *TIME*, something I might never have known about if Van Mullem hadn't given me his copy less than an hour earlier.

Paul came back into the living room wearing only his shorts. He took the tall drink I handed him, favoring me with a slight nod of thanks, much as a King might accept some humble offering from one of his serfs. Then he sat down where the breeze from the fan would hit him, and began to read the article.

I watched him impatiently, thinking he must have been the slowest reader ever to come out of Clarendon, Texas. I kept expecting to see some change of expression on his face, but there was nothing, deadpan. At last he looked up, tossing the magazine onto the coffee table.

That's what got you so fired up, for chrissake?" he demanded.

"Damn right it is," I said, "don't tell me you can't see it! Hell, man here's a way to get out of this rat-race, made to order."

"Sure, if you're lookin' to get your ass shot off," Paul said.

"What?" I couldn't believe my ears; I'd been certain that he would be as excited as I was about the possibilities.

"Look, R.T.," he said, "has it not occurred to you that those little buggers might get pissed off and start shooting back? Anyway, I thought it was the Germans you were mad at."

"Germans, Japs, what's the difference," I said heatedly, "the point is that when the U.S. finally does get into a shooting war, you and I are going to be stuck here, still sitting on our blistered butts trying to teach these knuckleheads how to do chandelles and lazy-8s from the back seat of a BT-9!"

"Yeah, you've got a point there," he conceded, adding, "I wonder what they're paying these idiots; the article doesn't say."

Something in his tone of voice convinced me that he'd merely been playing devil's advocate, that he was as interested in the whole idea as I was.

"Well, whatever they're paying can't be any less than what we're making now," I said. "I doubt if anybody's going over there with the idea he's going to get rich."

Paul took a long swallow of his drink, then grinned at me.

"So what are we waiting for?" he said "how do we go about getting into this screwball outfit?"

"Damned if I know," I laughed, "but I'm just before finding out!"

"I'll drink to that," Paul said, handing me his glass. "Here, old buddy, fix us another."

*　*　*

2nd Lt.s R.T. Smith and Paul J. Greene shortly before resigning their commissions in order to join the American Volunteer Group.

A Skip and a Jump

Greene and I soon discovered that "getting into this screwball outfit" was easier said than done. In the first place we didn't even know what the organization—if indeed there was such a thing—was called. The article in TIME had failed to put a name or a label to the project, and in the many inquiries we made around Randolph Field during the next couple of days nobody had the faintest idea what we were talking about. In fact, it seemed that we were the only ones in that part of Texas who had even seen the article. We drew a blank at the base adjutant's office and everywhere else we turned.

It was in a casual conversation at the bar in the Officer's Club that I finally got a clue. I was talking with one of the older instructors, a First Lieutenant, and asked him if he knew anything about an outfit being put together to go and help defend the Burma Road on behalf of China. Much to my delight he told me he'd heard a little bit about it from a friend who was stationed over at Kelly Field. Excited at this piece of news, and armed with the name of the officer at Kelly, I hurried back to the B.O.Q. It was Sunday night, and Greene had just returned from a date in San Antonio. I told him what I'd learned at the Club, then went to the desk and began thumbing through the little telephone directory that had listings for all the officers at the several Air Corps bases in the area.

"You going to call the guy right now?" Paul asked.

"Damn right," I said, finally locating the number.

"Don't you think it's a bit late?" He said after a glance at his watch.

"It's not even midnight," I said, and picked up the phone.

As it turned out, Paul was right, it was a bit late. A sleepy voice answered after several rings, and the guy was not terribly enthused when I apologized and explained the purpose and the urgency of my call. However, he did give me the name of a man to contact in Washington, D.C., and a mailing address. I asked him if he was going to join up, and his reply was to the effect that he'd been considering such a step, but that his wife took a very dim view of the whole idea and he'd decided he'd have to pass. I thanked him for his help, apologized once more, and hung up. We would later learn that a lot of other wives were also taking a dim view of such goings on, and consequently only a handful of married pilots signed up.

Paul and I got our heads together immediately and composed a telegram to send to the man in Washington, someone by the name of C.B. Adair. The message was brief and to the point. It said: *"We each have a thousand hours flying time and are ready to go." Signed:* 2nd Lieutenants R.T. Smith and P.J. Greene, B.O.Q. #207, Randolph Field, Tex.

The telegram was dispatched the first thing the following morning. Paul and I continued with our duties, of course, but it was difficult to keep our minds on regular business. Two or three days went by without any reply to our telegram, and we began to stew, wondering if the guy had received it. It wasn't until Thursday that we got an answer. A telegram addressed to the two of us arrived, saying, *"Will be at Gunter hotel, San Antonio, June 30, 31. Call me on 30th."* It was signed, C.B. Adair.

"Hot damn!" I said.

"My sentiments exactly," Paul grinned.

It was nearly six p.m. when Paul and I knocked on the door to room 419 of the Gunter hotel. It was Monday, the 30th of June. We had reached C.B. Adair by phone shortly after lunch, and he had said for us to come on into town at about that time and he'd be happy to talk with us.

The door opened and there stood a big, broad-shouldered man who appeared to be in his early thirties. "You must be Smith and Greene," he said, extending his hand.

"Not necessarily in that order," Greene laughed, shaking hands.

"Glad to meet you, Mr. Adair," I said, taking my turn.

"Skip," he said, "forget the Mister, call me Skip. Come on in, gents."

We entered the room and sat down on a couple of armchairs by the window while Adair moved to the makeshift bar he'd set up on the writing desk.

"Drink?" he asked, looking at us in turn. We hesitated, and he added, "I'm having one, if that means anything."

We laughed and indicated we'd be happy to join him.

Skip mixed the highballs and then sat down on the end of the bed nearby. "Damn," he sighed, "it's been a long day. I've been out talking to some of the troops at Kelly and Brooks all afternoon, and I'm about plumb wore out." His voice was deep, with a heavy southern accent, possibly from Virginia or one of the Carolinas. He took a big sip of his drink, then continued. "I guess you two would like to know what this thing's all about, so I'll give you my standard speech. After that I'll try to answer any questions you might have, and I'll have a few to ask of you. Okay?"

"Fine," we both said in unison.

Skip's speech was brief but covered a lot of ground. He gave us some background on the situation in China, telling of how the Japanese had invaded that huge country in the late thirties and now occupied a large part of it, including the entire coastline and all of its seaports. The only avenue of supply left to the Chinese was the Burma Road, a tortuous, unpaved, narrow highway winding for several hundred miles around the rugged mountain ranges between Lashio, the railhead in northern Burma, and Kunming in southwestern China. The major cities in China had been pounded mercilessly for years by the Japanese Air Force, and now that they had recently occupied French Indo-China and established air bases there, they were threatening to cut off this one remaining lifeline of supply. For all practical purposes the Chinese Air Force was non-existent, and the Japanese bombers were virtually unopposed. The Chinese had only a few obsolete fighter aircraft, ancient Russian-built biplanes which were no match for the faster and more maneuverable Japanese fighters. As for pilots, the Chinese had only a handful who could be considered capable despite recent efforts by a few former U.S. Air Corps pilots to train them for combat. Skip himself, he added, had been an instructor in China for the past two or three years, but it had become obvious to all concerned that this was not the answer to the immediate problem.

What was needed, Skip went on, was a group of top-notch pilots equipped with modern fighter aircraft, under the leadership of someone who knew what tactics should be employed and how best to thwart the Japanese threat. Only a few months ago had such a plan been set in motion; through a lend-lease arrangement, the United States government had agreed to fund the purchase of 100 Curtiss P-40 fighter planes and necessary supplies, and to allow 100 pilots to be recruited from the Army, Navy, and Marine Corps to fly them. These pilots were to be allowed to resign their commissions and be relieved from active duty, and as civilians would become members of the Chinese Air Force. In other words, soldiers of fortune. This was necessary from a diplomatic standpoint, since the United States and the Japanese were not at war although there were many signs pointing toward that eventuality at some time in the future. It was strictly a voluntary proposition, and in fact the name that had been chosen for the outfit was the *First American Volunteer Group*. It was hoped that additional such groups would be formed in the future, and numbered accordingly.

To be in command of the AVG, as Skip now referred to it, was a man named Claire Lee Chennault. He was a native of Louisiana, a former Captain and pursuit pilot in the Air Corps, who had been retired some years earlier due to partial deafness. A man now turned fifty, he had been hired shortly after his retirement by Generalissimo Chiang Kai-Shek, China's president, as an advisor to his Air Force. It had been Chennault, along with other influential people both in China and the United States, who had proposed the formation of the AVG, and after months of discussion and argument the idea had been blessed by our president, Franklin D. Roosevelt.

Once given the green light, things began to happen quickly. The Chinese had persuaded Great Britain to let them purchase 100 early model P-40s already scheduled to be sent to the RAF in exchange for a later and improved model of the same plane. A parent organization, called the Central Aircraft Manufacturing Corporation, had been set up to administer the details concerning supplies, personnel, etc. CAMCO was headed by a man named William Pawley, who already owned a small aircraft manufacturing and repair facility at Loiwing in southwest China near the Burma border. Pawley also had strong ties with the Curtiss-Wright company of Buffalo, N.Y., and had acted as their agent and sales representative in China for some years. His little factory at Loiwing would provide support to the AVG in repair and maintenance of the P-40s, many of which had already been delivered and were undergoing final assembly in Rangoon, Burma.

Skip paused long enough to freshen up our drinks, then continued. He told us that he was one of the several men with previous military and flying experience who were currently interviewing pilots at various air bases around the country. A couple of these, former navy men, were contacting young naval aviators at places such as Norfolk, Pensacola, San Diego, and Quantico. Others, himself included, had visited Air Corps bases at Mitchell Field, Selfridge, Langley, Hamilton, etc. They were looking for skilled fighter pilots from the navy and pursuit pilots from the Air Corps, trained in aerial gunnery and combat tactics, preferably with a couple of years or more of active duty. Those with P-40 experience, of course, were sought most of all.

My heart hit rock-bottom upon hearing what Skip was saying, but I kept listening, trying not to show how I was feeling although it was obvious that Paul and I didn't have a prayer of joining such elite company

Skip went on, telling us that there were to be three squadrons in the group, and three pay categories for pilots. The three squadron leaders were to be paid $750 per month, about one-fourth of the total number—the most experienced—would be paid $650 per month as flight leaders, and the rest, wingmen, were to receive $600 per month. He went on to say that while it didn't appear in the contract that each pilot would be required to sign, it appeared quite possible that the Chinese government might pay a bonus of $500 for each Japanese plane shot down and confirmed.

Others, of course, were also being recruited from the enlisted ranks of the various service branches; skilled engine mechanics, armorers, propeller specialists, parachute riggers, transportation, administrative, and communications personnel. There was to be a small medical staff, with flight surgeons, a dentist, a couple of nurses, and even a chaplain, for God's sake! In short, nearly two hundred well-qualified people in addition to the hundred pilots. The others would not be as well-paid as the pilots, since they would not be in actual combat, but still would earn more than twice what their previous pay-grades had provided while in the service.

Skip paused, then said, "That's about it, gents...how's it sound?"

"Great!" I said.

"Put me in, coach!" Greene nodded, "I'm ready!"

"What do we sign?" I asked, "when can we get going?"

"Hold on, now, not so fast," Skip grinned, "first, there's some information I need to know about the two of you. Like, out of that thousand hours of flying time, how much is in pursuit? How much aerial gunnery time?"

Greene and I exchanged sheepish glances, and Skip guessed the answer. "None, huh?" he said. We admitted as much.

"Ever *seen* a P-40?" Skip asked. We shook our heads, feeling stupid.

"Damn, that's too bad," he said, "I mean about your experience. I'm sorry gents, but I'm afraid we won't be able to use you."

We both protested, but knew that it was futile. It galled us to think that some of our former students, having completed their training and subsequently been assigned to pursuit squadrons, might even now be on their way to Burma. Skip had mentioned earlier that a couple of contingents were already enroute by boat, and that another would be sailing from San Francisco in two or three weeks. Now it was painfully obvious that we would not be among them.

"Look," Skip said after glancing at his watch, "I'm starving, so let's go get some dinner...it's on me."

We had dinner with Skip at a restaurant near the hotel, and while Skip was a pleasant, likeable guy, Greene and I were too discouraged at that point to enjoy it. Skip appeared to enjoy our company, however, and repeated how sorry he was that we didn't qualify. It was just that the "old man," as he referred to Chennault, had given him and the other recruiters instructions to sign up only pilots with pursuit or fighter experience; only in, rare cases could an exception be made, otherwise he'd sign us up immediately.   We drove back to Randolph feeling about as glum as we could possibly get, not even wanting to talk to each other, each of us nursing his disappointment in silence.

"Sonuvabitch!" Greene finally exploded, pounding the steering wheel, "I wish now we'd never even heard about that damn outfit!"

I didn't respond, just sat staring at the headlights of the oncoming cars, thinking, or to put it more accurately, scheming.

"What's goin' through that bird brain of yours?" Greene said after glancing in my direction.

I said, "Skip said he wasn't leaving until day after tomorrow. Let's go back in tomorrow night and have another crack at him."

"You're nuts, R.T.," he said, "what good would that do?"

"Well, I keep thinking about what he said, something about in rare cases they might make an exception. Dammit, if we're not rare cases I don't know who is!"

"Okay, so you're right, so why didn't he sign us up tonight?"

"I don't know, but maybe he can be persuaded. Hell, it's worth a try."

We plotted our strategy the next day. We figured Skip would be getting back to the hotel around five p.m., and armed with a brand new quart bottle of *I.W. Harper* we headed for San Antonio a little before five.

Skip was obviously surprised when he opened his door in response to our knock, but seemed glad to see us again. He invited us in, and I handed him the paper bag containing the bottle. He seemed pleased with the gift, and immediately began mixing drinks. We apologized for breaking in on him unannounced, but explained that since we were going to be in town that evening anyway, we thought we'd just drop by for a few minutes. We told him how much we'd enjoyed being with him the night before, how we appreciated his hospitality, asked about where he was going next.

The conversation never abated, interrupted only by Skip's frequent trips to his little desk-bar to fix more drinks. We questioned him at length about conditions in China, the Japanese Air Force, Burma, Chennault, everything we could think of to show our interest. As time went on, our soft-sell approach began to harden, and we insisted that he'd be making a big mistake not to sign us on for the AVG. And he kept insisting that, much as he'd like to, he was afraid the "old man" would chew him out royally if he did. It was becoming evident, though, that his resolve was weakening."

In the final analysis, I guess you could say that *Mr. Harper* was responsible for casting the deciding vote. By seven p.m. or so we had nearly killed the quart, and were feeling no pain whatever. That, and perhaps the fact that Skip was getting tired of arguing, made him finally throw up his hands and say, "Okay, gents, you've convinced me. I'll probably catch hell, but it won't be the first time." With which he dug into his briefcase and grabbed a handful of papers. He handed each of us a printed form and told us to read it carefully. It was a CAMCO contract, spelling out the terms and conditions that applied to the hiring of pilots for a period of one year. Greene and I scanned the pages hurriedly; there was lots of fine print, and in our present condition we probably couldn't have read it if we'd tried. Minutes later we had each signed a contract, accepting employment as wingmen in the Chinese Air Force, payment of $600 per month, with transportation to and from China to be paid by CAMCO. Skip signed each copy in a space provided, and it was done.

"See?" I winked at Greene, "nothing to it!"

"I oughta have my head examined," Skip muttered. Then he got some more forms from his briefcase, had us sign three or four of them. They were passport applications, requests for relief from active duty in the Air Corps, allotment forms indicating where we wished to have our paychecks deposited after deducting the amount of cash we wanted to draw in the Far East.

"I'll be taking all these back to Washington with me tomorrow, gents," Skip said after we'd finished signing. "CAMCO will handle everything there, but each of you get some passport pictures taken tomorrow and send them to that address in Washington, air mail."

We promised we'd do it, and asked how long it would be before we might be leaving San Antonio, and when we'd be sailing.

"You'll probably have orders relieving you from active duty in a week or so. By that time you'll be advised where and when to report in San Francisco, probably about the 19th or 20th of July. In the meantime, go home and see your folks and friends, do whatever you like. But you two better damn sure be on that boat when it pulls out or I will personally beat the living bejeezus out of you!"

***

Breaking Away

Greene and I went back to our regular duties with renewed enthusiam. Of course we told a few of our friends about what we had done, and were about to do; their reactions ran the gamut from disbelief to envy, but the majority of them seemed to think that we had simply lost our minds.

It was about the 7th or 8th of July that we each received a letter from CAMCO. We were advised that we could expect the orders relieving us from active duty, to be issued from headquarters in Washington, to arrive at Randolph Field momentarily. We were further told that we were to report to room 314 of the *Bellevue* hotel, San Francisco, by 3:00 p.m. on July 21st; a CAMCO representative would be there to give us further instructions. Also enclosed was a generous check to cover expenses and transportation, and a list of suggestions as to what items of clothing and personal effects should be taken along. Just like going to summer camp!

Paul and I were ecstatic; things were moving swiftly, just as Skip had promised, and it seemed almost safe now to stop pinching ourselves to make sure we weren't dreaming the whole thing. Then on the 10th, a Thursday, we were notified by the base adjutant's office that they had received a TWX from Washington stating that our orders had been issued on the 8th and were being forwarded via air mail. The adjutant's office promised to advise us the moment they received the documents. Our spirits soared, higher than any BT-9 could possibly fly.

With everything moving along so swiftly, some of our friends decided to throw a little going-away party for us at the Officer's Club that Friday night. It was to be a stag affair, impromptu, sort of an after-dinner open-house in the main bar. It turned out to be quite a party, lasting until they ran us out and closed the place. Two or three dozen of our good friends showed up at one time or another during the evening, even some of the older types, 1st Lieutenants and Captains, flight commanders and check pilots as well as ordinary instructors. Gabe Disosway, a Captain, would one day be a four-star general, and others such as George Dany and Freddie Gray would also wear stars. Future colonels were there in force; Van Mullem, Steadman, Bing Kleine, Curly Edwards, Huey Long, in fact everyone in the group would be wearing eagles in the not too distant future, although few would have believed such a prediction at the time.

The conversation, as might be expected, was centered on the subject of what Greene and I might be getting ourselves into. Some expressed concern for our safety, some for our mental condition, but most were envious and wished that they, too, could break away from the Randolph routine and get involved in something a little more dramatic. In any case, they all wished us well and meant it each time they proposed a toast to us and to "good hunting," an occurrence that seemed to happen with alarming frequency.

The next day, Saturday, we got a call from the adjutant's office advising us that copies of our orders had arrived from Washington. Since it was the weekend, however, we would be unable to clear the base until Monday, the 14th. Thus we still had a weekend ahead in which to say our goodbyes to our favorite girl-friends, taking them to dinner followed by dancing at the *Tower*, the closest thing to a nightclub that San Antonio had to offer. Its owner, a man named Wagner, and his wife and daughters had practically adopted Paul and me, so it was almost like a second home. They were fine people, and went out of their way to see to it that we always had a gay old time. I hope it's unecessary to add that I use the word "gay" with its original definition in mind, not the corrupted meaning it has been saddled with in recent years. In that "old fashioned" time and place, known homosexuals were a rarity, thought of as unfortunate people and often dismissed as "queers" or "fairies." If any existed among our peers, which I doubt, they somehow managed to keep the fact well hidden; to do otherwise would have meant instant dismissal.

Of course, those were terribly innocent times in many respects, judging by today's standards, as I believe most of my contemporaries will agree. But, for the enlightenment and amusement of later generations, consider: *Sex* was still a three-letter word, obscenity was frowned upon in mixed company, and more often than not a young lady would refuse to let a guy kiss her on that first date, much less go to bed with her. Graffiti, in effect, had not yet been invented, except perhaps for the time-honored custom of carving initials on wooden desk-tops with a jacknife in numberless high-schools, often with two sets of them surrounded by the shape of a heart.

Most of us had at least heard of a tobacco-like substance called *marijuana*, but not only had never tried the stuff but didn't know anyone else who had. *Fu Manchu* movies had made us aware of a drug called opium, but it appeared that its illicit and dangerous use was pretty much confined to China. Heroin and cocaine were simply words in the dictionary with no real meaning to most Americans. On the other hand, cigarette smoking was becoming ever more popular; even a few daring young women were taking it up, and of course it was considered relatively harmless. Beer and whisky were readily available and affordable, also considered relatively harmless, and most of us smoked and drank much more than was good for us, habits acquired in most cases as part of our college education. For entertainment we went to an occasional movie or sporting event, or simply stayed home and listened to favorite radio programs such as Amos 'n Andy, Jack Benny, Lum 'n Abner, or perhaps played a few hands of bridge or a little poker.

Sound like the nostalgic musings of an old fogie? Well, so be it, friends. I confess to the belief that our country and its people were much better off in many important ways during those years; frankly, I think it would be great if, through some celestial magic, we could return to the "good old days" of the early forties and start all over again, and maybe next time do it better!

Monday, the 14th, arrived in the nick of time after the hectic weekend; as Skip might have put it, we were just about plumb wore out. Clearing the

24

base was nearly an all-day chore. We had to take another physical exam to make sure everything was still in order, although this one was rather perfunctory and took only an hour or so to complete. That item checked off on the list of things to be done, supplied by the adjutant's office, we moved on; turned in our parachutes to base supply, paid our bills at the officer's club and bachelor officer's mess, picked up transcripts of our flying records from base operations and copies of orders placing us on inactive status from the adjutant. I had arranged with a young civilian employee at the base to drive my car to Los Angeles and turn it over to my parents. Meanwhile, the plan was for me to drive with Paul to his home in Clarendon, spend the night there, and fly to Los Angeles the following day via commercial airline from nearby Amarillo. And so, at mid-afternoon, we threw our bags into the trunk of Paul's Lincoln Zephyr and headed out toward the main gate without so much as a backward glance.

***

Don't Worry About a Thing, Folks

The captain applied take-off power and the DC-3 began to pick up speed as it headed west down the runway of Amarillo's airport. As always during those infrequent flights when I was merely a passenger I felt myself tensing up, listening critically to the sound of the engines, and trying through body language to help lift the plane off the ground. Perhaps there is no more nerve-wracking moment in the life of a pilot than to sit helplessly in the cabin of an airplane during take-off, unable to see up ahead and with some unknown person at the controls. This is ridiculous, of course, since that unknown person in most instances has had several years and several thousand hours more flying experience than the concerned pilot-passenger.

It was another hot and humid day as we lifted off and the sound of the landing gear being retracted could be heard. The pilot eased back on the throttles to climb-power, and we began the long ascent in the direction of El Paso. I glanced around the cabin once again, noting the plush interior appointments. Judging from its apearance and the new-plane smell, I guessed that this DC-3 had been in service only a few weeks. It was fully loaded, all twenty-one of the passenger seats being occupied, plus an attractive stewardess still strapped to a jump-seat by the little galley at the rear of the cabin. She had announced that she would be serving us lunch as soon as the plane reached cruising altitude, which promised to be a rather sporty undertaking unless the air was considerably smoother than it was at the lower altitudes through which we were climbing.

I pushed the little button on the armrest and leaned back, reclining the seat as far as it would go, and streched out my long legs with my feet under the seat just ahead. I was in the single row of seven seats, near the rear of the cabin. Across the narrow aisle were two more rows, the pair of seats opposite mine being occupied by a middle-aged couple who were engaged in a somewhat heated argument over whose turn it was to sit by the window.

I closed my eyes and mentally turned off the sound of their voices, glad to be alone with my thoughts and at long last to be headed for California. It would be a long flight, with a couple of stops, but it was good to know that I'd be arriving at the little air terminal in Burbank that served the Los Angeles area at about dinnertime. I had called the folks again from Clarendon the night before, and they had promised to meet me upon arrival.

Paul and I had driven as far as Brownwood after leaving Randolph Field on Monday, spending the night at a little motel. We were up early and on the road again the next morning, with still a long way to go. Clarendon was way the hell up in the Texas panhandle, and even though we stopped only for gasoline and to go the toilet, or to grab a quick hamburger, it was nearly mid-afternoon before we pulled up in front of the attractive two-story frame house and Paul announced, as if I were seeing the place for the first time, "This is it, R.T.—the Greene mansion, pride of Clarendon, featuring outstanding cuisine, comfortable beds, running water in the bathroom, and at a price even you can afford!"

Paul's mom and dad and brother Bill appeared on the front porch and hurried down the steps and sidewalk to greet us. I'd met them before during a weekend cross-country flight Paul and I had made earlier in the year, and now they treated me like another son. They were a typical middle-class salt of the earth kind of family, very similar in many respects to my own. Paul's dad owned a large dry-goods store and was highly regarded in this community of some 2500 souls. "Mom" was small and feisty, a bundle of energy and charm, and obviously devoted to her two boys as well as her husband. They hurried us inside the house and sat us down, and for the next hour or so we tried to answer their many questions about what we were up to, and why. Paul, of course, had called them a couple of times and written a letter or two, so they'd had at least some forewarning of our plans. Still, there was much to be discussed, and it was obvious that they were very much concerned about our future welfare. This fact was demonstrated most touchingly the following morning as we were about to leave for Amarillo where Paul was to drop me off at the airport. Just before we got into his car, Mrs. Greene kissed me on the cheek and whispered, "you take good care of Paul over there, R.T., hear?" I could see tears beginning to well in her eyes as I laughed and tried to reassure her, saying, "we're going to be fine, Mrs. Greene, now don't you worry about a thing!" Five months later those words were to come back to haunt me, my first thought upon learning that Paul had been shot down!

I guess it was only then, as we pulled away from his house, that I truly realized the degree of anxiety and apprehension to which Paul and I were subjecting our parents. We hadn't even considered them in reaching a decision which they must surely look upon as irrational and terribly dangerous, one which very conceivably could cost us our lives. The first real feelings of guilt came over me now as I thought of how, not for the first time, I had been thinking only of myself. My folks had made many sacrifices throughout my young life, many which they could ill afford, such as sending me to the University. Like so many others, they had been forced to endure the hardships of the depression of the thirties. Still, we were more fortunate than many, somehow managing on my dad's salary of $200 per month as superintendant of schools in Red Cloud. Unemployment was at a record level, long-established businesses forced to close their doors, and bank failures were commonplace. And all the while, countless farmers watched helplessly as their crops withered and died during the prolonged drought, and their farmland was literally blown away in the terrible duststorms that were to plague the nation's mid-section for years. We could see them coming well in advance, boiling gray-black clouds massed formidably on the horizon to the south, arriving an hour or so later driven by thirty to forty miles per hour winds, with visibility suddenly dropping to less than a hundred yards. Eight to ten-foot drifts of dust and tumbleweeds would pile up in the lee of wooden-slatted snow-fences that ran parallel to the country roads, while horses and cattle turned their backs to the storm's fury and waited it out, a few suffocating in the process. Weather-stripping had yet to be developed, so cracks around windows and doors were tightly stuffed with strips of cloth in a futile attempt to keep out the fine silt that soon covered everything in the house. A sardonic joke of the times might be heard when someone spotted a car bearing a Kansas license plate: "Probably some poor guy lookin' for his farm." But, at a point during those darkest days when people were most desperate, over the radio came the firm, reassuring voice of FDR, our new president, saying, "We have nothing to fear but fear itself," and people thought, *By God, he's right, things'll get better soon!*

I felt a gentle tap on my shoulder and opened my eyes to find the stewardess standing alongside. "Excuse me, sir," she said, "would you like me to serve your lunch now?"

I thanked her, but declined. I wasn't at all hungry after the big, late breakfast Mrs. Greene had fixed, and on top of that I had the firm conviction that the passengers about to have lunch would wind up with most of it in their laps. We had leveled off and were at cruising altitude now, probably about 6000 feet, but it was still very bumpy.

. I closed my eyes again and my thoughts returned to those adolescent years spent in Red Cloud from the age of nine until graduating from high-school at seventeen. With a population of 1700, Red Cloud was a fair-sized town by Nebraska standards, located in the south central part of the state just a few miles above the Kansas border. It was typical of hundreds of small towns scattered throughout the midwest farm belt, with a main street two blocks long, the usual stores and places of business, and quiet, shady, mostly unpaved streets lined with two-story wooden frame houses. There was a county courthouse, and a small jail with three or four cells that were seldom occupied by anyone more sinister than a wayward tramp: usually at his own request he'd be accomodated, given a hot meal, a bed for the night, and be on his way in the morning. Real crime, so far as Red Cloud was concerned, was practically non-existent. People never bothered to lock their doors at night, or remove the keys from their cars while parked in front of the Post Office or a store downtown, yet in all those years the number of burglaries could probably be counted on the fingers of one hand, and I don't remember ever hearing of a car being stolen. Oh, we heard and read about criminals elsewhere, since it was the era of the infamous John Dillinger, Bonnie and Clyde, and Al Capone, among others. But a young man named J. Edgar Hoover and his G-men were rounding them up on well-publicized occasions, and seemed to be gaining the upper hand.

Dust storms aside, the climate still left a lot to be desired. Summers were always scorching hot, and while the town couldn't boast of a swimming pool there was a fine though muddy swimmin' hole down on the Republican River just a couple of miles south of town. It was frequented by kids of all ages, usually unsupervised by adults, and miraculously nobody ever drowned. The river and creeks near town also provided places for ice-skating during those snowy, bone-chilling winters, when a two or three inch layer of ice could be depended on for weeks on end. Christmas was always a big occasion, of course, though often there were few presents that had significant monetary value. Still, kids were filled with hope that a new pair of skates might be found under the tree, or maybe even a shiny new *Flexible Flyer*, the Cadillac of sleds, and occasionally their prayers were answered.

Hunting of sorts was a favorite outdoor activity. Most boys made a sling-shot at an early age, graduated to a BB gun, and later, if they were lucky, acquired a .22 caliber rifle. A minor toll was taken of the plentiful supply of rabbits, squirrels, and crows to be found in the fields and groves of trees just outside town. Many of the farm kids ran trap lines during the winter, skin-ning and curing the hides of muskrats, skunks, raccoons, and even an occa-sional badger. Then, in the spring, they would bundle up the whole mess and ship them off to some firm in Kansas City in return for a few hard-earned dollars.

Transportation was primitive, which meant that a lot of people did a lot of walking. Many families didn't own a car, and those that did used them sparingly. Consequently it was every boy's ambition to own a bike, and eventually most of us managed to get one. Some of the farm kids had horses or ponies, and were the envy of all the rest. There were perhaps a half-dozen kids in the entire high-school who owned cars, nearly all of them dilapidated model-T Fords, and gasoline was often bought a gallon at a time with a hard-to-come-by dime.

Being the son of the superintendent of schools was not an easy role, although school itself was relatively easy for my sister June and me. Dad was an intelligent and well-educated man who still taught classes in civics and government, and my mother had also been a school teacher for a few years before they were married. As a result, we kids were constantly challenged over the dinner table and during infrequent automobile trips, with questions and information pertaining to every subject taught in school and many that weren't. Particular emphasis was placed on spelling and grammar; all I had to do to annoy dad was to casually use the word "ain't" in conversation. Other kids might get away with such a transgression, but not I.

Dad was a highly respected figure in the community, and naturally his kids were expected to set an example for the others. It was almost as bad as being a "preacher's kid," and of course I felt obligated to dispel any such comparison. I was, accordingly, about as ornery and full of mischief as any kid could be without actually getting into any serious scrapes. Far from getting any preferential treatment from my teachers, quite often the typical pranks perpetrated in the classroom or assembly hall resulted in my being ordered to report to my father in his office, usually with a hastily scrawled note from the teacher to deliver. There, depending upon the seriousness of my misdemeanor, I could expect punishment ranging from a stern lecture to having to give up the Saturday movie, and occasionally there was a good paddling meted out when I got home. Fortunately, I was aware that I deserved whatever punishment I got, and never brooded about it or held it against my parents; it was all part of the game, and not too high a price to pay for a certain amount of independence that sometimes bordered on rebellion.

Inevitably I got into my share of fights, both on the school grounds and around town; won a few and lost a few, usually with little damage inflicted on either party. While I wasn't belligerant or really looking for a fight, I was determined never to run from one for fear of being branded a sissy. Today, I suppose, a psychologist might nod his head knowingly and say that I was responding to "peer pressure," a term that none of us poor "peers" had ever heard.

I guess it was sometime during junior-high that I first started to pay much attention to the opposite sex. Red Cloud had its fair share of good-looking girls, and at about the usual time in most boy's lives I became aware of their charms; at one time or another I dated perhaps a half a dozen, never falling madly in love or feeling terribly serious about the whole thing. About as close as most of us ever got to intimacy was while dancing at the small parties that took place every month or so in someone's home, with perhaps a little "necking" on the front porch after seeing your date to her door. It wasn't that we didn't know about the birds and the bees, or speculate wildly about "sex," a word that was seldom spoken even by adults, it was just that most of us had been taught that certain activities would just have to wait until we were grown up. And so we waited, albeit impatiently!

Like many a kid of that day and age I was a member of the local Boy Scout troop, had fourteen merit-badges before giving up on ever becoming an Eagle Scout, and earned a dollar a week delivering milk for a dairy farm every evening from the back of an old Chevy coupe. I also had a disastrous fling at learning to play the slide trombone, and participated in whatever sport happened to be in season. As a Junior I became the regular center on the high-school football team, and at a mere 160 pounds on a six-foot frame got pushed around pretty good by some of those big, strong farm kids from the other towns. Still, we were the Republican Valley Conference champions that year, winning one game, losing none, and tieing four. Of course, some of the luster was dimmed a bit when we lost all three of our other, nonconference games, making our season's record read 1-3-4. Even our coach, who was also the principal, thought that was pretty funny and wasn't even worried about losing his job.

Not surprisingly, perhaps, I didn't half-appreciate those Huckleberry Finn-like years, and assumed that every other kid in the country was growing up under much the same conditions and circumstances. It was only in later years, after being exposed to the real, outside world, that I was to learn differently. Only one thing remained constant throughout that period, and that was my determination to become a pilot. Earlier I mentioned having had my first airplane ride with a barnstormer when I was ten years of age. What I didn't mention was the fact that it was free, and in direct violation of my parents' orders. I was punished for it, deservedly, but no conceivable punishment could have made me change my mind. A couple of years later I earned my second ride, this time with my folks reluctant permission; Inman Brothers Flying Circus, an itinerant bunch of barnstormers from Coffeyville, Kansas, came to town with three planes, one of which was a seemingly huge Ford tri-motor. I rode my bike out to the pasture early that Saturday morning and pestered the owner until he agreed to take me up later in the day in exchange for scrubbing what seemed like acres of corrugated aluminum.

I read everything I could lay hands on pertaining to airplanes and aviation in general, and of course built model planes with whatever crude materials I could find. The walls of my bedroom were covered with pictures of planes and famous pilots of the time culled from old magazines and newspapers. Eddie Rickenbacker, Clarence Chamberlin, Richard E. Bird, Wiley Post, Jimmy Doolittle and many others were familiar faces, not to mention the most famous of all, Charles A. Lindbergh. In my adolescent eyes they were all heroes of the highest order.

I was encouraged to read other things too, and was fascinated by the works of Rudyard Kipling, Joseph Conrad, and Jack London. Their stories did much toward creating a thirst for adventure in far-away places that only increased as the years went by. I was particularly intrigued by stories set in the Orient or Africa, and vowed that some day I would visit those strange and mysterious places. Of course, in my wildest dreams I could never have imagined just how and under what circumstances I would finally fulfill that vow.

Southern California seemed to sparkle as we made our way through San Gorgonio pass and began a gentle descent toward Burbank. Smog hadn't been invented yet, and the air was pure and clear. Looking down from my window seat I could see what appeared to be one gigantic orange grove from San Bernardino on toward Los Angeles, with a few grape vineyards thrown in here and there. Only a few cars could be seen on the roads connecting the small towns that dotted the San Gabriel valley. Much the same effect would be seen when we reached the San Fernando valley where Burbank was located, with still more citrus and walnut groves and hundreds of acres of vegetables growing in this fertile but sparsely populated area.

I pinched my nostrils and, with mouth closed, blew to equalize the air pressure; there was a satisfactory pop in my ears, and suddenly the noise of the engines sounded twice as loud as before. Now, as we continued our descent, I was becoming more and more excited at the prospect of seeing my folks again. They had spent a couple of summers in Los Angeles in the late thirties, and in 1939 had pulled up stakes and moved to California. Dad was now dean of men at Chapman College, a small private institution endowed by the Christian church, and also was a professor with a class or two in sociology. They had a small apartment in the dormitory on the campus, and were happy as could be. My sister, a year my senior, had also come to California, got married, and had a good secretarial job in Hollywood.

I spotted them standing in the small crowd outside the little terminal building before the plane had even come to a complete stop. Moments later there was the joyous reunion, the beginning of a few days of relaxation and catching up; during the past couple of years I'd seen them only two or three times, and never for more than a day or so at a time. I was relieved to find that they did not seem too concerned or upset with my plans, having adopted the attitude that if such a venture was what I really wanted, then it was the thing to do and they were confident I could take care of myself, somehow. I sensed that they were much more concerned than they would ever let on, and was thankful that all of us seemed determined to avoid any big emotional scenes when it came time to say our final goodbyes.

That time came very soon. Paul arrived on Sunday, the 20th, spent the night with us, and late the following morning my folks drove us back out to Burbank in time to make the United Air Lines flight to San Francisco. As I kissed them each goodbye, it surprised me to see that Dad was closer to tears than mother, and I was touched and terribly proud of both of them. It would be a long fourteen months before we'd be together again, separated by many thousands of miles but in a strange way perhaps closer than we had been for years. There were to be times when a single letter from them would mean more to me than all the tea in China. Literally!

***

Earl W. and Ulden Smith—Dad and Mom—Los Angeles, 1941

Welcome To San Francisco

Our lunch had barely settled when United set us down at San Francisco's airport on the bay. We collected our luggage and, feeling terribly affluent—we each had a couple of hundred dollars in cash—decided to take a taxi rather than the slower airport limousine into the city. Twenty minutes later our driver deposited us at one of the corner entrances to the *Bellevue* hotel in downtown San Francisco. Paul won the flip of the coin, and I reluctantly paid off the taxi driver while a bellboy materialized and grabbed our bags.

As we entered the lobby it was obvious immediatelty that the *Bellevue* would never be mistaken for the *Mark Hopkins*. It was small and filled with well-worn furnishings, but appeared to be clean and comfortable. At the reception desk we gave our names to the clerk, adding that reservations had been made for us. He nodded knowingly. *"CAMCO?"* he asked.

"Right," I replied.

He riffed through a small stack of registration cards that had already been filled out, then handed one to each of us.

"Just sign your names, please," he said, "you'll be sharing 507." He turned to the key rack at his back and extracted a room-key and a couple of envelopes. He tossed the key to the bellboy, then handed each of us one of the envelopes.

"Enjoy your stay," he smiled, "you'll find some of your buddies in the bar when you come back down," nodding toward a doorway on the far side of the lobby. Above the door was a small neon sign whose green message spelled out *Cocktail Lounge*.

Room 507 was a large and sunny corner room, with two big beds. A door in one wall obviously connected to an adjacent room. The bellboy checked to see that it was locked, opened a couple of windows, and seemed quite pleased when each of us tipped him a quarter before he withdrew.

Paul and I opened the envelopes given to us by the desk clerk; they contained identical messages advising us that CAMCO had an office in room 314, and requesting that we check in there immediately upon arrival, making sure to bring along our passports. We took time to visit the bathroom and hang a few items of clothing in the closet, then took the elevator back down to the third floor.

The door to 314 was open so we entered without bothering to knock. The room was sparsely furnished with a sofa and a couple of chairs, and a small desk. An attractive woman of forty or so looked up from her typewriter as we approached.

"Hi," she said pleasantly, "AVG?"

"Yup," Paul said, "we just got in."

"I've been expecting you," the woman smiled, "let's see, now," she glanced at a paper on the desk, then said, "you're Paul J. Greene and Robert T. Smith, right? Room 507?"

"That's us," I agreed.

"Fine, you're the last of the bunch. I'm Ruth Hamilton, by the way. May I have your passports please?"

We handed over our passports, and she glanced inside of them. Then she shook her head, laughing. "Well, Mr. Smith, I see your occupation is Plantation Foreman, and Mr. Greene is a salesman. I keep wondering who in the Washington office had to dream up all these fictitious job titles."

"We've been wondering about that, too," Paul said.

"Whoever it is has a wonderful imagination," she said, "I've seen about every occupation in the book go through here in the past few weeks, everything from meatcutters to missionaries. One little guy from Georgia—his last name was Moss but his buddies called him 'Moose,'—was supposed to be an acrobat." She put our passports in a desk drawer, adding, "We'll be keeping these for you until you're ready to sail."

"When'll that be?" I asked.

"I'm afraid I can't say, except that it won't be too long," she smiled again. From another drawer she withdrew a small stack of currency, counted out five twenty-dollar bills, then repeated the process. "Here's the hundred dollars expense money for each of you, as called for by your contract," she said, handing over the money. "Just sign this receipt, please." We signed and pocketed the money, a windfall that I had forgotten about. "Now then," she went on, "there's to be a meeting of your group at 4:30 this afternoon in conference room B on the mezzanine floor. Mr. Adair will give you a rundown on everything at that time."

"Skip is here?" I asked, surprised.

"He sure is," she nodded, then looked at her watch. "It's only three now, so you've got some time to kill. Have fun, guys, and if there's anything I can do for you, just let me know."

We went down to the lobby and homed in on the cocktail lounge. It was typical of thousands; dimly lit, L-shaped bar, a few booths along the opposite wall, and small tables in between. A couple of middle-aged men sat with elbows propped on the bar, while seated at one of the small tables were three fellows about our own age. Paul and I slid into a booth nearby and a moment later a cocktail waitress appeared at our side. She was a buxom blonde, dressed in a short skirt and low-cut peasant blouse about three sizes too small to contain her abundant charms. Somehow we managed to refrain from making any obvious comments, and each ordered a highball.

The waitress had no more than left with our order than one of the guys at the little table nearby turned to us and said, "Hey, you fellas AVG by any chance?"

"Yeah," I nodded, "you too?"

"Right," he grinned and reached across the space that separated us. "I'm Tex Hill," he said as I took his outstretched hand, "C'mon over and join the party." He turned away and grabbed another of the small tables and pushed it next to theirs, while Paul and I pulled up a couple of chairs and sat down with them.

34

The waitress reappeared with our drinks and put them down as I was saying, "I'm R.T. Smith, and this is Paul Greene, another fugitive from Texas."

"Well I'll be damned, put'er there," Tex beamed, pumping Greene's hand like that of a long lost brother. Then, remembering that he had assumed the duties of host, he said, "Meet Ed Rector, and Bert Christman here." We shook hands all around, and it was obvious immediately that we were among friends.

The five of us spent the next hour and a half in getting acquainted, comparing notes on previous military experience, and speculating as to what the future might hold in store. There were frequent and welcome interruptions on the part of the buxom waitress, whose eyes lit up like neon dollar-signs each time we called for another round. Nobody was paying for anything, of course, and the tab we were running up was the furthest thing from our minds.

It developed that our new-found friends were all former navy pilots. This was not unexpected, but what was surprising was the fact that none of them had any fighter experience; these guys had been flying navy dive-bombers, and like us had never even seen a P-40. Greene and I started to feel a lot better about the whole deal right then and there.

Tex Hill—David Lee Hill, to be precise—was from Hunt, Texas. He was about my height, a lean, rangy blonde with a permanent grin, outspoken and personable, the kind of guy who could charm the birds out of the trees. Then there was Ed Rector of Marshall, North Carolina; average size, handsome, an amused twinkle in his eyes. And Bert Christman, from Fort Collins, Colorado, quietest of the three, but friendly enough, blonde, and blue-eyed like his buddies. In no time at all Paul and I knew that we were in very good company. It wasn't anything that was said, really, just a comfortable feeling that we were all comrades-in-arms, and that no matter what the uncertain future might have in store we could each count on the others when the chips were down.

The time passed quickly until at last Tex looked at his watch.

"Damn," he said, "I hate to break up this little clambake, but I reckon we better get on up to that conference room."

He signaled for the waitress, looked at the check she handed him, and announced, "that'll be four bucks apiece, men." We each kicked in, Tex added his share, and handed the money and the check to the waitress. "Here you go, hon," he grinned, "you'll find a little somethin' there just for you." That "little something," as near as I could guess, was about five dollars. Ed Rector chuckled and shook his head. "You watch," he murmured, "that sonofa bitch'll be back here inside an hour and date her up for later tonight."

We filed into the small conference room and sat down in vacant chairs facing a table at the far end of the room. About twenty others, all appearing to be about our age, were already on hand. They looked us over with mild curiosity as we took our seats. Neither Greene nor I recognized anyone we might have met at an earlier time. Conversation in the room was strangely subdued, then died out as Skip Adair entered and closed the door. He strode to the small lectern at one end of the table, took some papers from his briefcase, then looked us over for a moment.

"Welcome to San Francisco, gents," he said. "For the benefit of the few of you I haven't met, I'm Skip Adair...come up and introduce yourselves when this meeting's over. Now, a few of you arrived just today...is there anyone here who has not checked in at the office in 314?" There was some head turning, but nobody responded. "Anybody who hasn't turned in his passport and collected his expense money?" Again no response.

"Fine," Skip said, "now we can get down to business. First of all, let me stress that whatever I say here is confidential, not to be discussed outside this room with anyone other than yourselves. The Japs already know enough about what's going on, and they've made official protests to our State Department recently, so the less said about what we're up to, the better." He glanced down at a paper on the lectern, and continued: "Everyone in this contingent has checked in by now, so I'm going to make a quick roll-call. Answer 'here' when your name is called, and hold up a hand so we can see who's who."

Skip proceeded to call the roll; inevitably there were a few "Yo"s as well as "Here"s, accompanying upthrust hands as the rest looked on with interest, trying to connect names to faces.

"Did I miss anybody?" Skip asked when he'd completed the list. Again there was no response. "Okay," he nodded, "now then, here's the poop, or at least all I can give you for the time being. You'll be sailing for the Far East within the next three or four days. You'll be aboard a Motor Ship called the "BLOEMFONTEIN" of the Java-Pacific Lines...she's a combination passenger-cargo vessel, with accomodations for about a hundred pasengers. This is a Dutch boat, and I'm told she's named after a city somewhere in South Africa, and that *Bloemfontein* means "flower fountain." Now, this is not exactly another *Queen Mary* by any means, but you'll find the accomodations and the food and service are excellent. She'll be putting into port three or four times before you finally arrive in Rangoon, Burma, which should be about a month or so from now. Chances are you'll be stopping for a couple of days in Manila and Singapore, as well as Honolulu. One more thing...since the Dutch are still at war with Germany, the ship will be blacked out at night; they tell us they don't think there are any Nazi U-boats or surface raiders in the Pacific at the present time, but it's a precaution just in case."

Skip paused for a moment; this last revelation had caused a bit of whispering and a few nervous glances were exchanged. Skip suppressed a grin, then asked, "any questions so far?"

One of the guys up front raised a hand. "What happens after we get to Rangoon? How do we get to China?"

"You don't," Skip said, "not right away, at least. You'll be staying in Burma for a few weeks for training; I can't tell you exactly where except to say that it's a couple hundred miles up-country from Rangoon. The RAF in Burma has turned a nice little airfield over to us for however long we want it; they're not using it and it's got all the facilities needed, so it'll be ideal. Later, after the whole group is assembled and we've done some training, everybody'll be moved on up to Kunming, China, where the main base will be located."

Another guy raised a hand, then asked, "Are you going over with us?"

"No, I'll be flying as far as Singapore on a Pan Am Clipper a day or two after you sail. I'll be there long before you fellows arrive, probably meet you in Rangoon."

"How many are already over there?" someone else asked.

"Only about thirty at the moment," Skip said. "That first contingent arrived a couple of weeks ago; they were all ground-crew types—aircraft and engine mechanics, and armorers, mostly. They've been getting things organized at the base, and helping with getting the airplanes ready in Rangoon. There are a hundred P-40s there now, either in crates on the docks or already assembled and flying. Now, a second, much larger group is due to arrive there about the middle of August; they sailed from here earlier this month, more than a hundred men, about a third of them pilots. There'll be two or three smaller groups to follow, and we hope to have everybody in place by the end of October."

Skip looked around the room, and when there were no more questions forthcoming said, "Okay, gents, I won't keep you any longer. Just one thing—you're free to do whatever you please for the next two or three days, but keep your noses clean and your lips buttoned up. Don't leave the Bay area, and every man is to check in at the office in 314 every day between one and five p.m. Incidentally, Mrs. Hamilton will be glad to help you with anything that requires typing; making out wills, mailing instructions, that sort of thing. Okay?"

The room seemed terribly quiet. It must have occurred to a number of us that we hadn't even thought about making out a will.

The meeting was adjourned without further ado. Greene and I went up to say hello to Skip, then trailed out behind the others. The entire group, consisting of fifteen pilots and ten ground crewmen, moved en masse down the wide stairway to the lobby. Everybody made a bee-line for the little cocktail lounge in the corner, filling up the small tables and the booths at random, with a few spilling over onto the bar. The place was jammed, buzzing with conversation, and our buxom little cocktail waitress jiggled and switched from place to place taking orders in her own peculiar style of shorthand, then rushing over to overwhelm the lone bartender. She seemed delighted at this sudden influx of business, and I noticed that Tex Hill was the first to be served.

I found myself jammed into a booth with five other guys I'd never seen before the meeting. Except for one pilot, a good-looking and personable guy named Bill Reed, they were all former enlisted men from the army and navy, ground-crew types. This little get-together could never have happened in the service, of course, where the caste system prevailed at all times and socializing between officers and men was strictly taboo. But here, all of a sudden, we were all civilians and for all practical purposes rank had flown out the window. Well, not completely, perhaps. Long-ingrained habit still dictated a certain amount of deference and respect toward former officers, particularly those who flew. I suppose this was largely due to the fact that the ground crewmen were well aware that in the final analysis, after they had tuned the engines and loaded the machine-guns and checked the radios, the pilots were the ones who were going to have to fly the planes and get shot at, while they sweated things out in relative safety on the ground. While this subject was seldom discussed, it was a fact of life understood by all concerned.

So there in our crowded booth I was meeting and rubbing elbows with four such men, more or less typical of those upon whose skill and dedication my life, and the lives of the other pilots, would in large measure depend. There was Keith Christensen, former navy armorer who, like Bill Reed, came from a small town in Iowa; Alex "Mickey" Mihalko, radioman, former navy petty-officer, short and stocky and with a voice like a bullhorn; Jasper Harrington, former crew-chief and sergeant from the Air Corps; and finally, also ex-Air Corps, Harold Osborne, parachute rigger. Bill Reed, it developed, had been three of four classes behind me in flying school but had been flying P-40s ever since being commissioned.

It was a relaxed, congenial group, already bound together by the promise of still unknown and mysterious adventure that lay ahead. And for the first time in a long while I felt completely at home; these were my kind of guys, all of them, seeking adventure and willing to accept the risks and pay the price. Fortunately, we couldn't know how high that price would be: of the fifteen pilots gathered there in the little cocktail lounge, four would be dead in less than a year, and a fifth would be a prisoner of the Japanese. Three more would be killed later in the war that was fast approaching. A lucky eight would survive to celebrate V-J day. Flip a coin, heads or tails. But even had we known the odds in advance, it's doubtful that it would have changed our outlook. We were all aware of the danger to be faced, but it was a case of thinking, perhaps subconsciously, *Sure, somebody's going to get killed, but it won't be me!*—the age-old philosophy that has sustained men in combat since wars began.

We carried on for an hour or more, moving freely from one small group to another and meeting others for the first time. There were a few older, and perhaps wiser, heads among us, but even so the average age of the group as a whole was probably about twenty-four. They came in a wide variety of shapes and sizes, and from an equally wide range of social and ethnic backgrounds. We were what many in the year 1941 A.D. might have thought of as a representative cross-section of young American males, ignoring the fact that there was not a single black or Hispanic among us. That situation would be rectified in the years to come, of course, when America belatedly realized that blood was red no matter what a man's skin color might be, and that other races were capable of producing fine soldiers, technicians, and yes, even pilots.

Paul and I got together again as the group began to break up in twos and threes and head for points unknown. We decided to go back up to the room and relax for a while before going out for dinner. A couple of the other pilots got in the elevator with us, then got out on the 5th floor when we did. They were Maax Hammer, from Cairo, Illinois, and Ed Leibolt of Camden, Ohio. Both were short, solidly built, and obviously buddies of long standing. We walked down the hallway, and when Greene and I stopped at 507 they went only a few steps beyond to 509. It was their room that connected with ours, so we threw open the door and spent the next few minutes in getting better acquainted.

We soon learned that Hammer and Leibolt had gone through the Air Corps flying training program together as cadets, but had been several classes behind us. They'd served in the same pursuit squadron somewhere back east for the past few months, flying P-40s. The moment they discovered that we had been nothing more than instructors all this time their reaction was about what might be expected if we had suddenly announced that leprosy ran in our families. They acted as if they didn't know whether to laugh at us or pray for us. Hammer pointed out how much we had to learn, and how difficult the transition would be from BT-9 to the P-40. Naturally, his superior attitude irked the hell out of Paul and me.

When they finally left, we closed and locked the connecting door.

"You think maybe we better resign while we still have a chance?" Paul laughed. "According to Hammer, we're never going to make it."

"That little piss-ant," I growled, "just let me get five hours in a P-40 and I'll wax his smart ass!"

Down in the lobby a few minutes later we ran into Bill Reed and George McMillan, whom we'd met earlier. They were just heading out for a steakhouse that somebody had recommended, and asked if we'd like to join them. We accepted the invitation, and the four of us walked the couple of blocks to the restaurant.

The steaks were good, and so was the opportunity to get better acquainted with a couple of pilots who were destined to become close friends and squadron mates. George McMillan was the kind for whom the expression "tall, dark, and handsome" might have been coined. He was a couple of years older than the rest of us, and had put in a couple more years of active duty in the Air Corps. He was from Winter Garden, Florida, and like Bill Reed had flown P-40s for the past several months. But, unlike Hammer and Leibolt, both of our new-found friends assured us that we should have no trouble with the P-40; they called it an honest airplane, a bit demanding at times, but a hell of a lot of fun to fly. Reed, from Marion, Iowa, was as handsome as McMillan, though not as tall and with a more athletic physique. Both were completely outgoing and friendly, and each of them possessed a great sense of humor.

We kicked around a couple of smoky night-clubs after dinner, staying just long enough to have a drink at each place before deciding to move on. Knowing we had three or four more days in San Francisco, we decided to make an early evening of it and returned to the hotel.

Paul and I had been sound asleep for an hour or two when suddenly we were awakened by a god-awful racket coming from the adjoining room. There were heavy thuds, shouts and curses, the unmistakable crashing of furniture followed by a furious banging on the door connecting our room to that of Hammer and Leibolt. Someone on the other side began screaming, *"Hey, open up, lemme in! Jesus, open the door, hurry!"*

"What in the hell's going on?" I mumbled groggily, switching on the lamp beside my bed.

"Sounds like they're tryin' to kill each other," Paul said, getting out of bed and going to the connecting door. The frantic pounding and shouting continued until the door was opened and Hammer, wild-eyed and bloody, burst into the room, slamming the door shut and locking it in a flash. He was in pyjama bottoms, blood running from a cut above an eye and another on his upper lip, panting from lack of breath.

"That goddam Leibolt's trying to kill me!" he managed to gasp. Now there was more pounding on the door, and Leibolt's muffled shout, "Lemme in there, I'm not through with that sumbitch!"

"Jesus, don't open it!" Hammer pleaded, "he's probably found his .45 by now, the bastard'll shoot me!"

The whole thing struck me funny as hell. "Maybe you ought to go in and reason with him, Paul," I suggested, laughing hilariously.

"No!" Hammer screamed, "for chrissake don't open the door!"

"Don't worry, friend," Paul said, "I may be crazy, but I ain't stupid."

I stopped laughing long enough to ask, "what's going on, Hammer...what's it all about?"

"Hell, I don't know," Maax said, still panting but starting to relax a bit. "We made the rounds, had a pretty good snootful, and came back to the room and got ready for bed. Then we got into an argument—I don't even remember what it was about—and the next thing I know I'm fighting for my life. Jesus! I never saw him like this before."

Leibolt finally stopped yelling and pounding on the door, and we guessed he must have decided to wait until later in the day to kill Hammer. Greene suggested that it might be safe for him to return to his own room now, but Hammer was having none of that. "Listen," he said, "if you guys don't mind, I'll stay right here, sleep on the floor."

We found a couple of extra blankets in one of the closets and Hammer built himself a nest. Paul and I got back into bed and I switched off the light. There was complete silence for a minute or so, then Paul's voice saying, "Just one thing, Hammer...I hear a single snore out of you, I'm gonna finish what Leibolt started!"

There was no reply from Maax.

***

On To The Orient — And On, And On...

Aboard M.S. Bloemfontein
Java-Pacific Line
July 27, 1941—10 P.M.

Dear Folks:

Well, here we are out in the blue Pacific and having a wonderful voyage. We are due to pull in to Honolulu tomorrow. I guess I'll be pretty busy taking in the sights then, so thought I'd better scratch out a couple of lines now and mail it when we get in.

The whole trip so far has been very interesting and enjoyable. The first day out we hit some rough weather, and took plenty of water over the bow. Several passengers got seasick, but I only felt a little woozy for a time. The group is a very congenial bunch of guys and we all get along fine. We play deck tennis, shuffleboard, etc., and get our excercise. The food and service aboard are wonderful. We gorge ourselves as never before, and I believe I've already gained back all the weight I lost before leaving.

According to the Ship's News, we may have a little trouble getting on from Manila if the Japs go into the East Indies as threatened. We are blacked out every night even now. Had quite a thrill today when 9 ships hove into sight on the horizon. They blinked signal lights at us, and one broke away and came right up alongside. It was a U.S. Navy destroyer, and the rest were heavy cruisers and other destroyers. They just wanted to know who we were and where we were bound.

Must go to bed now, as I have an appointment with the Engineer to see the engine-room in the morning. This afternoon I was up on the bridge and saw how they run this tub. Some fun!

Love to all,
Bob

We had sailed from San Francisco at about noon on the 24th, a Thursday, past the federal prison on tiny Alcatraz island in the bay, and under the majestic span of the Golden Gate bridge. Once outside the entrance to the bay, all hell broke loose; we ran into heavy seas, with what appeared to be at least fifteen-foot waves, and the old "Bloom," as we had immediately nicknamed our ship, began to bob like a cork. At least half of the complement of passengers got sea-sick, even some of the old salts from the navy. The other half, myself included, merely felt woozy and uncomfortable. There were several who would have given a month's pay to be put ashore immediately, while the rest began to wonder what in hell they'd been thinking of in knowingly asking for such torture, and how they could survive the next several weeks enroute to Rangoon. Fortunately, by late afternoon we had sailed into relatively calm water and things began to look a lot better.

Those last couple of days in San Francisco had been busy but enjoyable. There was shopping to do, sights to see, and for me a chance reunion with my best pal from high-school days, Bob Copley. We'd kept in touch through occasional letters, and Bob was now a Flying Cadet undergoing basic training at a new base in central California only a hundred miles or so from San Francisco. I had called him before leaving Los Angeles, and somehow he managed to get a few hours off and showed up at the hotel the day before we were to sail. It was great to be together again after so many years, and we reminisced about Red Cloud and old friends as well as current topics. Bob was going through the agonies that all cadets must endure, and wondering if he'd ever make it all the way through. He did, as it turned out, and a few years later flew B-29s on some of the heaviest raids of the war against Japan.

Bob went with me on one of my shopping expeditions, this one to a big sporting goods store on Market street. Skip had told us that there was excellent duck hunting in the Kunming area, and I had decided to buy a shotgun in addition to a handgun. I'm afraid I got a bit carried away, and before I was through I'd bought a 12-guage Remington pump, a .38 Colt Police Special revolver, and a .22 caliber Remington semi-automatic rifle, plus several boxes of ammunition for each gun. Of course my little arsenal cost a small fortune, nearly a hundred dollars as I recall, but I figured it was money well spent.

I didn't see much of Greene during this period. One of his former girlfriends, a raving beauty from Seattle, had come to town to wish him *bon voyage*, so his time was well occupied. Meanwhile, things had settled down next door; Hammer had moved to a single room on a different floor, and while there were still some hard feelings, at least it appeared that Leibolt was no longer intent on taking him apart piece by piece.

We were all notified on the evening of the 23rd that we were to sail the following day at noon, and that transportation by bus would be provided for the short trip to the pier. All of us were on hand in the lobby at 10 a.m., eager to get going.

We were rushed through the formalities at Customs and Immigration offices in a corner of a huge warehouse where our passports were checked and stamped, and our baggage was delivered directly to the ship at the pier outside. Moments later we were out on the pier and heading for the gangway of the Bloemfontein. She was a good-sized vessel of about ten thousand tons and perhaps three hundred feet in length, predominantly black in color with areas of tan and white on her superstructure. The name BLOEMFONTEIN appeared in large block letters on her stern, and just beneath in smaller letters the word *Batavia*, her home port in Java. A single stack, or funnel, slanted back at a rakish angle amidships, and her Dutch ownership was reflected in her neat, clean appearance. This was definitely no tramp steamer, and we clambered up the gangway buzzing with excitement. For most of us, except for the navy types, this was to be our first experience with anything larger than a sailing or fishing boat.

The ship's purser was seated at a desk opposite the gangway as we came aboard single-file. We had been told that he would give us our cabin assignments, with three men to a cabin, and Paul and I had learned that we would be sharing one of them. The purser, a roly-poly Dutchman, glanced at our passports, checked our names against his passenger list, and said what sounded like, "Der two uff you vill pee in gabin noomber serty-zigs, choost down der corridor und on der ride...your paggage vill pee broad down lader."

Greene gave me a quizzical look, and I said, under my breath, "It's okay, I think I got it."

We found number 36 and entered our little home away from home. Paul took one look and said, "Good God amighty, I've had bigger closets than this!"

- He was exaggerating, of course, but not by much. The cabin was the size of a very small bedroom, about ten feet by twelve. There was a double-deck bunk along the outer bulkhead, with a couple of portholes between. A single bunk was just opposite; there was also a small writing desk and a couple of chairs. A narrow door opened onto a tiny bathroom equipped with a sink, shower cubicle, and toilet. Paul shrugged after our cursory examination, then laid claim to the single bunk. I sat down on the lower bunk opposite, bounced a couple of times, decided it was reasonably comfortable, and staked it out for myself. We wondered who might have been assigned to share the cabin with us; whoever it was would be stuck with the upper bunk, whether he liked it or not.

We didn't have long to wait before discovering his identity. There was a rap on the door. Paul got up and opened it, and there stood a smiling Maax Hammer.

"Hi, roomies," Maax said. Paul and I groaned inwardly but decided we'd just have to make the best of it.

"You're in luck, Hammer," I said, "we saved the top bunk for you."

He came on in and looked around the little room as Paul closed the door. He spotted the single bunk and said, "How about this one?"

"That's mine," Paul said, and sat back down on it.

"Well, wait a minute," Maax protested, "how about we draw straws?"

"Screw the straws," I said from my lower bunk, "it's first come, first served, old buddy, and you're dead last."

"Unless you'd rather move in with Leibolt," Paul suggested, "maybe that can be arranged."

"Very funny," Maax said, "it's okay, I'd rather have the top bunk anyway."

"Wonderful," I said, "now we'll all be happy."

Our baggage was delivered by a couple of Javanese cabin boys. They were barefoot, and dressed as they did in their native island of Java; loose-fitting white shirts, long wraparound sarong-like skirts, and small turbans wrapped around their heads. They were brown as almonds, with fine features and sparkling black eyes, typical of dozens who performed the various services for the ship's passengers.

We had nearly finished unpacking and stowing things away in the single closet and the three large drawers under the bottom bunks when we felt a slight vibration underfoot, the throb of the two huge diesel engines running through the ship. We dropped everything and raced down the corridor, up a flight of stairs and out onto the main deck. The ship was easing slowly away from the pier; at long last we were under way.

The next few days went by quickly and pleasantly. We discovered that

Skip hadn't exaggerated a bit about the food and the service; both were excellent. Meals were announced by one of the Javanese boys making the rounds and tapping on a set of chimes. There was a well-stocked bar which proved to be very popular with most of our little group, a spacious passenger lounge equipped with a piano, and there was even a small swimming pool near the stern on the second deck. The dining room sparkled with fine glassware, silver, and spotless linen.

We had each received a copy of the passenger list from the purser and it looked like a future United Nations roster. Of the eighty-five passengers aboard, only a handful besides our group were Americans. The rest were mostly Dutch, Chinese, East Indian, and Swedes, with strange-sounding and often unpronounceable names such as Djabber Sahlehnia, Hsu, Huang, Paramasany, Elfstrom, Saligupta, and my favorite, a real Dutch Baron: *A. Steengracht van Mooiland!* About thirty of the passengers were missionaries, both male and female, enroute to various outposts to convert the heathens. The rest were mostly businessmen or low-level diplomatic officials. Quite a conglomeration, and before this long trip was over we would get to know some of them well.

Early on the morning of the 28th the island of Oahu could be seen in the distance, and a couple of hours later we were off Diamond Head and could see the Aloha tower on Honolulu's waterfront. We had been told that we'd be sailing at 4 p.m. the following day, and until that time we could do as we pleased.

George McMillan and Bill Reed joined forces with Paul and me, and we spent the rest of the day enjoying the relaxed atmosphere and beautiful scenery of the small city of Honolulu. There were probably a few hundred other tourists around, brought over by the cruise ships operated by the Matson Line, American President Lines, and a few foreign steamship companies. There was no commercial air travel between Hawaii and the States, of course, except for the infrequent flights of the big Boeing Clippers of Pan American.

Our little foursome wandered into the *Royal Hawaiian* hotel, a huge pink palace that was considered the finest of the three or four hotels on Waikiki beach. We had drinks at an outdoor lanai bar, listened to the soothing strains of Hawaiian music accompanying a couple of beautiful girls dressed in grass skirts as they swayed and gestured in their native dance. The beach itself was relatively deserted, but we couldn't resist it; we rented trunks and splashed in the surf like a bunch of kids, and marveled at the skill of a handful of Hawaiian teenagers as they rode their surfboards in just ahead of the breaking waves. Boy, this was living!

Later in the evening, while making the rounds of the night spots, Paul and I decided to call an old friend whom we knew was stationed at nearby Hickam Field, a large Army Air Corps base. Ralph Wanderer had been in our upper class throughout flying school, and was a terrific guy. He'd been lucky enough to be assigned to Hickam immediately upon being commissioned, and was now in a bomber squadron being equipped with B-17s. He seemed delighted to hear from us, and insisted that he'd pick us up at eleven the following morning and show us around Hickam Field, then have lunch with his wife in their quarters on the base. We readily agreed to the plan.

Ralph showed up at the pier alongside the Bloom at the appointed hour and we exchanged gossip while he drove to Hickam. It was there that Greene and I got our first glimpse of the kind of plane we hoped to be flying soon; two or three dozen P-40s were neatly parked wingtip-to-wingtip in front of a couple of large hangars. They looked beautiful, and we were itching to get into a couple of them and take off. Not far away were a dozen or more B-17s, also neatly parked, belonging to the bomb group to which Wanderer was assigned. They were beautiful machines, too, and Ralph raved about their performance and flying characteristics, but they were not the sort of thing that could hold much appeal for Paul and myself; too big, too many people involved, too restricted to the straight-and-level or gentle turns type of flying that had to be boring.

Ralph's wife was a lovely and gracious hostess, and fed us a fine lunch in the attractive little bungalow provided for them near the edge of the base. Then he drove us back to our ship shortly before sailing time, and a few minutes later the gangway was hoisted and the throbbing of the engines could be felt once again. We stood at the rail as the Bloom slowly gathered headway, watching as the Aloha tower gradually became smaller; in the distance we could see a few planes buzzing around the big naval base at Pearl Harbor, and the superstructures of a half-dozen battleships rising toward the clear blue sky. It was beautiful, a scene to remember, so peaceful. December 7 was just over four months away.

August 9, 1941
Somewhere on the Pacific Ocean

Dear Folks:

I don't know exactly how to start this letter, as I don't know where in hell we are, where we're going, or anything else. But I will give you a summary of events following our departure from Honolulu.

After we were about three days out of Honolulu, supposedly headed for Manila, the Captain of the ship called a meeting of all passengers and made a little speech, which went something like this:

"My friends, due to the war situation, namely the presence of German surface raiders and the tense situation between Japan and the East Indies, we have been forced to change our course and take a route to Manila which will take about a week longer, making a 3-week trip of it. Please cooperate in the blackout of the ship at night. Do not strike matches on deck, keep portholes closed, etc. Also, please economize on the use of water, or it will be necessary to ration it before long."

That was about it. He didn't tell us what new route we were to take or anything. We are now eleven days out of Honolulu and have seen only two or three islands to date. We have been heading southwest, and crossed the equator about 5 days ago. There has been much speculation about where we are, where we are going, etc.; some of our navy guys who have studied celestial navigation go on deck at night and gaze at the stars, and they insist we're heading for Australia. This morning we were told that all cameras had to be turned in to the purser's office, so it looks as if we may be getting close to somewhere. At any rate, when we do get into a port I'll mail this and tell you in a P.S. what the dope is, hoping it won't be censored.

Things have been pleasant enough aboard, but we're all getting bored as the devil with the same old routine day after day. The damn missionaries—"Holy Joes" to us—are driving us nuts with their constant gatherings around the piano and singing hymns by the hour. So we drive them nuts by playing hot swing records on the phonograph; Goodman, Dorsey, Artie Shaw, et al.

The weather has been nice most of the time, altho the last couple of days have been kind of chilly, and they tell us it's winter down here now, wherever the hell "here" is. Food is still plentiful and good, I'm in the best health ever, and gaining weight. Am enjoying everything, and sure glad I got to make this trip. Imagine a "Cook's Tour" like this, and getting paid for it!

Aug. 10. Sure enough, we pulled into Brisbane, Australia, early this a.m. I'm writing this aboard ship as we are now in the process of going through customs and quarantine; we should get ashore in a little while. We're looking forward to seeing the town, although they say most everything is closed up tight on Sunday. We saw some planes this morning and I'd give anything to get in and fly again for a while.

All my love,
Bob

Brisbane was not much to write home about; it turned out to be Australia's answer to Philadelphia. It was an attractive enough city, but it was closed up tighter than a drum; there was practically no traffic on the streets, few people to be seen, and not even a pub open. I'd seen more activity in Red Cloud on a Sunday than Brisbane displayed, but at least it was good to get back on land and stretch our legs a bit. We looked in vain for a hamburger stand, but when we finally found a little place that was open and looked promising, it turned out that all they served was fish 'n chips.

Our stay in Brisbane was brief, just long enough for the ship to take on fuel and water and some fresh vegetables. We sailed at about noon the following day, August 11, this time headed north, and once again our next port of call was said to be Manila, capitol of the Philippines. A glance at the large map of the world in the purser's office was discouraging; it appeared that Manila was nearly as far from Brisbane as it had been from Honolulu.

We settled back into the routine of shipboard life, resigned to the fact that we would be at sea for another eight or nine days before reaching Manila. By this time the members of our little group had become fairly well acquainted with each other, being on a first-name basis in most cases. Skip Adair had named one of the more senior pilots to be nominally in charge of our group. This was Ed Goyette, former navy Lieutenant and fighter pilot, who was four or five years older than most of us. He supervised the brief sessions devoted to calisthenics a couple of times each day out on deck, helped to settle the occasional arguments that occurred, and acted as an intermediary between some of our more boisterous members and the missionaries who by now had about given up on ever saving us.

We whiled away the time by reading, swapping books and magazines that had been brought aboard, and usually there was a small-stakes poker game going on in one cabin or another. Some of the navy guys had brought along their Backgammon boards and dice, and introduced the rest of us to their favorite shipboard game called Acey-Deucy, the navy's version of Backgammon. Greene had taken it up with a vengance and played for hours on end; usually his opponent was Robert P. "Duke" Hedman, an experienced P-40 pilot who had been in class 40-A, three months ahead of Paul and me in flight training. Duke was a modest, stocky fellow from Webster, South Dakota, and the only one of our group who could play the piano. Inevitably, some of those dice from the Acey-Deucy games were used for another purpose; ever heard of a floating crap game?

In addition to those already mentioned, there were three other former Air Corps pilots, all with P-40 time. They were Frank Schiel of Prescott, Arizona; Bill "Black Mac" McGarry from Los Angeles; and Matt Kuykendall of San Saba, Texas. Ben Foshee, still another ex-navy pilot, hailed from Red Level, Alabama. Former enlisted men included Preston Paull, a crewchief from Idaho; Leon Colquette of San Diego; Robert "Caribou" King, radio operator from Palestine, Texas; Jack Cornelius, crew-chief from Commerce, Texas; and a couple of guys from San Diego named Durbin and Dyson with whom I never had more than a nodding acquaintance.

We had lots of time to get to know each other, and there were some interesting characters among us. One such was "Black Mac" McGarry, of Los Angeles. Like several of the others, he had been a few classes behind me in flying school, but had gone on to a P-40 squadron at some base back east upon being commissioned. Black Mac, not to be confused with plain old "Mac" McMillan, was black-haired, blue-eyed, and slender of build. He was a quiet type, but intelligent and with a wry sense of humor. One day, shortly after leaving Honolulu, we were sitting on deck and Mac glanced to either side, as if afraid of being overheard, and then in a lowered voice said, "There's something damned strange going on here, R.T." "Oh?" I said, "how so?" "Well," Mac replied, "they told us we were going to the Far East, right?" I agreed that that was what we'd been told. Mac glanced around once more, then said, "Okay, so how come we've been heading *west*, for god's sake? Think about it!" His expression was completely deadpan, and for a moment I thought he was serious and obviously a mental case. Over the next few months, those of us who knew him well learned to expect the unexpected from Black Mac.

The days seemed to drag by endlessly, but the weather was good and as we worked our way back toward the equator the temperature rose. We spent most of our waking hours on deck in athletic shorts and continued to get nearly as brown as the little Javanese stewards. Now and then we would attend a lecture in the lounge; a few of the other passengers, mostly from India, China, and the Malay states, spoke frequently about the customs and conditions to be found in their native land.

We rounded the northernmost tip of Australia and headed northwest with New Guinea somewhere off to our right. Islands were seen frequently now on the horizon, none of them identifiable, of course. A Dutch crew member pointed far off to the left one day and confided, "That's Celebes island over there, and just beyond is Borneo. We'll be in Manila in another two or three days. Don't tell anybody I told you."

Naturally, I couldn't wait to tell the rest of the gang. We were getting pretty fed up with all this hush-hush stuff, as if there were any possible way anyone could communicate with the enemy if indeed there had been spies among us. At any rate, we all agreed that our arrival in Manila couldn't come too soon. The cramped quarters, and now the heat and humidity as we crossed the equator again, plus the constant presence of others, the same faces day after day, were starting to get to us. We were becoming considerably more testy with each other, more apt to take offense at some imagined slight. The only one in the entire group who seemed to retain his sunny disposition was Tex Hill, but then Tex had a project that was occupying much of his time. There was a missionary woman of about thirty, single, reasonably attractive and built along the lines of Dorthy Lamour, whom Tex was doing his damndest to convert. She, of course, was trying equally hard to make him see the light and give up his fun-loving ways. I'm not sure how the contest finally came out, but knowing Tex, I'd never have bet against him. At least they seemed pretty chummy by the time they finally parted company in Singapore.

We arrived in Manila on the 19th of August and for the next couple of days spent most of our time ashore. It was our first exposure to a country peopled by the brown race, and we found them to be friendly and generous toward Americans. We took in the more interesting sights, and on one occasion Paul and Bill Reed and Mac and I hired a taxi to take us out into the countryside. Everything was terribly primitive, but interesting; thatch-roofed houses made of teak and bamboo and rattan, supported a few feet above ground level by log stilts, a necessary precaution against flooding during the rainy season. We saw our first water buffaloes, the workhorse of the Orient, pulling crude wooden plows through the flooded rice paddies. We stopped at one point and got out of the taxi to watch. The old man guiding the plow, wearing nothing but a loin cloth and a conical straw hat, gave us a toothless grin, but the buffalo's look appeared anything but friendly. Our driver explained that water buffalo didn't like the odor of white men, with which Bill Reed sniffed the air and said, "Frankly, I'm not real crazy about the way *they* smell."

We went to the famous old Manila Hotel, a landmark that reeked with atmosphere, and which would one day soon become the headquarters of the conquering Japanese army of the Philippines. There we found fresh milk, perhaps the one item of food that was missed the most by all of us, unavailable aboard ship for more than two or three days after sailing. We each had a couple of glasses of it along with our lunch. We also sampled the night-life of Manila, night-clubs with an abundance of beautiful hostesses who charged by the hour just to sit with us, and got a cut of the price charged for the watered booze that was served. They were also available for other activities, for a price of course, but strangely enough many of them seemed disinterested in the economic aspect and would settle merely for the pleasure of your company if necessary.

We sailed from Manila on the morning of August 22nd, expecting to arrive in Singapore about three days later. The old Bloom was soon up to her cruising speed of about seventeen knots as we crossed Manila Bay and headed for the South China Sea. Off to our right we could see the island of Corregidor just below the southern tip of the Bataan peninsula; it vaguely reminded us of Alcatraz, the prison island that we had passed as we steamed out of San Francisco Bay just a month earlier, but of course instead of being occupied by desperate criminals, Corregidor was an impregnable fortress manned by U.S. and Philippine army troops.

We settled back into the familiar routine of life aboard ship; this time our heading was southwest in the direction of Singapore, last stop before going on to Rangoon. Our spirits soared with the thought that we would finally arrive in Burma within another eight or ten days. Like junkies desperate for a fix, all of us pilots were craving to get into an airplane and fly once again; already we had been deprived of that ultimate "high" for much longer than any other period since we had first begun training.

Our soaring spirits took a nose-dive after we'd been back at sea for nearly three days. With Sarawak and Borneo now off to our left, and Singapore dead ahead and less than a day away, the Bloom changed course to a heading of due south. Our navy guys spotted the change in direction immediately, and Ed Goyette made a trip to the bridge to ask the captain what was going on. When he returned he gave us the bad news; the ship was heading for her home port of Batavia, on the western tip of the island of Java. The captain guessed that we'd be in port there for two or three days, and then proceed to Singapore.

We received this news with mixed emotions. The non-pilots were happy; another strange new land to visit, another part of the great adventure. But to most of the pilots it meant still another delay in getting on with the business of flying and fighting. Again there wasn't a damned thing anyone could do about it, and again we shrugged and decided we might as well make the best of it.

Batavia (now Djakarta) was the capitol of the Dutch East Indies, an island archipelago that stretched some 2500 miles from east to west. When we arrived on the 26th of August the Dutch influence was obvious immediately; there were canals as well as streets, interwoven like a spider web, and the houses and buildings occupied by the colonials looked European with their steep slate roofs and gabled windows. Of course, on the outskirts of the city and in the countryside the native Javanese lived much like the Filipinos, with most families devoted to tending their rice paddies and vegetable gardens. Naked children played their simple games, oblivious to the many pigs and ducks and chickens that were part of every household and which were free to roam wherever they pleased. They were an attractive race of people, curious and friendly and uninhibited, and seemingly content as could be.

So we saw the sights and heard the sounds and smelled the smells, as visitors to a strange land have done for centuries, but we were more than ready to set sail once more on the evening of the 30th. As always just before sailing, Ed Goyette got us all together for roll-call, only to discover that two of our group were missing; Durbin and Dyson, two ground-crew men, were nowhere to be found. A couple of others who knew them said they'd heard them complaining often and bitterly about the whole setup, and were convinced that the two had simply jumped ship. So the old Bloom headed out to sea once again, and our little group was now down to twenty-three in number.

We arrived in Singapore on the morning of Sept. 1. A small island, connected by a causeway to the lower tip of the Malay peninsula, Singapore was another impregnable fortress, Britain's bastion in the Far East known as the Pearl of the Orient. Ships of the royal Navy were lying at anchor, and planes of the RAF could be seen buzzing around the area, the whole scene being somewhat reminiscent of what we had seen in Honolulu.

It was in Singapore that we were to part company with the Bloemfontein. Ed Goyette had learned while we were still in Batavia that our ship would not be going on to Rangoon, and that transportation beyond Singapore was in the process of being arranged. Meanwhile, reservations for most of us had been made at some famous old hotel known as the *Raffles*.

We arrived in the midst of a torrential downpour, one of many that we had experienced during the past week or so. The Asian monsoon season was still in full swing, with perhaps another month to go, which meant that we could expect plenty of rain. Sometimes it came down in brief but frequent showers, often with sunny spells in between; at other times it would rain steadily for hours on end. Rain or shine, it was hot and humid as hell.

Other than during our brief stopover at Brisbane, Singapore was our first experience with British colonialism. Their officials and businessmen all wore white linen suits and pith helmets, and took a no-nonsense approach to everything. More often than not they were terribly proper and officious, but at the same time maddeningly slow about getting things done. Getting through Customs and Passport Control took nearly and hour; there were endless questions about where we'd come from, how long would we be in Singapore, what was our next destination, why were we going to Burma, and on and on. One official frowned as he looked at my passport, then asked, "And what kind of plantation are you to manage, Mr. Smith?" "Uh, rubber," I replied. "Odd," he said, "the last I heard, there were no rubber trees in Burma." "Oh," I said, "well, how about teak, then?" "That would seem a bit more likely," he replied with a trace of a smile. I wondered later what sort of explanation Moose Moss, the "acrobat", might have come up with if he'd run across this joker.

Paul and I gathered our luggage and hailed an ancient taxi. Our driver was a tall Indian Sikh, with full beard and turban, who drove as if he were practicing for the next Indy 500. In a matter of minutes he had deposited us at the front entrance to the Raffles. It was a large, rambling hotel, probably built around the turn of the century if not before, and turned out to be one of the focal points of social activity among Europeans living in Singapore. There were two or three comfortably furnished lounges where tea and drinks were served at the proper times, facing spacious gardens filled with a wide variety of beautiful flowers and shrubbery. The atmosphere was terribly subdued, people talking with lowered voices, and servants moving silently about their chores. The place had all the charm of a funeral parlor, but things were about to become a bit livelier now that our little group had arrived.

Paul and I were given a room on the ground floor, and after our confinement in the cramped cabin aboard ship it seemed huge. It had a high ceiling with a couple of large fans suspended from it, their blades turning barely fast enough to stir the air. There were two big beds, each equipped with an overhead mosquito bar and netting for use at bedtime. The bathroom was also large, with a marble floor and a big bathtub that was supported by stubby legs shaped like lion's paws.

That first night in Singapore was one to remember. We had all been invited to a dinner party in our honor, hosted by the Chinese Consul General, in a private dining room of a large Chinese restaurant. There followed about a fifteen-course dinner with everything from soup to nuts, dishes that most of us had never seen or heard of before, but in the true spirit of adventure, and not wanting to offend our gracious host, we were all determined to try everything in sight. For most of us it was also our first experience with chopsticks; we decided that they were inventions of the devil, designed to promote starvation. Of course the eating was frequently interrupted by toasts to our future success, to our great President, to good health, to

China, etc. There was a bottle of *Johnny Walker* scotch between every two guests at the long table, and little ceramic cups that were constantly being refilled with rice wine. Naturally we responded to each and every toast, and managed to propose a few of our own. For the benefit of those who have never tried it let me advise that shark's-fin soup and scotch whisky do not mix at all well. At one time or another, before that dinner was finished, it seemed that every one of us had excused himself from the table and made a bee line for the restroom. When we returned, usually a bit paler and sweating profusely, we sat back down and started all over again, having learned very little from the experience. I guess we were being just plain stubborn, or stupid, or perhaps both, as evidenced by massive hangovers the next morning.

Between rain showers the next few days we managed to do some shopping and sightseeing, and at night visited some of the many taxi-dance halls that featured some of the most beautiful girls imagineable. Singapore was a true oriental melting pot, the majority of its people being Chinese but with large numbers of Malays, Portuguese, British, Dutch, and other nationalities as well. Racial intermarriage, while frowned upon by most of the whites, was still a common practice and produced some truly exotic "flowers of the Orient." Hundreds of them wound up in their late teens and twenties as "hostesses" in the dance halls, performing the same services as the girls in the night-spots of Manila, or for that matter Manhattan.

Once again the time began to drag by, and once more we got impatient. with delays. We were stuck in Singapore, and it began to appear that we'd been entirely forgotten, but then one rainy day Goyette got the word that transportation had finally been arranged, and that we were to leave the following day on a coastal steamer for Rangoon. Our spirits rose immediately, and the next morning, the 10th of September, we said goodbye to the staid old Raffles hotel and headed for the docks. The manager of the Raffles didn't seem at all reluctant to see us go; I'm afraid there had been a few occasions when we had been a bit boisterous, upsetting the quiet decorum of the lounges and drawing frowns from the proper British patrons. It might be fair to say that we mixed with the British about the same way that shark's-fin soup mixed with Scotch.

It may be worth noting that the Raffles, like the Manila hotel, was destined to play host to some terribly unwelcome guests in the months to come, namely the staff of the Imperial Japanese Army which poured down the Malay peninsula and entered Singapore by the back door. The huge batteries of coast artillery, all pointed out to sea, proved to be worthless, and the impregnable fortress turned out to be "pregnable" as all hell.

***

The Last Lap — At Last!

The *Penang Trader* was a small coastal steamer of only a few hundred tons, a mere fraction of the Bloemfontein in every respect, and one glimpse made it obvious that the final leg of our long voyage would be anything but a pleasure cruise. There were frowns aplenty as we boarded her, particularly from the ex-navy guys who were not accustomed to seeing rusted metal and grime such as the Trader displayed in abundance. After the spit-and-polish of the Bloom, the thought of spending the next few days aboard this little tub was not the least bit inviting. With about 1300 miles still to go, and at a speed of only ten knots or so, we could look forward to the better part of five days aboard a ship that looked as if crossing the bay from San Francisco to Oakland might have presented something of a challenge. Mickey Mihalko, our hard-bitten little ex-navy petty officer, put into words what most of us were thinking when he growled, "I hope to hell the definition of 'coastal steamer' means this bucket never loses sight of land!"

The accommodations lived up to our expectations; a far cry from what we had become accustomed to. There were a half-dozen small cabins, each designed to house five passengers in about the same amount of space that three of us had occupied aboard the Bloom. Five of the cabins were taken over by our group, the other being shared by a couple of missionaries and their wives whom we hadn't seen before.

The Captain, First Mate, and Chief Engineer were Norwegians, which was somewhat reassuring. The rest of the crew, perhaps a couple of dozen in number, were a mixture of Malays, Lascars, and Chinese, a crew that could be described as "motley" in the fullest sense of the word. They were about as mean a looking bunch as might have been assembled by Warner Brothers; I had the feeling they'd have been more at home aboard a pirate junk in the South China Sea, and that even Errol Flynn would have had the good sense to say "be my guest" as they drug Olivia DeHavilland off, kicking and screaming, to a fate worse than death.

The *Penang Trader* finally got under way and began steaming through the many small islands that dot the entrance to Singapore, then proceeded on the northwesterly course into the Malacca Strait which separates Sumatra and Malaya. A sudden rain squall drove us all to our cabins late in the afternoon, an occurrence that was to be repeated may times during the next few days. The heat and humidity inside were the worst yet, but we soon discovered that a refreshing shower could be had simply by stripping down to our underwear and stepping out onto the deck while the rain pelted down. Since this was the only way to get a fresh-water bath, we made the most of it on frequent occasions despite the disapproving frowns of the missionaries.

The little dining salon could accommodate only half the passengers at one sitting, so we were divided into port and starboard sections and ate our meals in two shifts. We were pleasantly surprised to find that the food was quite good; plain, but wholesome, and plenty of it, although there was much less meat and considerably more fish than most of us would have preferred.

Later that first evening as we steamed through the calm sea, its surface broken only by the dozens of flying fish that broke free and skittered along for a few feet before plunging back, Bill Reed and I stood on deck enjoying the sunset. We'd seen many gorgeous sunsets from the Bloemfontein, but this one was the most spectacular yet; there were layers of broken clouds low on the horizon far off to our left, and the many shades of red and pink and purple were unbelievably beautiful.

Bill and I wandered forward, beyond the small deck area aft of the bridge that was strictly for passengers. We stopped near the hatch of the number one hold; a few feet beyond, up close to the forecastle, four or five crew members were squatting on their heels. They were gathered around a small charcoal brazier, apparently about to cook something and obviously intent upon the proceedings. Curious, we watched them, and found that they were either unaware of our presence or simply chose to ignore us. One of them stuck the end of a wire rod into some substance that he'd been rolling between his fingers into a little ball about the size of a small marble. Then he held it over the glowing charcoal, twisting the wire slowly between the palms of his hands.

"What the hell is he doing?" I whispered to Bill.

"Beats me, pal," he shrugged.

We continued to watch. A moment later the crewman, a Chinese, took the glowing ball from the end of the wire and quickly placed it into a tiny metal bowl that was fastened atop a thin bamboo tube. Then he sat up straight and put the other end of the tube into his mouth; we could see his cheeks sink in as he sucked hard on the tube, inhaling deeply.

"Jeez," Bill whispered, "I think we just found us an opium party."

The crewman passed the pipe to the man next to him and the process was repeated, then the others in turn took deep drags from the long pipe. By the time it had made the rounds, the first man was already cooking still another little ball of opium over the charcoal.

"Hey, maybe we oughta go over and join them," Bill chuckled softly.

Oh, sure," I whispered, "they look like such a nice bunch of fellas."

We retreated quietly and returned to our own deck area. Bill was still chuckling. "You may not believe this, R.T." he said, "but we didn't see a hell of a lot of that sort of thing back in Marion, Iowa."

"Come to think of it, Red Cloud wasn't exactly noted for its opium dens either," I laughed. "You think that's really what they're smoking?"

"I dunno, " Bill grinned, "but I'm willing to bet it's not *Prince Albert!*"

Again the days seemed to go by in slow motion. We continued to plow through intermittent rain squalls, rarely saw the sun now, and only occasionally got a glimpse of the long, narrow stretch of the Malay peninsula off to our right. Sometimes the wind would be at our back, just strong enough to keep us surrounded with smoke and soot from the belching stack that rose some twenty feet overhead. At other times there was little to do except envy the flying fish, or watch the dorsal fins of a couple of sharks that seemed to be escorting us throughout the voyage, usually trailing the wake astern, patiently waiting for the cook's helper to throw garbage overboard.

Most of us, now wise to the game, had bought more books and magazines in Singapore, so for a while at least we had some fresh reading material. But it was soon exhausted, and the business of swapping with each other began all over again. And as before, there were a few poker and crap games, not to mention Greene and Duke Hedman's never-ending Acey-Deucy marathon. And of course there were letters to be written to parents, wives, or sweethearts, to be mailed when the ship reached port.

We finally entered the mouth of the Rangoon River, an offshoot of the Irrawaddy, early on the morning of September 15th, then steamed slowly up the wide channel for the fifteen or twenty miles to Rangoon. It was a Monday, seven and a half weeks since we'd sailed from San Francisco. It was hard to believe that we had at last reached that fabled land which had so inspired Kipling and Joseph Conrad and others, and that we had traveled nearly halfway around the world in the process.

The *Penang Trader* dropped anchor in the stream, there being no dock space available at the moment, and soon the customs and immigration officials came out in a launch and boarded our little ship. A couple of Britishers were in charge, aided by three or four Burmese civil servants. By the time they had finished processing all the paper work involved it was nearly noon, but finally we were put aboard a couple of launches and taken ashore. We couldn't know whether or not Rangoon was ready for us, of course, but we were damned sure ready for Rangoon!

Skip Adair and William D. Pawley, the head man of CAMCO, were at the pier to greet us. They took us to the *Strand* hotel nearby, and after a drink or two we had lunch. Most of us also received some pay, the amounts varying according to what we had previously specified would be drawn in cash each month while in the orient. We were paid in Burmese currency which, as in all British colonies, came in a variety of sizes and denominations. The basic unit was the *rupee*, which was worth about 32 cents in American money and made the conversion problem easy; rupees were three-for-a buck.

Skip Adair made one of his brief speeches while we were at lunch in a small private dining room. "Welcome to Rangoon, gents," he said. "You'll be happy to know there's only another 170 miles to go." This was greeted with a collective groan from our travel-weary group, but Skip ignored it and continued. "The rest of the trip will be by train, gents...we've booked first class accommodations on the beautiful *Mandalay Express* as far as

Toungoo, your final destination. The train leaves at four p.m., and everybody will meet here no later than three-thirty so we can all go to the station in a group. Until then, have a look around, do some shopping, whatever you want. Just don't get lost and miss the train!"

After lunch we began to drift out of the Strand in small groups. There were ominous looking clouds overhead, not surprisingly, and both the temperature and humidity were over ninety. Duke Hedman, George McMillan, and I wandered toward what seemed the center of the business district. The population of Rangoon was said to be about four hundred thousand, but it didn't give the impression of being that big a city. The tallest buildings were only four or five stories high, and traffic was negligible; there were more bullock carts than trucks, more horse-drawn *gharries* than antiquated taxis, and only an occasional vintage bus. There were no traffic lights, but in the center of some of the busier intersections uniformed traffic policemen, most of them turbaned Indians, could be seen directing traffic by hand signals while standing on a small, raised platform with a little umbrella-shaped roof overhead. Considering the climate, it was understandable that everything and everyone moved at a very leisurely pace.

The sidewalks were generously splattered with dark red spots that looked suspiciously like dried blood. However, by now we knew that they were caused by the many Burmese who chewed *betel* nut and spit about as often as Reggie Jackson or many other major-league baseball players. We were told that the leaf or nut of the betel palm, when chewed, has a mild narcotic effect similar to that of the cacao plant of South America. We also saw a few Burmese, both men and women, smoking the fat *cheroots* that hadn't changed since Kipling's day.

Most of the native Burmese, regardless of sex, wore colorful ankle-length wraparound cotton skirts, and simple white blouses or sleeveless shirts. Nearly all had jet-black hair and eyes, with fine features and bone structure, though their skin color ranged from brown to black. Most were either barefoot or wore the simple thong-type sandals common to the Far East.

We discovered that many of the shopkeepers and salesmen, even those owned by British merchants, were Indian. They dressed more in the European style, and seemed much more aggressive than the Burmese when it came to doing business. Often they stood in their doorways soliciting casual passersby, and not infrequently came out onto the sidewalk to try to steer customers into their shops, extolling the wondrous bargains to be found inside in their peculiar sing-song manner of speaking.

By this time, of course, we had become accustomed to the varied and mysterious smells of the orient, and Rangoon was similar to Manila and Batavia and Singapore in that regard. It was simply an indescribable blend of odors, ranging from the hot curried dishes of the sidewalk vendors to the horse manure in the streets, with dozens of other more or less subtle fragrances mixed in. Most of the streets were broad and lined with trees, with occasional areas set aside for colorful flower-beds. And, seeming to dominate the city, we could see the huge golden dome of the Shwe Dagon pagoda on the crest of a low hill a mile or two away. It was one of the largest and most revered Buddhist shrines in all Asia; its bell-shaped dome rose high into the air, and was completely covered with untold layers of pure gold leaf applied over many decades by the faithful. There were said to be literally tons of gold there, and at one point I said, "I wonder how much all that gold would be worth in dollars?"

Duke sort of giggled and said, "Buddha only knows, R.T."

Mac shook his head in disgust, saying, "Smart ass!"

We browsed through some of the shops along the way, but didn't buy a great deal. My purchases were limited to a daily diary, about the size of a small book called *"Guide to Burma,"* that I also bought, plus a couple of tins of English *Players* cigarettes, fifty to the tin. Most of the merchandise we saw in the shops was of British origin, and indeed the Crown's influence was seen and felt everywhere. We didn't see many Englishmen around, but were told that at this time of day most of them could be found lingering over lunch at one of their private clubs, or perhaps having "a bit of a nap" at home. Here, as in Singapore, the British residents lived at a very leisurely pace in comparative luxury. Most had spacious, comfortable housing provided by the government, in the case of civil employees of the Crown, or by the many companies engaged in commerce. Native servants could be hired for the equivalent of fifteen or twenty dollars per month, and most British households had at least three or four of them. Food and clothing were plentiful and inexpensive, and considerable time off was allowed for vacations in the highlands of northern Burma during the hottest part of the year, which must surely include the present. Later we learned that much the same sort of thing applied to the British in India and other colonies, and it was easy to see why so many chose to accept employment in the Far East. This far from the action and the struggle going on in Europe, it was hard to believe that England was fighting for her life against Nazi Germany.

The three of us moved back in the direction of the Strand, our steps quickened by the threatening rumble in the dark sky above. We found ourselves sprinting the last couple of blocks as it began to rain again, and by the time we gained shelter there was a downpour in progress with lightning and thunder all around. Most of the others had already returned and were crowded into the little bar stuck off in a corner of the Strand's lobby. Thirty minutes later, when it was time to head for the railway station, the storm had passed and the clouds were beginning to break up.

Bill Reed began to break up, too, as we approached the only train in sight upon reaching the railway station.

"This is the 'beautiful *Mandalay Express*?'" he chuckled. "That goddam Skip Adair has a weird sense of humor, you know that?"

By this time we were all shaking our heads and laughing; from the look of it, our train might easily have been inspired by the *Toonerville Trolley* cartoons. Up front was this little antiquated engine, hissing and puffing, for all the world like something the Union Pacific might have junked at the turn of the century. It looked too small to pull its own weight, let alone the tender and six little box-like wooden cars strung out behind. The tender was stacked high with three-foot lengths of split logs to feed the fire beneath the steam boiler; with no coal and an abundance of forest, Burma Railways had used wood for fuel since the first track was laid, and obviously wasn't about to change.

We were herded toward the last two cars of the train, told that the middle two were for second-class ticket holders, and the first two for those who were traveling third-class. In addition to the fact that our first-class seats were thinly padded and covered with worn and cracked leather instead of being bare wooden benches, there were a couple of other advantages; being that far removed from the engine meant a little less soot and smoke, and first-class passengers were not allowed to carry animals aboard. A number of the natives entering the third-class cars up front were carrying bamboo cages and baskets containing chickens, ducks, small pigs, and no doubt other forms of animal life. The railway cars were of the European style, just like we'd seen in the movies, with compartments designed to hold six passengers and with doors opening directly onto the station platform.

We moved in small groups toward the four empty compartments that had been reserved for us. Greene, Reed, McMillan, Hedman, McGarry and I got into one of the compartments. We stowed the small bags or bundles carried aboard in the overhead racks and settled down. A few minutes later, promptly at 4 p.m., the train jerked to a start and slowly began to pick up speed. Finally, we were indeed on the very last lap of our long journey.

We had been told that we would arrive in Toungoo at 9:30 that night, and for the first time it occurred to us that five and a half hours was rather a long time to cover a mere 170 miles. We soon discovered the reason; while the *Mandalay Express*, as Skip called it, couldn't accurately be called a milk-run, since there was no milk involved, it made frequent stops along the way. Most of the stops were for only ten minutes or so, but were obviously the big event of the day for the villagers of such places as Pegu, Nyaunglebin, Pyu, Kywebwe, and other towns with equally unpronounceable names. The station platforms were invariably crowded and noisy, as if everyone in town had turned out for the occasion, though few people seemed to be either getting on or off the train except to stretch their legs and be jostled by the many vendors hawking their wares at the top of their lungs.

During the brief stop in Pyu—or "Pee-yoo" as Green called it—a Burmese carrying a wicker basket the size of a beach-ball approached McGarry. "Sahib," he said, his lips parted in a red-toothed smile, "I have something most unusual for you, only thirty rupees, sahib."

McGarry stopped, curious. "What you got there, buddy?" he asked.

The Burmese smiled again, saying, "Is most beautiful cobra, sahib...here, I show you!" He started to remove the lid of the basket, but Black Mac was back-pedaling already and screaming, "No, for chrissake get that sumbitch outa here, go away!" The rest of us were doubled up with laughter, but we too beat a hasty retreat into the safety of our compartment. "Jesus," Mac was mumbling, "that's all I need, a goddam pet cobra!"

Our journey took us through the rich, flat bottom-land of the Irrawaddy delta, formed over the centuries by the annual flooding of that great river just to the west. The elevated roadbed of the narrow-guage railway was surrounded on either side by flooded rice paddies as far as the eye could see. There was little change as we entered the broad valley of the Sittang River and headed almost due north for the remainder of the trip. Everywhere we looked were paddies of different sizes and shapes, broken up occasionally by dikes wide enough to accommodate a bullock cart, narrow roadways that led to the many small villages or walled compounds that contained a few thatch-roofed houses surrounded by palm and banana trees. Water buffalo were also to be seen everywhere, often with children no more than six or seven years of age perched happily on their broad backs.

As we went farther north the valley of the Sittang River became progressively narrower, and as darkness came on we could see to either side the dark green of the jungle, the dense rain forest that blanketed the low mountian ranges that defined and paralleled the course of the rivers of Burma. It was not a very encouraging sight to a pilot, no matter how adventuresome he might be; an engine failure over that kind of terrain, with no flat or clear areas in which to attempt a forced-landing, left only one alernative, and it was somewhat less than appealing at best. Bailing out under such circumstances seemed to offer only a very temporary solution to the problem. We were all aware that the jungles of Burma were the natural habitat of tigers and wild elephants in abundance, to say nothing of quite a wide variety of venomous snakes. This wasn't the sort of thing that many of us might dwell on or lose much sleep over, but it was always there in the back of our minds, and in the coming months a few of us would have first-hand experience with just such a problem.

Despite its leisurely pace, our little train chuffed into the station at Toungoo right on time, 9:30 p.m. We all piled out and onto the crowded platform, and immediately our ears were assailed by the sound of a brass band that had been hired to help celebrate our arrival. The musicians, if they could properly be called that, were playing their hearts and lungs out, obviously convinced that volume was everything. There were only three of them, Burmese, dressed in ragged black and red uniforms that looked like something the Salvation Army had cast aside. One was playing a battered cornet, another an equally beat-up trombone, while the third beat the hell out of a bass drum. They were blasting away with their own unique interpretation of *Stars and Stripes Forever*, which must have had John Phillip Sousa doing snap-rolls in his grave. Still, corny as it was, it made us feel good to know that some of the earlier arrivals were glad to welcome us, and a half-dozen of them were on hand for that purpose. There was much back-slapping and hand-shaking, and it was apparent that our welcoming committee had been celebrating our arrival in the station's little bar-restaurant for some time before we got there.

The little brass band was determined to earn its pay, and upon finishing the stirring Sousa march immediately broke into an equally interesting rendition of *There'll Be a Hot Time in the Old Town Tonight*. Somehow amidst all the confusion our baggage was gathered together and put on a tarp-covered truck, and we were herded into Studebaker station-wagons and sedans brought in by our welcoming committee. We were all dirty and exhausted, and anxious to get out to the little airfield that would be our home for the next few weeks, and to bed. We'd been up since shortly after dawn, most had had too many drinks in Rangoon and aboard the train to be in the mood for further celebration, but there was a tremendous feeling of relief in knowing that at long last we had arrived at our destination.

The eight-mile trip to Kyedaw, the name of the small RAF airfield next to the little village of the same name, took only a few minutes. The cars carrying the pilots stopped outside a large thatch-roofed wooden building that turned out to be the pilots' mess. We went inside and were welcomed once more by all the other "old timers" who had been on hand for a month or so, about thirty in all. A bar in the corner was doing a thriving business in dispensing drinks of scotch or gin, and we were supplied immediately. It was a festive occasion, all right, and we newcomers were greeted like long-lost brothers.

Old acquaintences were quickly renewed. Some of our former navy pilots found others they had known at Pensacola or on duty with the fleet, and the ex-Air Corps pilots were going through much the same process. Greene and I were soon talking with three or four pilots whom we recognized from earlier days, particularly Arvid "Oley" Olson, Neil Martin, and Parker Dupuoy who had been in 40-B, our upper class during cadet days. And there was Sandy Sandell, now the Squadron Commander of the AVG's 1st Pursuit Squadron, who had been one of my instructors during advanced training. It developed that Olson was the C.O. of the 3rd Squadron, and he soon informed us that Greene and I, along with Reed, McMillan, Hedman, and Ben Foshee were to be in his squadron. We were all delighted with the news, as by this time we had become good friends and we couldn't have planned things better ourselves.

Skip Adair, who had come up on the train with us, banged on a table with one of his huge fists and shouted for attention. When the noise had subsided, Skip said, "On behalf of Colonel Chennault, I just want to welcome our new arrivals to Kyedaw, the garden spot of Burma." There was an immediate chorus of boos and catcalls from the old-timers, and even Skip was forced to chuckle.

Skip held up a hand for quiet, then said, "The old man's up in China and won't be back for a day or two, but he wanted me to tell you that he's glad you're here and he's looking forward to meeting you the minute he gets back. Meanwhile, you've been told what your squadron assignments are, and you'll be taken care of by your own people. That's it for now...the bar closes in five minutes!"

Olson and the dozen or so other 3rd squadron pilots led the way to the barracks only a hundred yards from the mess hall. It was a long, thatch-roofed wooden structure with a wide veranda that stretched the entire length of the building. The inside was dimly lit by a couple of small light bulbs suspended overhead. Our baggage had been stacked in the wide aisle that separated the two long rows of native-type "charpoys," narrow teak-wood beds with a lattice-work of rope that supported thin straw mattresses. Above each bed, suspended from the rafters, was a wooden frame that held the mosquito netting which had to be dropped and tucked in under the mattress when it was time to retire. Already we had discovered that the place was alive with mosquitos about the size of wasps, and with dispositions to match.

We were told to pick out any of the many beds that obviously were available. Bill Reed and I claimed a couple near the center of the building, and Hedman and Greene took over two more directly across the aisle. We gathered our belongings together, then paid a quick visit to the latrine out back; it was a four-holer that also had a tin trough for a urinal. A few yards away was another small building which we learned was the "bathroom;" unheated rainwater was supplied from a tank atop a ten-foot tower to the four or five sinks and showerheads inside, with bamboo pipes for plumbing.

Back in the barracks, we got ready for bed. Due to the heat and humidity, even during nighttime hours, nearly everyone slept in his underwear, or in nothing at all. We wasted no time in getting into bed, carefully tucking the mosquito netting under the edge of the mattress, and stretching out for what we hoped would be many hours of rest. I did take time, however, to scratch a few lines into the diary I'd bought in Rangoon, having resolved to do this at the end of each day from then on, no matter what.

"Hey, will somebody down there turn off the goddam light?" a voice I didn't recognize shouted from one end of the barracks.

"Bite my ass, Wallace!" another of the old-timers yelled back.

But a moment later the light went out, and within minutes it's doubtful that a herd of wild elephants stampeding down the center aisle could have awakened anyone within the 3rd squadron pilots' barracks in the garden spot of Burma.

***

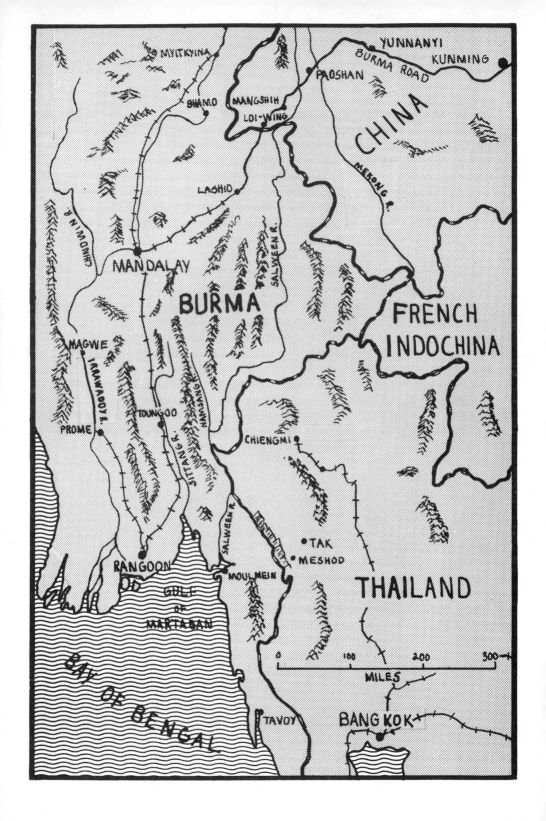

COLLINS
INDIAN
ROYAL DIARY

FOR

1941

**Containing Postal Information for India, Burma,
Ceylon and Malaya**

No. 53.   Quarter bound, paper sides, stiff
No. 52.   Full cloth, stiff, lettered black
No. 52½ Quarter bound, cloth sides, stiff

LONDON AND GLASGOW
COLLINS
CLEAR-TYPE PRESS

Manufactured in Great Britain

Well, we pulled in to Rangoon at dawn, and had to wait until 10 a.m. to go ashore. Skip Adair and C. B. Pawley were there to meet us. Went to the Strand Hotel and had lunch there at noon. Also we got paid!

Left Rangoon on the train for Toungoo, known as Point A, where we are to be training for a few weeks.

Arrived Toungoo at 1:30, where a bunch of the boys already here met us with a 3 piece brass band. Ha! Piled in station-wagons & went out to the field, an R.A.F. Base turned over to us for the time being, about 8 miles from town. Found several guys here already whom I knew at Randolph as cadets — Olson, Cook, Wallace, Atkinson, and also Sandell, the C.O. of the 1st Pur. Sqdn., my old Brooks instructor. I was assigned, along with Reed, Greene, MacMillan, Foshee, & Redman, to the 3rd Pursuit Squadron. Olson is C.O.

After a few Beers at the Pilots Mess we went to our Barracks & to Bed.

Tuesday 16
(259-106)

Up at 5:30 a.m. (what an ungodly hour) and over to Breakfast.

After breakfast we all went into Town to buy shorts, shirts, long socks, etc. Also over to the line for a little cockpit time in a P-40, or tomahawk, to be technical.

They tell us we will check out in them tomorrow — happy day.

They are only working mornings here, 6:30 to 12:30, due to the heat in the afternoons — and I mean it's plenty hot.

The mess here looks like it's going to be lousy. It's done by native contractor, as is everything else around here.

We have 16 pilots in our squadron now, counting us, and all live in one barracks. Bunks are hard as hell, and each is equipped with mosquito netting.

Perhaps I should mention here that most references to the Tomahawks that we flew identified them as P-40Bs, and in fact that is the model designation we ourselves used. However, the purists in the aviation fraternity who concern themselves with such things insist that ours more properly should be called P-40Cs. While they had started out as B models, there had been enough changes made in the 100 planes received by the AVG, particularly in fuel cells, communications equipment, and armament, to warrant their being known as "C"s. I tend to go along with the experts for a change,

3rd squadron pilot's barracks at Toungoo

Well, friends, so much for my initial resolve to faithfully write in my new diary each day; that resolution seems to have carried about as much weight as many that I've made on New Year's Eve. The entry for Sept. 16th was to be the last until the 5th of October, but from that date on I *did* stick with it every single day until the AVG was officially disbanded in July of 1942. I don't know why I allowed this lapse to happen, unless it was simply because I had never before kept a diary and hadn't summoned the necessary discipline required of such a project. Which is a nice way of stating the obvious: I was being lazy.

A lot happened during that gap of more than two weeks, and for that matter a lot had happened even before our little group from the Bloom reached Burma. So perhaps this is a good place for a very sketchy account of what had taken place before our arrival, as well as a bit of background concerning some of the people, facilities, and living conditions which made up the overall picture in late September.

The first contingent of AVG personnel, all ground crewmen, had arrived in Rangoon by ship about the middle of July. This little group, only twenty-five or thirty in number, was made up primarily of aircraft and engine mechanics and armorers. Some of them stayed in Rangoon to assist in the assembly of the P-40s, while the rest went on up to Toungoo to help get things organized at the little airfield.

The second, and largest group had reached Rangoon in mid-August aboard the *Jaegersfontein*, a sister ship of the Bloom. This bunch consisted of about thirty pilots and nearly a hundred ground personnel; they proceeded to Toungoo and settled into quarters readied for them at Kyedaw. Thus, by the time we arrived a month later, the nucleus of the three squadrons had been formed, each with about ten pilots and perhaps thirty-five ground crewmen, and each with a handful of planes.

Flying activity got under way in late August, although it was hampered a great deal by the seemingly ever-present rains. Between storms the pilots got in as much flying time as possible, becoming familiar with the flight characteristics of the P-40, practicing formation flying, and sharpening their skills in mock combat, one-on-one dogfights.

The first fatality of the AVG occurred on September 8th, a week before our arrival. Two former navy pilots of the 2nd squadron, John D. Armstrong of Hutchinson, Kansas, and Gil Bright from Reading, Pennsylvania, had a mid-air collision while engaged in a dogfight high above the field. Bright managed to bail out and parachuted to safety, but Armstrong was not so fortunate and died in the crash of his plane. He was buried in the little RAF Airmen's Cemetery in Toungoo, with our chaplain, Paul Frillman, conducting the service.

There had been a number of other accidents as well, with no serious injuries, resulting in considerable damage to the planes involved. Most of these were landing accidents, and nearly all attributable to pilot error due to faulty technique or poor judgment, sometimes both. Many of the former navy pilots, used to hitting a carrier deck with the nose high and in a stalled condition, learned the hard way that this was definitely not the recommended procedure for the P-40; at best it often resulted in a ground-loop and dragging a wing-tip, and at worst it meant wiping out the landing gear and sliding to a stop on the plane's belly, prop blades bent back like a pretzel and extensive damage to the fuselage. Others landed too long on the 4,000-foot macadam strip and, being unable to stop in time, nosed up due to hitting the brakes too hard, or were forced to deliberately ground-loop the plane. Let me hasten to add that some of the ex-Air Corps pilots, including a few with previous P-40 experience, were equally guilty in putting a number of our limited supply of aircraft out of commission, some of them permanently.

On the morning of September 17 I couldn't wait to finish my breakfast and get on over to the flight line. This was the day I'd been told I would be checking out in the P-40, weather permitting, and as if by divine providence the sun was shining.

Neil Martin, of Texarkana, Arkansas, gave me a final cockpit check.

I'd already read the pilot's manual and spent some time in the cockpit, becoming familiar with the location of the many switches, valves, levers, and instruments, and was impatient to get going after a two and a half months layoff. Neil was another of my upperclassmen as a cadet, and was flying P-40s in a pursuit squadron at Mitchell Field, Long Island, when a AVG recruiter visited the base. Blonde, slender, and a fine athlete, Martin was now our 3rd squadron operations officer, and one of the most likable guys in the entire group. Now he squeezed my shoulder and said, "Have fun, R.T., there's nothing to it," then jumped down from the wing.

The Allison, sometimes cantankerous to start, fired up immediately and soon I was taxiing out to the end of the narrow runway. There was nobody in the little wooden control tower, so after stopping just long enough to check the mags I closed the canopy and turned onto the runway, got lined up, and firmly eased the throttle forward. That big prop began to bite into the humid air as eleven hundred horsepower thundered a message I'd never heard before. We began to accelerate rapidly, manifold pressure guage showing 48 inches, 3,000 rpm on the tachometer, now holding lots of right rudder to counteract the powerful torque that was trying to pull us off to the left, forward pressure on the stick to get the tail up. Now there was a clear view over the nose of the runway ahead and in a matter of seconds the airspeed indicator was showing 100 mph; a little back pressure on the stick and we broke free of the runway and started to climb. A quick upward tug on the landing-gear lever, and a moment later a glance at the position indicator on instrument panel showed that the wheels were retracting. More back pressure on the stick, nose pointed skyward; reach down quickly and crank in a little nose-up elevator trim; now back off on the throttle and prop-pitch control until the proper manifold pressure and rpm for climb showed on the guages. A quick glance at the other instruments; airspeed now up to 150, rate of climb indicator at about 3,000 feet per minute, altimeter needle winding steadily clockwise, oil and coolant temperatures in the green, and up ahead of that long nose a big patch of blue sky showing through broken clouds.

At this point I was grinning and chuckling to myself like a kid with a beautiful new toy, and feeling terribly self-satisfied. Somehow I'd managed to beat the system and the eggheads in the pentagon with their silly rules. Granted, the P-40's cockpit was a pretty tight squeeze for my six-feet four, even with rudder pedals fully extended and seat lowered as far as possible, but it really wasn't as bad as I'd expected and certainly nothing that, with a little luck, I couldn't live with.

I'd been told to fly around the local area for an hour, getting accustomed to the feel of the airplane, so I climbed on up to about 8,000 feet while making a series of turns. The controls were not quite as sensitive as I'd expected, in fact they felt very much like those of the BT-9. I spent the next few minutes doing both power-on and power-off stalls, found plenty of warning in either case before the full stall occurred, and recovery was swift and easy when the nose was dropped and power re-applied. I did a couple of three-turn spins, and again the recovery procedure and response was much like the BT-9. And finally, of course, I began to really wring the old girl out, the stuff I'd been itching to do for all these weeks; slow-rolls, snap-rolls, loops, and Immelmanns, so much easier and so much more fun with all that power up front. About the only real surprise, however, was the tremendous speed that could be picked up in a dive in a matter of mere seconds; this thing dove like the proverbial streamlined brick, a characteristic for which all of us were to be extremely thankful in future months.

If you're partial to puns, you'll forgive me for saying that it was a case of love at first flight; that near-new P-40—or *Tomahawk*, as the British had dubbed it—not only felt good, it even smelled good with that rich aroma found only in certain airplanes, a not-too-subtle mixture of hot metal, exhaust gases, and paint that most pilots preferred to Chanel No. 5. I stretched the time to an hour and a quarter, and even then was reluctant to land.

The landing itself was uneventful, though the recommeded procedure was unlike that for the BT-9 and most other airplanes of the time. Attempting a three-point landing with the P-40 was asking for trouble, as some of the ex-navy pilots learned to their chagrin; with the tail down and nose high, engine throttled back, there was insufficient airflow to provide good rudder control, a sure invitation to a ground-loop. The cure for the problem was to land in an attitude that more nearly resembled level flight, touching down with the main wheels only at about 90 mph, and holding the tail up with forward stick pressure until the speed had slowed considerably, after which directional control could be maintained by judicial use of the brakes. Even so, there were to be ground-loops galore in the next few weeks, even a few on takeoff!

As I taxied back to the parking area I saw Greene taxiing toward the end of the runway. He also checked out uneventfully, was every bit as enthused about the airplane as I was, and like me couldn't wait for another flight the next day. Unfortunately, our flying activity was severely limited during the next few days due to the weather. We managed to get in a few flights between storms, but it was obvious that not much could be accomplished until the rainy season came to an end, supposedly about the 1st of October, still a couple of weeks away. And even when we did fly it was often hazardous; visibility was seldom good, we had no maps or navigational aids, and the mountains and jungle stretched as far as the eye could see except for the Sittang river valley nearby. Getting lost was real easy, and, to add a bit of spice, we wore Chinese parachutes without survival kits.

It was on the 22nd of September, just a week after we had arrived, that the first pilot from the Bloom "bought the farm." Weatherwise, it was one of those marginal days for flying, meaning lousy. I was in the barracks, writing a letter, while a half-dozen others whiled away the afternoon hours reading or playing cards. McMillan came in from the veranda, having just returned from Operations, and stopped by my bunk, saying, "Have you heard the bad news, R.T.?"

"Sure," I laughed, "they're predicting rain."

"No, seriously," Mac said, "Hammer's been killed."

"Oh hell, no!" I groaned. I hadn't seen much of Maax since we'd arrived; he and Leibolt, once again fast friends, had been assigned to the 1st squadron, along with Matt Kuykendall and Black Mac McGarry.

"What happened?" I asked Mac as others within hearing gathered round.

"Nobody knows for sure," Mac said. "The RAF office got a call from the headman of some village a few miles south of here; he said one of our planes had crashed during a thunderstorm and they'd found the body of the pilot in the wreckage. Hammer's the only one they can't account for over at operations."

Maax Hammer was buried at the Airmen's cemetery in Toungoo the following day. Again our Chaplain, Paul Frillman, conducted the brief ceremony beside the wooden coffin draped with a U.S. flag. Ed Leibolt, who'd been mad enough to commit mayhem a couple of months earlier, took the loss of his buddy harder than anyone, and was not entirely successful in fighting back the tears.

We could only speculate as to the actual cause of the crash, but the most likely theory was that Maax had tried to fly through a thunderstorm instead of around it, and in the severe turbulence usually found within those dark and boiling cumulo-nimbus clouds—capable of tossing a P-40 around like a leaf—became disoriented and unable to control his plane. A P-40 was not the easiest thing to fly on instruments even under ideal conditions, and often the updrafts and downdrafts encountered in most thunderstorms could be unbelievably violent. He could have wound up in a spin, or in a vertical dive from which recovery was impossible

Since our arrival, each of the three squadrons now had about fifteen pilots and perhaps thirty-five or forty ground crewmen. There was a single barracks to house the pilots of each squadron, and a couple more for its ground personnel. Most of the 1st and 3rd squadron pilots had come from the Air Corps, while nearly all of those in the 2nd squadron were ex-navy pilots. Future arrivals were assigned in much the same way, although eventually the 3rd squadron wound up with about a dozen former navy or Marine Corps pilots.

The 1st squadron was commanded by Robert "Sandy" Sandell, who had been one of my instructors in advanced flight training at Brooks Field, Texas. He was three or four years older than most of us, small, dark, and intense. I knew from first-hand experience that Sandy was an excellent pilot, but I also knew that he'd never win any popularity contest. He was a bit too much of a disciplinarian to suit a bunch of guys such as the AVG was composed of, and often rubbed people the wrong way. Sandell's deputy, or vice squadron commander, was just the opposite. This was Robert H. Neale, former navy pilot, who was as likable as they come and a born leader.

The 2nd squadron was commanded by Jack Newkirk, a personable ex-navy fighter pilot, and Tex Hill was appointed his deputy shortly after we arrived. Ed Rector, Bert Christman, Ed Goyette, and Frank Schiel were also assigned to the 2nd.

As mentioned earlier, Oley Olson, a Chicagoan, was our 3rd squadron commander. He had been in our upper class as cadets, and Greene and I remembered him as a fun-loving guy with a great sense of humor. His deputy was Parker Dupouy, also in our upper class, from Seekonk, Massachusetts. Parker was a quiet, very capable guy who was well liked by all. Of the six key squadron leaders named above, only Olson and Dupouy were to remain in their respective positions throughout the life of the AVG.

Each of the squadrons had a small office in the operations building near the flight line, which also had a classroom where lectures were held. There was a good-sized hangar where major maintenance or repair could be performed on half a dozen planes while protected from the weather. Otherwise our crew-chiefs and armorers did their work outside, regardless of the weather conditions. Theirs was not an enviable task, but they were tough and seemed to thrive on adversity, though they had plenty to complain about and didn't hesitate to sound off frequently. Strangely enough, in later months when things were *really* rough, they worked their tails off day and night with fewer complaints than before. Crew-chiefs and armorers and other technicians alike, they were extremely proud of their ability to "keep 'em flying," and of the individual pilots who flew "their" planes. A good thing, too, for without them we'd have been grounded in no time; I doubt if one pilot in ten was capable of properly loading a machine-gun, or even changing a set of spark plugs without help, a fact which was occasionally pointed out to us with delight by those who could and did. Here again, the absence of "rank" as it existed in the army or navy permitted a much more democratic atmosphere, which in the case of our little group worked very well and was seldom abused. Actually, I think it tended to keep us on our toes; I well remember a couple of occasions when I'd made a bad landing, maybe bounced two or three times and come close to ground-looping, only to be greeted by my crew-chief after I'd parked with some sarcastic comment like, "Beautiful job, R.T. — you think you're ever going to get the hang of landing one of these things?" Imagine something like that happening in the Air Corps or on the deck of a carrier!

For those of us who had arrived on the 15th of September, our first glimpse of Claire Lee Chennault was some three or four days later. He came flying in aboard the little twin-engined Beechcraft that had been provided for his use by the Chinese government, and that evening had dinner at the pilots' mess. He made a brief welcoming speech for our benefit, and later we all met him in person.

Much has been written about Chennault's appearance, which seemed to invite cliche's such as "face chiseled from granite," etc., many of them quite appropriate. A man now fifty-one, he was dark, with black hair and flashing brown eyes, short of stature but wiry and tough as nails. (See what I mean about the cliche's?) His face was indeed leathery, pockmarked and deeply lined, weatherbeaten. Winston Churchill, in his inimitable way, summed it up nicely after meeting Chennault at a high-level conference many months later when he whispered to an aide, "Thank God that man's on our side!"

He was not a man to waste words, and his manner was rather gruff but not unpleasant. He spoke in a low voice, with a Louisiana cajun-country drawl that took a bit of getting used to before being completely understood. He was a physically active man, loved to hunt and fish, and often took part in our softball games late in the afternoon. He would play cribbage by the hour when possible, hated losing and seldom did. He drank very little, and had only one bad habit that I know of; he was a chain-smoker, about three packs of cigarettes per day up to the time of his death in 1958. In case you may be wondering if he died of lung cancer, the answer is Yes!

Except for occasional references to "the Old Man" when he was not within hearing, Chennault was usually called "the Colonel," the title that had been conferred on him by the Chinese. Thus, unless otherwise indicated, any future mention of the Colonel refers to him.

Chennault's chief aides were Skip Adair and Harvey Greenlaw. Skip was in charge of supply and transportation for the group, while Greenlaw, an old China hand and former Air Corps type, was the old man's executive officer who doubled in Operations. They and a small staff of administrative personnel had offices in a small building on the base. Harvey Greenlaw was about Chennault's age, a big, jolly character who was married to a White Russian woman several years his junior whom he'd met in Shanghai or some such place. Olga Greenlaw was enough to turn the head of any red-blooded young man whose genes were properly distributed; she was a very attractive female of about thirty, bearing a resemblance to Paulette Goddard, only with a better figure. In future months there was to be considerable gossip concerning Olga and a couple of our more romantic types, but at the moment she and Harvey lived in a rented house in Toungoo and we didn't see much of either of them. Olga was put on the payroll later on and charged with keeping the official diary of the AVG activities.

Another staff member was a little be-spectacled guy named Joseph Alsop, said to be a distant relative of president Roosevelt. Joe was about thirty, and assisted Skip Adair as a supply officer, particularly in the difficult job of procuring spare parts for the planes. Although his background was as a writer, Joe had met Chennault in Washington, had been deeply impressed by the man and the cause, and volunteered to help in any way possible. With his good connections in Washington and other qualifications, Chennault gladly took him aboard. Years later, Joe and his brother Stewart Alsop became famous as a team of Washington political columnists.

In addition to those already mentioned, there were a number of other buildings scattered around the little base meant to accomodate other personnel and the various functions of a para-military group such as ours. One of the most important of these was the dispensary, a building with a couple of doctor's offices or examining rooms, plus a small infirmary containing five or six beds. The medical staff was headed by Thomas Gentry, aided by flight surgeons Sam Prevo and Lewis Richards, and dentist Everett Bruce, all with previous military experience in their respective fields. Equally important were our three nurses, two of whom were attractive and dedicated females; Jo B. Stewart and Emma Jane "Red" Foster. Bob Gallagher, a very capable male nurse, later went on to become a fine doctor.

Paul Frillman, our Chaplain, was a helluva guy. Stocky and blonde, he was an ordained Lutheran minister from Minnesota, not much older than most of the pilots. He had spent a couple of years in China as a missionary, learned to speak Chinese fluently, knew their customs, and could act as an interpreter when necessary. Frillman conducted services every Sunday in a little makeshift chapel for a less than overwhelming congregation, but he was liked by everyone. There was to be a rather strange twist to his career, however; by the time the AVG was disbanded it was apparent that he had given up on converting this wild bunch to his ways, and instead we converted him to *ours*.

I don't quite know how this came about, whether it was being so much closer to us day after day than most ministers are to their flock, or having to conduct funerals for so many who had become good friends, or what. It was a gradual thing, of course, but in time an outsider might have guessed that our "Padre" was another pilot or mechanic rather than a chaplain, as occasionally some mild profanity began to creep into his conversation, and often in the evening he would join others at the bar for a few highballs and singing ribald songs. In any event, when the AVG was disbanded he accepted a commission in the Air Corps and stayed on as highly competent Intelligence officer. After the war ended he returned to civilian life, this time not as a preacher but as a successful businessman. Like I said, Paul Frillman was a helluva guy.

The RAF had a small contingent there at Kyedaw, mainly to keep an eye on their property and to supervise what might laughingly be called "base security." They had a platoon of Gurkha troops, tiny but tough soldiers from the Himalayan province of Nepal in northern India, who guarded the entrances to the field night and day. The problem was that they knew only about a half-dozen words of English. Sometimes at night when three or four of us approached the main gate, usually after an evening in Toungoo, the procedure could be hilarious; the little Gurkha, rifle at the ready, would stand in the middle of the road and in a strong voice issue the challenge, *"Halt! Who goes there?"* And as often as not one of our clowns would yell back, "Japanese spy!" With which the little Gurkha would lower his rifle and sing out cheerily, *"Poss, Jopponese spy!"* and we would enter the base, laughing and leaving the poor sentry wondering what the hell was so funny.

By the end of September we probably had about 40 P-40s on hand in various states of repair. The rest were in huge crates awaiting assembly in Rangoon under the supervision of a couple of Curtiss-Wright technicians, after which each plane was given a test hop by Byron Glover, a Curtiss test-pilot. Once Glover had put his stamp of approval on the plane by signing off on the Form 1, the airplane's flight log, operations at Kyedaw would be notified and one of our pilots would be sent down by train to ferry it back. Often there would be a couple ready at the same time, as the assembly operation in Rangoon was now cranking out four or five per week. These ferry trips were highly coveted, of course, for it usually meant an opportunity to sample the night-life of Rangoon, maybe even have a steak dinner, before having to return. The center of activity was a place called the *Silver Grill*, a night club that served good food as well as drinks, had a little band that played for dancing, and lots of beautiful Anglo-Burmese and Anglo-Indian girls who seemed to prefer Americans to Britishers. Since we much preferred *them* to Britishers, things often worked out very well indeed.

Toungoo was a city of some 25,000 Burmese with a small colony of Britishers, mostly minor government officials or businessmen engaged in the harvesting of teak logs from the jungle forests. The heavy labor on the teak plantations, moving the huge logs to the rivers, was performed by elephants that had been captured, domesticated, and trained for the job. Teak trees grew at random throughout the area, but the rugged terrain and thick jungle made it impossible to use tractors or trucks for work that the elephants seemed to accomplish with ease. There were other British commercial interests in Toungoo such as various minerals, precious gems, and rice, but the city had little to offer by way of recreation.

Transportation for the group consisted of a half-dozen Studebaker sedans and station wagons, and a few small trucks. Nearly all of us bought bicycles on our first trip into Toungoo, lightweight British jobs with hand-brakes. Occasionally we would ride them into Toungoo, a distance of seven or eight miles, but mostly they were used just to get around the base. On our trips to Toungoo most of us visited one of several tailor shops to order khaki shirts, shorts and bush-jackets, and had ankle-high mosquito boots made by a local bootmaker. While we had no official uniform, and wore no insignia of rank, these items were inexpensive and reasonably comfortable, and became sort of the unofficial uniform of the day.

We also discovered that the heat and humidity were slightly more bearable without a mop of hair, so most of us got crew-cuts from one of the Burmese barbers who moved from one barracks to another. It was also a time for experimenting with mustaches, and a few even went so far as to grow beards. I succumbed to the temptation of a mustache, and kept it thoughout the war and for a few years thereafter. I doubt if it enhanced my appearance any, but I was sure it couldn't hurt it much, and it was something to do.

The climate, of course, was something none of us had ever experienced before, and it took its toll on both health and morale. The constant heat and humidity were enervating, to say the least, and coupled with the abundance of rain led to frequent summer colds and sinus problems. Malaria and dengue fever began to crop up among a few of the more unfortunate; we learned that we were in the middle of one of the worst areas in the world for those two mosquito-borne diseases. Dysentery and diarrhea were a couple of other less than charming illnesses that beset most of us with embarrassing frequency. Of course, we were assured that once the rainy season ended things would be much better, and indeed they were. But it seemed the dry season would never come as the rains continued well into October.

Perhaps the biggest gripe of all was the chow provided at the mess halls. The food was bought, prepared, and served by a Burmese company run by a man named Yusef under contract to CAMCO. Obviously there were limitations as to what could be obtained that might suit Americans, but even so Yusef had some pretty weird ideas. Beef was not available in Burma, but Yusef insisted that boiled water-buffalo tasted just as good. It didn't! We couldn't quite stomach buffalo milk either; the only way it resembled cow's milk was that it was white. Vegetables, such as they were, had to be boiled, there was no such thing as a fresh green salad, the bread was coarse, often stale and moldy, and... well, you get the idea. Sometimes I'd look at my half-finished plate and think back to the days when I was a kid; I wasn't allowed to leave the table until every scrap had been cleaned up, my parents shaming me by saying something like, "Remember the starving Armenians." I could never quite figure out how my eating was going to help *them* in the slightest, but I dutifully ate whatever I'd wanted to leave.

Now, in Burma, I often doubted that even the starving Armenians would have been game enough to eat such leftovers.

As you have gathered, morale was at a pretty low ebb and it would get worse as time went on. Conditions at Toungoo were a far cry from the "summer camp" that many seemed to have expected. By the end of September at least a half-dozen pilots, including a couple from the 3rd squadron, had quit in disgust and left for Rangoon, there to buy passage back to the States aboard some ship passing through. These were the chronic bitchers and moaners, a few of whom can be found in any organization, and the rest of us were glad to see them go. There would be still more in the future, and being civilians there was no way they could be forced to stay; the contracts we had signed were mere scraps of paper in that respect. Chennault, of course, wanted no part of them anyway, saying that it was best to weed out the malcontents and cry-babies before we got down to the serious business of fighting the Japs.

And so, for whatever their reasons, before the year was out a dozen pilots and half that many ground crewmen were to turn tail and return to the safety and comfort of the USA. Still another ten pilots and nearly forty others either resigned or were discharged as undesirables during the months following the Japanese attack on Pearl Harbor. Thus approximately 25 percent of the entire group who signed up originally failed to live up to their part of the bargain, and while they were in fact civilians, all were given the military equivalent of a dishonorable discharge. In fairness, however, I should point out that many of them returned to active military service upon their return to the States, fought and sometimes died, and a few had distinguished careers indeed. Not the least of these was my friend Greg "Pappy" Boyington, who was something of a misfit in the AVG but went on to become the outstanding Marine air ace before being shot down and taken prisoner in the South Pacific.

To complete the cast of characters that made up the 3rd squadron pilots roster following our arrival on Sept. 15, in addition to Olson, Dupouy, and Martin were former P-40 pilots Bob Brouk, Lacy Mangleburg, and Fred Hodges. The pair who quit and left for home late in September were Elmer Cook and S.H. Wallace. Three more, Estes Swindle, R.H. Walroth, and Albert Criz, all with P-40 time, decided they'd had enough a few weeks later and also pulled out, Criz just a couple of days before Pearl Harbor. They would be replaced in time by others more dedicated and responsible, but many of the late arrivals were terribly inexperienced and had very little time to get trained for the combat that was imminent. No matter; those who stuck it out, now and later, were great guys, every last one of them.

So much for background; it's high time to get on with events as they happened, so let's see what I wrote down on October 5th as I resumed the task of keeping a diary. And rest easy, friends, future interruptions will be much more brief.

***

OCTOBER 1941

17th after
Trinity

Sunday 5 ☺

(278-87)

Summer Time ends
(subject to alteration)

Slept late this morning —
that is until 8:30 anyway.
Spent the day in reading,
listening to the phonograph,
and just idling away the hours.
Rained plenty hard this p. m.
again. — And we thought the
rainy season was over.
Tonite ends the Yusef regime,
so maybe we'll get some decent
food from tomorrow on. —
I hope!
Early to bed on account of
it's up at 5:30 in the mornin'.

Instrument panel of a P-40.

Monday 6
(279-86)

Up and at em at 5:30 a.m. to start another week.

3 hours of tactical formation — plenty for one morning too.

We are having one helluv a time with in-place turns. Ships all over the place every time.

Had a pretty good string and some nice slow rolls & loops in string.

My Auto. prop. control went haywire on the last hop on takeoff and I flew formation on manual. Some fun!

Good ol' Ginger Rogers was with us this evening at the pitcher show. "Bachelor Mother" & pretty good altho I'd seen it only a year or so ago.

The P-40 was equipped with a Curtiss-Wright 3-bladed constant-speed propeller, Changes in pitch were actuated by an electric motor in the hub, unlike the more common hydraulically-actuated system of the Hamilton-Standard props. Normal operation was in the Automatic mode which maintained a constant engine RPM once the desired setting of the prop control lever next to the throttle had been established. Thus the engine speed remained the same regardless of changes in the throttle setting or whether the plane was diving or climbing. Occasionally, however, this automatic feature would malfunction, forcing the pilot to switch to the manual mode and make necessary adjustments repeatedly of prop-pitch lever as well as throttle. This made for a very busy time when frequent changes in attitude and speed occurred.

Tuesday 7
(280-85)

Flew 2 hours of formation tactics in the morning.

Pete Atkinson noseup up taxiing.

After lunch slept + read until 4:30 at which time we had a soft-ball game.

Paul and I got word to go to Rangoon by train tonite to bring back two new Tomahawks.

We left Toungoo at 9:30 p.m., with Rushton, played poker till midnite, and went to Bed. The damn train stopped at every town and the jabbering natives kept us from sleeping all nite.

P.S. I almost forgot. Schiel got in one of those "nasty" inverted spins at 8,000 ft. in a good dogfight with Shilling. Bailed out at 4,000 + landed in a swamp — OK. Shook him up quite a bit. Plane completely buried. Natives held out for 30 rupees to row him to dry land. Ha!

Inverted spins were not common, but when they did occur the P-40 tended to flatten out and flight controls were ineffective. Without a lot of altitude to play with, a pilot was wise to hit the silk before it was too late.

Wednesday 8

Got to Rangoon about 8 this a.m.,
had breakfast at the station, and
then went into town.

Went shoping and then reported in at
the Intercontinent offices. Saw
the Pawleys and Col. Chennault.
Went out to the field, got in our
ships and took off at 12: noon for toungo
We had no maps & were told to fly the
R.R. north. We did, and turned back
after about 35 min. due to weather.
Took off again at 3: p.m. and started
up the tracks again. Flew for 1 hour and
10 min. and ran out of railroad. No toungoo!
Sooo, we came back to Rangoon again
and landed in a blinding rain.
Found out then that there were two R.R.'s
north & we had taken the wrong one - an
open switch, so it were. Col. Chennault
took us to town. Stayed at Mints Mansions
Went to dinner & partying with Keller,
Cruikshank, & Kennedy - some of the boys
working at that end. Had a good time
far into the night.

Thursday 9
(282-83)

Got up and went out to the field after breakfast. Met Glover, the Curtiss test pilot. All the guys talking about our formation slow rolls of the day before. I hope the good Col. doesn't hear of it.

We took off at 11:00 a.m. for Toungoo for the third time! Anyway, we got on the right railroad this time. Up the valley all the way, nothing but rice paddies — some change from the dense jungles we flew over yesterday. Landed at 11:40, and got quite a ragging from the gang. Slept & read again this afternoon. It's about dinner time now so enough of this.

In our attempts to reach Toungoo the day before, we ran out of railroad at Prome. At that point we were only about 70 miles due west of Toungoo, but without a map to show us that, and the weather forcing us down to low altitude, there was nothing to do but return to Rangoon.

Friday 10
(283-82)

Went over to the 6:30 lecture and heard a talk by Wing Commander Darley who has seen a lot of action with the R.A.F. in England. He gave a very interesting talk, with some good pointers for us which may be of use soon now. No flying at all today as we are giving the men a chance to do some much-needed maintenance on the ships.

Some of the boys went to Rangoon last night for the week-end. The next bunch of guys is supposed to get here tonite. I understand we are getting 3 new pilots in our squadron — all marines — out of this batch.

This may be as good a time as any, since there's some space available, to do a bit of name-dropping that might be of interest to trivia buffs and help to avoid confusion later on. Now, admittedly the name Robert Smith is about as common as they come, but it still came as quite a surprise when I discovered there were *four* of us in the AVG. There was Robert H. Smith, a great little guy and fine pilot in the 1st squadron whose nickname was "Snuffy." Another was Robert A. Smith, sometimes called "Big Bob," a husky six-footer who was a crew-chief in the 3rd squadron. And there was Robert M. Smith, a quiet, capable radio/communications technician. I was the last of this strange quartet to arrive.

Saturday 11
(284-81)

Lecture this morning by the Col. on pursuit tactics etc.

No flying again today — a continuance of maintenance.

Slept + read most of the day, there being nothing else to do.

Went into town after dinner and met the 9 o'clock train on which the new bunch came up from Rangoon.

Brought our 3 marines out and got them settled. Seem to be very nice fellows.

They will check off in the P-40's tomorrow I guess — or rather monday.

Another load of mail in, but still no letter for me.

I can't understand why in hell I don't get a letter once in a while.

Our three former Marine Corps pilots turned out to be Chuck Older of Los Angeles, Tom Haywood from St. Paul, Minnesota, and Ken Jernstedt of Yam Hill, Oregon. Older and Haywood were both short, Older with dark hair while Haywood was blonde. Jernstedt was a six-footer, also dark. My first impression that they seemed to be "very nice fellows" was absolutely correct, all three being wecome additions to the 3rd squadron and well-liked from the beginning.

Here it is Sunday — a day of rest — Ha! Another day of reading + sleeping.

Tis now 4: p.m. and raining slightly.

Boy, what I'd give for a Hamburger + a malt!

Tomorrow we go back to work in earnest. Mostly individual combat and 6 ship attacks on target ships I understand.

Guess I'd better start addressing a few Xmas cards now, as the time is drawing near.

Anyway, all's quiet in camp, altho the natives in town are still raising hell in celebration of the end of the rainy season. Ha, again!

I wish to hell I'd get a letter one of these days. Even a bill would be better than nothing.

So far I haven't recieved one letter since I got to Toungoo!

The natives were indeed premature with their annual celebration of the end of the summer monsoon, although ordinarily the rainy season was over early in October. This didn't seem to matter to the two or three hundred Burmese who lived in the little village at the edge of the airfield, and each night they would sing and dance and beat the hell out of their drums until well past midnight. This did nothing to endear them to us when it came time to get to sleep, but then they probably wondered why *we* weren't entering into the spirit of things. And so they carried on with their ancient custom, celebrating the coming of the dry season during which time the flooded paddies, solid green with waist-high rice, would dry out and the abundant crop could ripen and be harvested. This, after all, was what they had worked so hard for, and was the basic food upon which their lives depended.

Those of us who had arrived on the 15th of September had been here four weeks now, and it had rained an inch or two nearly every day. It was impossible to schedule flying activity with any degree of certainty; we simply flew when it was at all possible, and even then conditions were hazardous. Morale, not surprisingly, was deteriorating with each passing day. The rain and humidity and heat simply drained us of energy, clothing was always damp and mildewed, and the change in operation of the mess halls had resulted in very little improvement in the quality of the food. As a result, most of us had lost weight, and very few were overweight to begin with. And then there were the insects; swarms of mosquitoes, battalions of beetles, moths the size of sparrows, and occasionally the sinister scorpion nesting for the night in a boot or pantleg. With unscreened window-openings, bamboo shutters always open to allow whatever circulation was possible, the nights turned into nightmares. Even the ritual of simply going to bed was a challenge, trying to make sure all the insects were on the outside before quickly tucking the bottom of the mosquito net under the edges of the thin straw mattress.

Recreational activities were practically non-existent. There was little to do in Toungoo, and getting there and back was difficult. Movies, always several years old, were shown two or three times per week after dinner in the mess hall, but the 16mm projector broke down frequently, and the sound was often scratchy and out of sync with the action. The bar was open in the evening until ten p.m., and as the days went by was doing more and more business in the dispensing of Scotch whisky, gin and barely cool Australian beer.

By this time our little base at Kyedaw—which had been designated "Point A" for communications purposes—often seemed like a masochist's paradise. More of our people were saying "The hell with this rat race" and quitting, or threatening to do so.

Now, on this dreary Sunday, the rain began to come down a little harder. I put aside my diary and looked over at Bill Reed on the bunk next to mine; he was completely absorbed in trimming his toenails. It was getting along toward that time of day when someone would suggest that a few hands of poker or a crap game might be in order; you could almost set your watch by it.

Down at one end of the barracks the scratchy hand-cranked phonograph was playing the sad refrain of *"I'll never smile again"* for the third consecutive time; perfect for the mood of the day. Across the wide aisle that separated the two long rows of bunks Greene and Hedman were engaged in their ongoing Acey-deucy feud, and as usual arguing.

"Fearless Fred" Hodges, so named because of his unreasonable fear of insects of any kind, came sloshing in from the veranda. He was scowling, his skinny torso dripping wet after what must have been about his ninth trip of the afternoon to the "Four-holer" out back. Fred was one of those currently afflicted with the old "Toungoo Trot."

Reed glanced up from a big toe as Fred went by. "Everything come out okay, Fred?" he asked innocently. Hodges made an obscene gesture with a finger and shuffled on down the aisle, ignoring our laughter.

Lacy Mangleburg got up from his bunk on the other side of Reed's and looked in my direction. "You got anything to read that I haven't seen, R.T.?" he said.

"Sure, Lace," I said, "I've got a best-seller my grandma gave me to bring along. I'm nowhere near through with it yet, but I'll loan it to you."

"Hey, great!" Lacy said. I dug it out of my foot-locker and handed it to him, chuckling as I saw his jaw drop about six inches when he saw the title, *Holy Bible*, stamped in gold on the black leatherette cover.

Mangleburg laughed and handed it back to me. "Thanks just the same," he said, and moved down the aisle. Lacy was from Athens, Georgia, a good-looking and likeable guy who had been in a cadet class that I had instructed at Randolph. He'd had nearly two hundred hours in P-40s before joining the AVG, and was considered by the others to be about the hottest pilot in the squadron

Reed got up from his bunk, streched and yawned noisily, then moved to the open window nearby. He stood there silently for a moment gazing vacantly across the veranda into the sheet of water pouring from the edge of the thatched roof and at the sea of mud beyond. Then he turned to me. "You know, R.T.," he said, "I read an article by some guy who said that Calcutta, India, is the left armpit of Asia. Now, if that's so, what the hell does that make Toungoo?"

"Don't tell me," I laughed, "let me guess...uh, the left testicle?"

"Wrong," Bill grinned, "But you're damned close, pal!"

Monday 13 ☾
(286-79)

Up and to work at the usual time.
Lecture given by Col. Chennault
on Squadron tactics and night
fighter operations.
Two hours of flying today.
Engine cut out and was missing
very badly on first take-off.
Circled the field & landed holding
my breath all the time. Got another
ship and joined the formation.
Second hour I acted as target
ship, representing an enemy bomber
while flight of 6 made gunnery
runs at me.
These babies look plenty mean
coming down at you in a dive,
one after the other.
I am now Asst. Squadron
Operations officer.
About time for dinner now, after
which I shall go see Deanna
Durbin in "It's a date." Ho Hum!
P.S. It's been raining practically all day!

Tuesday 14
(287-78)

Rain, rain & then some rain! It's still going strong after an all day siege.
We didn't fly at all today as it didn't let up for a minute.
Stayed around the Ready Room getting Squadron duties cleared up.
I am coming down with a cold that looks like a honey.
Damn this rain anyway!

My squadron duties as Assistant Operations Officer didn't amount to much. Neil Martin, our Ops officer, and I made out the flight schedules for the following day, and kept records of flying time logged by each of the pilots, etc. Group Operations assigned the new planes arriving from Rangoon to each of the squadrons, at which time the large fuselage numbers were painted on either side just forward of the tail assembly. The 1st squadron was to use numbers 1 thru 33, the 2nd to have No.s 34 through 66, and the 3rd No.s 67 through 99. One of the hundred planes had been dropped in the drink while being unloaded in Rangoon, and except for some spare parts couldn't be salvaged.

When it came time to assign individual planes, by number, to each of the pilots in the 3rd squadron, Martin asked me to do it. I asked Neil if he had any favorite number that he'd like, and he said no. Then he asked me the same question, and I told him I'd like No. 77. He laughed, and said, "You think a pair of sevens'll be lucky, huh?" I agreed that such a thought had occurred to me, but also it was the jersey number that had been worn by a football hero of mine when I was a kid, the *"Galloping Ghost"* himself, Red Grange. Martin laughed again, but told me if that's the number I wanted to help myself. Old 77, as things turned out, was luckier than most and brought me back safely on every occasion that we flew. Let me add that much of the credit must go to my outstanding crew-chief, Jesse R. Crookshanks of Jonesboro, Tennesse. Having him to look after us was the luckiest break of all.

Wednesday 15
(288-77)

Lecture this a.m. by Col. Hoyt, U.S. Air Corps, who is head of the American Military Mission in the Far East. He's been here several days observing our activity. His job is to report on the use of lend-lease equipment + personnel, and progress of same.

Flew two-hours of 6 ship gunnery runs (dry) on target ships. Got in some good passes, but this damned head cold is giving me trouble. My ears stop up in steep dives, and my nose bled twice today in pull-outs etc. Went to the hospital for pills. The new boys all checked out today — uneventfully.

I finally got mail today — 3 letters in fact. My first ones. So now I can write some myself.

The only air mail service was by Pan American's infrequent Clipper flights as far as Manila or Singapore. From there the mail was transported by boat, and letters were usually a couple of months enroute before finally reaching us. Knowing this didn't boost our morale a great deal.

Lecture & discussion on the
Allison engine this a.m.,
conducted by Mr. Lett, Allison
representative.

Flying as per schedule.
I flew one hour, and on
coming down got a terrific
pain in the head, sinuses.
It hit me at about 1500 ft. and
scared me plenty. Eyes watered etc.
Landed & decided that was enough
for today.

Held an 18 plane review this
P.M. in honor of a visit from
the Rt. Hon. Duff Cooper & wife.

Went over to the hospital after
dinner & Doc Richards stuck
Argyrol swabs about 3 inches
up my nose. Some fun but
it helped.

Home & to bed early.

Friday 17
(290-75)

Continuation of discussion on engines this morning.

Reed & Mc Garry left last nite for Rangoon to bring up 2 new ships. They should be in soon.

I didn't fly at all today, as my cold is hanging on still.

No flying except for the new men tomorrow—maintenance day.

Went over to the hospital after lunch where Doc. Richards again swabbed out my nose. I think its getting better now my cold, I mean.

Harvey Greenlaw and Chennault flank a British visitor who is pointing at Olga Greenlaw. Sandell and Olson look on, while I kibitz from my bike at far left.

Saturday 18
(291-74)

Slept late this morning as I
had no duties, and only the new
men flew.

Reed, Mangleburg, + I went over
for late breakfast at 7:30.

Wrote a letter to the Wagners
after breakfast.

Reed + I went to town after
lunch to do some shopping
and fool around a bit.
Doc Richards drove us in.

Some of the boys are going
in tonite to see the natives
dance & put on a play.
They're still celebrating the
end of Rainy season.

Think I'll go to the show
here tonite + to bed early.
My cold is definitely better
now, — hope it's o.k. to fly Mon.

Just a routine diary day.
Nothing of event to record.
Sat around the barracks
most of the day. Addressed a
batch of Xmas cards, & wrote
notes inside the cards.
Still have a bunch to do.
My Cold is almost gone now,
and I plan to fly 3 hours tomorrow.
The R.A.F. is supposed to
send some bombers up on a
couple of missions this week.
We're to intercept them & defend
Toungoo against their attacks.
Should be some fun.

R.A.F. Blenheim bomber

Monday 20 ●
(293-72)

Well, things seem to be picking up a bit around here. Col. Chennault lectured to us this morning, and said we were in a precarious situation here, due to the tension between the U.S. and Japan, and their interests in the far East. Said Japan was massing troops on the Thailand border.

Sooo— it looks very much as if we might be attacked any day. We are arming all the ships now, and start keeping an "alert" crew on duty all during daylight hours. Each squadron to have the duty every 3rd day. Plan to have 12 ships fully armed and ready for battle at a moments notice. If the Japs do come, we probably wont know of it until about the time they get here.

We are supposed to intercept a flight of R.A.F. bombers tomorrow in a practice maneuver.

Tuesday 21

We received word this a.m. that
3 Blenheims had taken off at 9:23
from Rangoon. The 1st Sq. was
on alert today, and we were
the secondary alert. So Sandell
took his gang off at 9:45 to
intercept them. Oley, Martin,
MacMillen, Hedman, Greene, +
myself took off right after they did,
+ we were supposed to stick around
and defend the airdrome here.
The 1st Squadron missed the
bombers completely, never saw them
at all, but we made contact about
8 miles south of the field. Broke
into 2 ship elements and attacked.
I don't think they would have
lasted long had they been Japs.
We go on alert thursday.
I must address some more Xmas
cards now,

Wednesday 22
(295-70)

Another routine day, with a
few exceptions. Merritt lost
an elevator in combat, but
brought the ship in, landed on
the runway at 150 m.p.h., rolled
off the end into a batch of tree stumps
and stuff. - A neat job. - He wasn't hurt.
Had an hour's combat with Greene,
and gave him a good waxing.
The formation as planned for the
last hour fizzled out, so Manbeburg
and I went up for Combat.
And, surprise! - I whipped him
nicely 2 out of 3. He even
admitted it. Hope I can do
as well next time.
Our Squadron goes on alert
tomorrow, and we expect to
have another attack maneuver
with the R.A.F. from Rangoon.

I meant to mention earlier that China Defense Supplies, which had been
the procurement agency that purchased our P-40s, had been unable to buy
military radio sets as regular equipment. Instead they were forced to settle
for small commercial transceivers, the type that you would expect to find in
a light private plane. These radios, not surprisingly, didn't stand up very
well under the rugged conditions encountered in combat, had a very limited
range, and were difficult to maintain.

Thursday 23
(296-69)

Flew target ship one hour, and
then waited for the Bombers to come.
6 men + ships from each sqdn.
went out on 3 flights to intercept
them. Our Squadron, on alert,
was first off. But, the B's came
in and nobody saw them until
they got here. I wasn't on this
mission, + the way it turned out
~~I'm~~ glad I wasn't.
McMillan + I went up for an
hour of combat and I waxed
him good — 6 out of 6 in fact,
+ I had wing guns + he didn't.
Now Manglesburg is screaming
for a rematch, ~~so~~ guess I'll
have to prove to him that
yesterday was no accident. Ha!
Afternoon ~~spent~~ as usual,
sleeping + writing more messages
on Xmas Cards. Have 48
people to send them to.

Friday 24
(297-68)

Only flew one hour this a.m.
Mangleburg & I had another combat,
on equal terms as far as ships go,
and I think I whipped him again,
altho he wanted to settle for a draw.
Got on him good the first pass, and
got the most shots on him the second
pass until about 5 min. had gone by.
He finally got on my tail however,
so claimed that round.

Started on a little party about
4:00 p.m. in preparation for the
big dance tonite. An R.A.F.
benefit dance, with imported
babes from Rangoon.

We're about ready to shove
off now for said dance.

Sat. Last night's party & dance
were quite a success. Everyone
had a big time, but we're feeling
pretty low this morning. Ha!

Saturday 25
(298-67)

I was lying in bed this a.m., about 9:00 o'clock, halfway asleep & half awake. All was quiet, several of the others were still in bed. Then I was brought out of my daze by the most God-awful sound I ever expect to hear. An unearthly screaming roar, going up very suddenly to a high pitch and then a sound like an explosion. Helman & I ran outside but could see nothing. Found out in a few minutes that Pete Atkinson was testing a ship, dove from 10,000 ft. towards the field. Some of the men saw him coming down and at about 800 ft. the tail section came off & the whole ship disintegrated in the air. They estimate he was doing about 600 m.p.h. Pieces fell over an area of several acres. He was found dead still strapped to the seat, but none of the rest of the ship within 100 yds. of him. Crash was about a mile from the barracks. I didn't go look.

Peter W. Atkinson, of Martinsburg, W. Va., was our third fatality. Pete was the Group Engineering officer, an experienced P-40 pilot, and a great guy

Sunday 26
(299-66)

Up at 4:30 a.m. and over to the "Alert"
shack by 5:00. Martin, Manglebury,
Reed, Greene, & McMillen & myself on duty
About 10:00 a.m. a strange silver ship
sighted over field at about 6,000 ft. We all
took a quick look at it and raced for our
ships & took off. Reel's engine cut out
on take-off & he didn't get up. O.K.
The rest of us went tearing off to
the North in the direction of the strange
ship, went into search formation,
but never sighted it again.
Everyone is wondering where it was
from, of course, & whether or not
it was a Jap ship.
We were glad we had the alert
shift, as we were the only ones so far
to get a chance to go after
anything.

We were all convinced that the strange unidentified planes that we were sighting occasionally now were Jap observation planes, probably coming from new bases recently established in neighboring Thailand. I'm not sure just what we'd have done if we had caught up to one of these, since no state of war existed at the time. Of course it would have been fun to at least identify it, if nothing else, and maybe scare the bugger a bit.

Monday 27 ☽
(300-65)

Lecture this a.m. by the Colonel.
No flying at all scheduled for
today, as all ships are being
inspected, especially the tail-
sections and wing roots.
Trying to see if any are loose
and ready to fly off, as that appears
to be what caused Pete to get his.
And Merritts ship lost an elevator
Went back to barracks early this
morning. About noon another
silver ship flew over and
Shilling took off to see if he could
catch it. Lost sight of it but
did see five other strange ships
flying around. Never got close
enough to identify them, as
his oil temperature went way
up & he had to return.
Lots of speculation again, and
I guess our alert duty will
continue. Letter from the folks
today. Happy day! Mom, Dad, & June
all wrote.

Tuesday 28
(301-64)

The old man lectured more on
Jap tactics this a.m.

No flying except engineering hops.
All ships are being inspected
carefully, as the elevator fittings
on both Merritt's & Atkinson's ships
were found to be broken in someplace.
Started boresighting today on the
new range.

Alert duty is to continue and we
have orders to take-off and force
down any ship flying around here
that we see. We still don't know
where the strange ships came from,
but it seems pretty obvious.

Went to town this afternoon with
Merritt & Mangleburg.

Took in the show here after dinner.
"Strike up the Band" was the name.
I had seen it, but enjoyed it again.

Wednesday 29
(302-63)

More lecture on the Japs by the Col.
Still no flying due to inspections.
Went over & watched them bore-sight
Helmons ship after lecture.
We are using a speed of 300 mph
and range of 300 yds. for sighting.
These 6 m.g.'s really pour out a
stream of slugs.
We're still having trouble getting
a good arrangement of the optical
sights.
Rumor has it that we will move
up North within a couple of weeks
We're to send up our excess
baggage Monday.
Another new bunch of men due
in tonite. Ten navy pilots and
18 men. We are to get 3 pilots
for our Sqdn.
I must go in to meet the train
to see if my trunk is coming
on this one.

Our three new pilots, all former navy types, were Henry "Hank" Gilbert from Lovell, Wyoming; Robert J. Raine of San Francisco, and Edwin S. Conant of San Diego. Gilbert, just twenty-one and fresh out of flying school, was the youngest pilot in the entire AVG.

Thursday 30
(303-62)

Met the train last night. My
trunk came + am I glad!?

All my woolen uniforms etc. in it.

No lecture this morning.
Went to the range + watched some
more bore-sighting.

Gen. Archibald Wavell dropped
in on a C.N.A.C. transport about noon.
We put on an 18 ship review for him,
but I wasn't in it! I had already
come back to barracks.

Slept thru lunch, but got up
a little later + wrote the folks.

Quite a little excitement in the
landings this a.m.

Sandell started to ground-loop,
drug the left wing, gunned it and
took off again... Made it OK.

Then Moss came in and a tire blew
out, but he kept it straight + no damage.
Sawyer also blew a tire + ground-
looped with little damage.

Some thrills for Archie. Ha!

Friday 31
(304-61)

Went to the show last night.
Got up + went to the line after
breakfast. Our three new Navy
men checked out in the 40's this a.m.
And how they did check out!
We gave them cockpit checks + then
sent them up.

Gilbert made it OK. Then
Conant came in, levelled off at
about 25 ft., stalled and dropped
in. Bounced up, collapsed the
landing gear, came down on one wing
and the belly and turned around
180° on the runway. He wasn't hurt
but the ship was a complete washout.

Mc Millan took off and got a
wing clipped off 3 ft. by Hebold's ship
which was sitting at the edge of runway
Prop. on L.'s ship clipped it right off.
Mac went on up, felt it out, and
brought it in plenty hot with no
more damage. A damn nice job.
I think I'd have jumped tho.
Never a dull moment.

Only the new men flew this a.m., and there were no mishaps, although many a breathtaking moment during most of the landings. This last bunch of men were all Navy pilots, some big-boat men too, and they are having a bit of difficulty with these ships.

I substituted part of the morning on Alert Crew, and spent the rest of the a.m. at operations getting some work straightened out.

Spent the p.m. re-packing my trunk and wardrobe case.

We are sending our excess baggage on up to Kunming Monday, and some of the men go up too.

I think we pilots will go within ten days or 2 weeks. We'll fly our own ships up when we go.

By this time Greene and I were laughing about how much bourbon mixed with persistence had been required before Skip Adair, protesting our lack of fighter and gunnery experience, finally signed us up. Recent arrivals included a number of navy pilots whose only active duty flying had been in PB-Ys, lumbering twin-engined flying boats. Ed Conant was one of these. Most of the others had been assigned to the 2nd squadron, among them being Robert "Buster" Keeton, George "Pappy" Paxton, Bob Layher, Freeman Ricketts, and Tom Cole. They discovered that landing a P-40 at 90 mph on a narrow runway was considerably different than skimming onto the vast ocean's surface with a PB-Y at much slower speed.

Up at 9:00 a.m. and to breakfast.
After that Greene, Mangleburg, & myself
went over to the gun butts on the
firing range, and shot a few
rounds with our guns. I took
my .22 Automatic Rifle and my
.38 Colt and had a big time.
The guns work fine — wish I
could say the same for my shooting.
Spent the p.m. in painting
my name and organization on
my baggage.
All in all, a very quiet
Weekend.

3rd squadron pilots, Toungoo, November 1941
l to r, seated: Older, Conant. 2nd row, kneeling: McMillan,
Greene, Hodges, Mangleburg, Jernstedt, Criz. Standing: Gilbert,
Reed, Martin, Raine, Smith, Olson.

Monday 3
(307-58)

Boy, what a day this has been.
A lecture this a.m. by a Chinese ace who
has been in the war since it started and
has shot down several Japs. Very good too.
Then came the flying. I led a 3 ship
formation attack on target ship first period.
Last period had a combat with Reed. We
broke about even, if anything he had the edge.
But my ship was fully loaded with
ammunition, weighing about 400 lbs., so he
had quite an advantage.

Gohant, the "P" boat man, tried to land on
the last 3rd of the runway, & couldn't stop.
Nosed up + bent the prop.

Ramies had a tire blow out on take-off,
ran off runway across a ditch, landing
gear folded, bent prop & wing.

A mech. taxied one ship head-on into
another and ruined both props.

Sandell ground-looped on landing
after returning from K-C to Lashio.
Five ships put out of commission
in one day. Some stuff.

Sandell, 1st squadron commander and one of the most experienced pilots
of the bunch, took quite a ribbing after his ground loop. It made a few
others who'd had the same misfortune feel a lot better.

Tuesday 4 ☺
(308-57)

Another talk by Major Wong this a.m.
Told more of his experiences in
the Sino-Jap. war.

Flew one hour target ship
this morning. We have grounded
all ships with more than 40 hrs.
because the tires are going out
fast due to the hot landings on
the runway.

Reed nosed one up when he landed
too long. Rolled off the mat and
hit a stump — another prop
shot to hell.

Gilbert, one of our new Navy men,
let a prop run wild and revved
the engine up to about 3500 r.p.m.
Burned out the bearing in the
engine. Luckily it was a ship
belonging to Sqdn. 2.

Our abysmal accident rate was taking a heavy toll on our limited inventory of P-40's. I think it was Erik Shilling of the 1st squadron who said he'd figured out that at the current rate of attrition if we continued "training" at Toungoo for another six weeks the Japs wouldn't have a thing to worry about, we'd be completely out of flyable planes. While his remark was admittedly humorous, the situation was definitely not funny and Chennault was fit to be tied.

Wednesday 5
(309-56)

Well, the Colonel gave us a talk on the Chinese warning yret we will use up North, and then a rather cutting speech regarding our flying around here, accidents, etc. I hope it sinks in on some of these would-be hot shots!

Conant came in to land, his left tire blew out, landing gear gave way, and he slid in on his belly, making a total loss of the ship. His third crack-up in four days of flying. Two ships completely washed out, + one prop bent on the other. This one wasn't his fault tho. Too bad.

Manglebury + I went to town & got our boots, + called on the McLauis after dinner. We were supposed to be there for dinner the Monday after the big party, but forgot. So we had to apologize.

The Boneyard—A few P-40s wrecked in training accidents at Toungoo

Thursday 6
(310-55)

Colonel Chennault lectured on night-fighter tactics in the war, and how we would operate at night in China.

I flew an hour of acrobatics and really wrung the ship out. Got some good 90° immelmanns, as well as loops, rolls, etc.

Buzzed the Mc Lains house in Toungoo just for fun. They are to be out here for dinner at our mess with some R.A.F. people tonite.

The Beechcraft took a load to Singapore yesterday on business.

M angle - & I are trying to get Mr. Mc Lain to arrange a Tiger hunt for us over the week-end. There is a man-killer on the rampage about 40 mi. north. He has killed two native women + two elephant calves in the past 2 weeks.

Friday 7
(311-54)

Flew an hour this a.m. A combat
with Cruz, and I waxed him good.
We had four passes, and I got 3 out
of four but he wouldn't admit defeat.
Made me sore because I whipped
him decisively, but he has been
beaten before and wouldn't admit it, so
guess he's just that way.

Mangles & I went to town this afternoon
to see Mr. McLain. He took us over
to see a Mr. Rosemeyer about the
tiger hunt. Mr. R. is in the District
Commissioner's office, and he is going
to contact the head-man of the village
near which the tiger is raising hell.
We are to go up there Sunday and
make arrangements to hire beaters,
guide, etc.

Jones got lost on an X-c to Leslie
today, ran low on gas, and was forced
to land about 40 mi. N.W. of Leslie.
Cracked the ship up, but wasn't hurt.

Saturday 8
(312-53)

No flying this morning. Just fooled around the ready-room and line, and got a little work done on my operations job.
We start firing on the ground gunnery range Monday. So far we have 7 ships from our Sqdn. boresighted.
Six Brewster Buffalos flew up from Rangoon this morning + landed. They're from the R.A.F. base there.
The head-man of the village where the tiger is raising hell is gone now, so we have to wait a few days before we can make arrangements for the hunt.

It's hard to believe that Lacy Mangleburg and I were serious about going after that man-eating tiger, but we were. Ah, the audacity of youth! Neither of us had ever hunted anything more ferocious than a rabbit, but it sounded like it should be a lot of fun and we were confident we could do the job. We planned to borrow a couple of .30 caliber British army rifles, take a couple of days off, and bring back that tiger's hide as well as winning the undying gratitude of the natives in the area. Just like that!

After dinner last night Maggle-
McMillan, Kirk, Wright, Shilling,
Schwartz + myself sat on at our
table and talked of stuff + things
and had a few sociable rounds.
I was lucky + didn't get stuck
for a single round. Wright +
Schwartz + I got into quite a
heated argument, each insulting
the others, + we chased around the
table, knocking over chairs and
having a big time. We all had
a lot of fun.

Slept late this a.m., and spent
the afternoon in writing to
Grandma Smith and just idling
around. Not much excitement
around these parts.

Jones isn't back yet from his
forced landing. Ha!

Almost forgot, but I lost a few
Rupees in a flashlight crap-game
last nite.

Monday 10
(314-51)

Today I was Control Officer and spent the whole morning in the tower. Didn't fly at all. Observed the rest flying, especially landings. Nothing of importance came up, altho I had a few notes in general to report at the noon staff meeting.

Did absolutely nothing this p.m. just lay around sleeping & reading.

Tomorrow we have the gunnery range, so I should get in some firing time.

RAF Brewster Buffalo fighter

Today our squadron had the gunnery range, and I went over and flew on the first mission. We, Olson, Criz, + myself, gunned for an hour. It was the first gunnery mission on the range. We all did lousy, partially due to our own lousiness, and partly because they hadn't been fired in before, and some didn't work so hot. My 50's worked fine, but the 30's were terrible. My score was worse. The next batch of men is due in tomorrow. Looked at the list of names, and was surprised to see — A. M. Wright is on the list. A classmate of Greene's + mine.

After dinner went to show.

Another pilot from the 3rd squadron, Estes Swindle, decided he'd had enough and planned to leave the next day. Within the past three weeks several pilots from the other squadrons had already pulled out, including Morris Bohman, Edwin Rushton, R.H. Walroth, and Richard White. This made a total of eleven pilots who had quit since mid-September, and three more had been killed in accidents. We had lost about ten planes—complete washouts—due to various kinds of accidents, and perhaps another ten were scattered around the base in need of major repair. Altogether a pretty grim picture!

Wednesday 12 ☾
(316-49)

Flew one hour of 6-ship formation this a.m. all in all it went pretty well. We did attack on target ship and then formed in "string" and Martin led us thru a good rat-race.

Spent the p.m. trimming my nails, shaving, bathing, etc. Really exciting!

Haywood + Ferrell brought in two new ships from Rangoon and said the new guys are on the way up now. They should get in on the 9:30 p.m. train. Am anxious to see Al Wright + talk over old times.

The new bunch of men due to arrive had pulled into Rangoon only that morning aboard the Boschfontein. Of the thirty or so arriving in this last shipment, about two thirds were pilots and most of them from the navy or Marine Corps. Two of these former Marines, both older and more experienced than most of us, were Curtis Smith and Greg Boyington. "Pappy," as Boyington was called, was assigned to the 1st squadron along with Dick Rossi, Bob Prescott, and ex-Air Corps pilots Charley Bond, George Burgard, and Jim Cross who had been ferrying bombers to Canada for the RAF prior to joining the AVG.

Thursday 13
(317-48)

The new bunch got in last nite, and we met them and got them settled. Wright didn't come up from Rangoon. It seems that he has signed up for a 2 year hitch of instructing in China, and isn't going to fight with us. Personally, I should think he'd had enough of instruction.

I didn't fly this a.m. at all. Spent most of the morning bore-sighting my ship. Fired in all six guns 50 rounds each. My ship, 77, is one of the first to get an optical sight installed. It works fine and she's all ready to go battle now. We still don't know when we leave.

We got 8 new men in our Squadron. All navy or marine pilot. Seem to be a good bunch.

Our eight new men were former navy pilots Lewis Bishop, John Donovan, Herb Cavanah, Cliff Groh, Ralph Gunvordahl, and Frank Adkins, and Marines Curtis E. Smith and Chauncey "Link" Laughlin. They were all fine guys, but here again was a group with practically no experience whatever in flying single-engined high performance planes. It was becoming increasingly obvious that the AVG recruiters had been unable to find and sign up more than a fraction of those whose job description fit the requirements for the task ahead.

Friday 14
(318-47)

Flew on a gunnery mission this morning. I had a ship with an optical sight and had a pretty good run. Got some in the bull and all around it. There is sure a difference in sights. Hedman got on my target for 3 runs so can't tell just what my score was.

Wright, a. m., came up from Rangoon this morning. We had a good bull session. He will be here for a few days & then up to Kunming as a check instructor. He says Loane, Sheppard, Shamblin etc. are on their way over to do the same thing.

Got a letter from the folks today. Enclosed was a clipping telling of a B-17 crashing on takeoff at Duncan Ill. "Dutch" Reichstadt killed in it. One of the best friends I ever had.

Robert "Dutch" Reichstadt, son of a prominent Omaha doctor, and I had become close friends from the start of our days as flying cadets. He'd been assigned to a B-17 squadron at Hamilton Field, California, and was killed while on a cross-country flight to Duncan Field, San Antonio, Texas.

Saturday 15
(319-46)

Not much doing today. Got up at the usual time, and over to the line after breakfast. We all damned near mutinied at breakfast when they tried to serve us cabbage and sausage. Claimed they had no eggs, but we raised such a stink that they brought out some eggs anyway. Another one of Joe Alsop's great ideas, the cabbages I guess. Imagine — Cabbage!

I inspected my ship at the line, and she's all set to go.

The Col. came back on CNAC from Kunming this a.m. I hope he has some good news as to when we go up North. Rumor is rampant here about various things. Spent the afternoon reading & sleeping. Nothing in view for tonite.

CNAC was *China National Airways Corporation*, owned jointly by the Chinese government and Pan American Airways. Most of the captains on their little fleet of DC-3s were Americans, the co-pilots Chinese. Their routes served Chungking, Kunming, and a few other cities in China, as well as Calcutta, India, and Rangoon, Burma, with occasional stops now at Toungoo. Their pilots were incredible, flying over the most formidable terrain in the world, often in the worst kind of weather, and with practically no navigation aids whatever. Under the cirmumstances, their safety record was simply amazing.

Mangleburg, Raines, myself + a few others celebrated Sat. nite at the mess last nite, and had quite a time; about 1:00 a.m. we took off on our bikes and rode out to inspect the guard, which has been tripled due to sabotage scares.

We were challenged about 10 times in two miles, and had collisions with each other + ditches etc. and a lot of fun. Lace + I took some good spills.

Got some breakfast at 9:00 a.m + came home and read.

After lunch wrote to the folks. Hope the Col. gives us the dope tomorrow and it will be good news.

It was at about this time that the three squadrons decided to establish their individual identities and insignias. I don't recall much discussion about it, but somehow the 3rd squadron chose the name "Hell's Angels," featuring an insignia in the form of a shapely nude female figure, bright red in color and with white wings and a halo. Stan Regis, one of our crew chiefs and a talented artist, designed this basic insignia, then made a number of variations for individual pilots showing the Angel in different poses. The name itself had its origin in the title of the movie, "Hell's Angels," a World War I air epic of the thirties. This, of course, was at a time when the first members of the notorious motorcycle gang that was to adopt the name many years later were still in diapers.

Charley Bond, a recent arrival who'd been assigned to the 1st pursuit squadron, designed its insignia. It consisted of a large green apple as background for stick-figures of a woman chasing a man; Eve chasing Adam, mankind's first pursuit. So the 1st squadron became the "Adam and Eves."

I don't know whose idea it was, but the 2nd squadron adopted the distinctive black and white Panda—native to China—as its insignia, thus becoming the "Panda Bears."

Monday 17
(321-44)

Up again at 5:30 and to the line at 6:30. Greene + I had a combat this morning and I waxed him 3 out of 8. Twice we worked down to 1500 ft. which is too low for safety. Anyway, there was no room for doubt as to the outcome.

Most of the new guys checked out today and there were plenty of thrills again, all tho all went pretty well. Only trouble was Cross' ship caught fire at 1000 ft. and he made a belly landing in a rice paddy and wasn't hurt. Put fire out.

Mangle + I haven't been able to get anything set for the tiger hunt.

It was also about this time that we decided to paint the nose of each plane to resemble the business end of a shark. Credit for this idea was claimed by both Erik Shilling and Charley Bond of the 1st squadron, and since they're both good friends of mine I'm not about to argue with either of them. Matter of fact, I think it's possible they came up with the idea at the same time, having seen a picture in a newspaper or magazine of an RAAF (Australian) P-40 painted in such a manner. So, either way, it wasn't original with the AVG.

There was no stencil used for making the shark's mouth, so each pilot simply drew the outline with chalk and then painted the lips, teeth, and eyes according to his own taste. As a result, of course, no two were exactly alike.

Tuesday 18
(322-43)

Dammit, I caught the "dog-watch"; 12 midnite to 3 a.m., on the gate last night after drawing lots. So at 11:30 I piled out + went out to the gate. Nobody came in and all was quiet, and at 3:00 Conant took over.

Slept till 8:30 and went to the line. Didn't fly any today but got started painting up my ship. We are making Shark-heads out of the front end. Looks mean as hell.

Ricketts, one of the new guys, landed with his wheels only part-way down, and they folded and he skidded along on his belly + washed out another ship. Stupidity!

Rumor has it that they are going to suspend training of the new fellows until we leave, so to conserve ships. I hope they do.

Spent the afternoon at the line painting some more on my ship.

Wednesday 19 ●
(323-42)

Flew an hour of gunnery this morning. It went pretty good altho still not good enough. A couple of my 30's didn't work so hot. Had Greene's ship.

I went over to the range at 10:00 to relieve Greene.

Scored targets till noon and came home.

Spent all afternoon at the line again doing some more work on 77, my ship.

It's looking good too.

Shilling went up this afternoon in a P-40 and combatted an RAF pilot in his Brewster Buffalo. Shilling beat him but we all agree the R.A.F. guy did a lousy job of flying. Looked like he wasn't trying and he made some lousy mistakes.

I must go see Paulette & Bob in Ghost-Breakers tonite — specially Paulette.

For the benefit of those not on first name terms with the movie stars, I was referring to Paulette Goddard and Bob Hope.

Thursday 20
(324-41)

I had a sore throat last nite at bedtime, + Doc. Richards painted it for me, but this morning it was still sore so I stayed in bed. Two or three others complaining of the same thing.

Tom Jones is having a tough time with his Malaria. He's in the hospital and half-delirious most of the time.

I've been around the barracks all day, + my throat is better I think.

Got a letter from the Harlans today + it sure looked good.

The Col. has called a meeting for tomorrow morning. Maybe he'll spend a little time in giving us the dope on when we go.

Friday 21
(325-40)

Lecture this morning by the Col.
Told us about customs and conditions
we would meet in China.
No flying except for new men.
Maintenance day for the rest of the
ships + men.
I did a little more painting
on my ship.
Tex Hill took off on an engineering
hop and his motor was cutting out
pretty bad. He just barely cleared
the trees at the end of the runway.
Moss started to ground-loop + had
to gun it + take off again — about
400 off of the runway course.
Almost hit a native house.
My nose is running today + it
looks like I'm in for a good cold.

Saturday 22
(326-39)

Spent the morning in bed trying to shake my cold. My head is all stuffed up and I feel lousy. Seems to be an epidemic, as lots of the guys have colds. Nothing to do but read and shoot the bull this afternoon. There seems to be no news at all except the rumor that Spare tires and solenoids for the guns are being shipped via Clipper from the states — We hope

Burmese woman about to kiss a Cobra

Up for breakfast at 8:30
Spent the morning reading and
gossiping.
After lunch Ed Overend and I
went to the line and shot a
bunch of pictures - some in color.
We're going to see if Criz will
take them to the States + deliver them
to the folks for developing. He goes
back next week. We also went out
and rode up the road to a temple
and took more pictures. I used
Reeds' Camera.
Tonite another bunch of men are
supposed to arrive. Most of them
instructors who will go to China to
instruct - Loane, Hall, Shapard, +
Shamblin are arriving - men I knew
in the Army at home.
I am going in to meet the train
if possible.

Al Criz was the latest pilot from our squadron to decide the AVG was not his cup of tea. He did take our rolls of film back with him when he finally left Rangoon, but the color pictures were not very good.

"Bus" Loane, Les Hall, Van Shapard, and Arnie Shamblin were all instructors at Randolph with Greene and me. They, and Allen Wright, had been hired by CAMCO to train young Chinese pilots at Yunnanyi, though they transferred to the AVG a few weeks before we were disbanded.

Monday 24
(328-37)

Flew two gunnery missions this morning — 1 hr. each.

I got hot as hell finally, and wound up with 4th high score for the day.

My optical sight was way off tho' and I had to use the iron ring sight.

Spent the afternoon reading and sleeping.

My ship is being worked on in the hanger now, new plugs and timing & valve clearances checked up.

The new guys didn't come in last nite and aren't expected until tomorrow night now.

Our P-40s, as delivered, were equipped with only the old-fashioned externally-mounted ring sights. However, the newer and better optical sights had been procured for installation at Toungoo. This sight, not originally planned as part of a P-40's equipment, projected a bright ring of light with a dot—or "pipper"—in the center of the ring, onto a piece of glass mounted behind the windshield. It was a difficult job to get it installed and working properly, but our armament men managed it somehow. Joe Poshefko, 3rd squadron armament chief, was a big happy Polack from Pennsylvania; our other armorers, all highly competent, were Charley Baisden and Clarence Riffer, also from Pennsylvania, ·Paul Perry from Virginia, and Keith Christenson of Iowa. These five guys did the work of a dozen or more who would be found in any pursuit squadron back in the States.

Tuesday 25 ☽
(329-36)

Flew an hour of 6 ship attack formation on a target ship this morning. All went OK.
Spent the rest of the morning tuning up my ship. I'll get to fire it in on the range thurs.
Meeting of flight leaders today and now the story is that we really will go to Kun Ming in a week or ten days. I sure hope so.
The new guys arrive tonite.
I leave at 9:30 tonite for Rangoon to bring back the last P40. When I get up here with it there will be no more, it being the 100th one.
Have some business to tend to in Rangoon too.

My business in Rangoon included plans to visit a British-owned jewelry shop with the idea of ordering a hand-made copy of the gold Air Corps flying school graduation ring which I couldn't afford at the time I graduated. Most of my classmates had bought one, for twenty-five or thirty bucks, but I was flat broke at the time. Greene had loaned me his to have copied, and I arranged for it to be done when I visited the shop the next day. It was to be hand-crafted of 22 karat gold, an exact copy of Paul's, and I was told that it would be ready in a couple of weeks. The price: 90 rupees, less than $30.00.

Wednesday 26
(330-35)

Got into Rangoon at 8:00 a.m. after a hell of a train ride all nite. Saw the new bunch at the Toungoo station just before I left. Did a lot of shopping and errands for some of the guys. Bought a camera for 87 rupees and a batch of film.

Reported to the office and they said the ship wasn't ready to go yet, & that Glover, the Curtiss Test pilot would bring it up later.

Sooo, I was free to come back on the train with Paxton. But we missed the 4:00 p.m. train, had a party at the Clifton and the Strand for late dinner & caught the 10:00 pm train. Arrived Toungoo at 4:00 a.m. Thurs.

George "Pappy" Paxton, from Abilene, Texas, was one of the former PB-Y pilots from the navy. He was a likeable and gregarious sort, and one of the older pilots in the group, probably in his early thirties. He would later give up combat flying and become finance officer.

Thursday 27
(331-34)

After arriving at 4:00 a.m., we found nobody to meet us at the station so went to Greenlaw's + slept until he got up to go to work at 6:00 a.m.

Went to the line after breakfast and flew my ship, no. 77, two periods of gunnery. My guns didn't work worth a damn, but it hadn't been fired in the air before. My scores were relatively good for the no. of rounds fired. Slept in this p.m. to make up for lost time! Guess I'll go to the show tonite.

Jim Cross, 1st squadron pilot, with Adam & Eve insignia

Friday 28
(332-33)

Well, more tires developed blisters today, and all flying for our Sqdn. suspended after the 1st. period. They say our new tires are to arrive in Singapore via Clipper on Dec 2. We should get them up here soon after.

Got a letter from the folks today, with enclosures from June, Ross Worthington, and about all the relatives from Nebr. It was sure nice to hear from so many.

Slept most of the p.m.

Nothing exciting to report.

I hope we get out of here in a week or so.

Saturday 29
(333-32)

Spent the morning on the line
tuning up my ship and finishing
the paint job. Also Cleaned all
over, especially the glass in Canopy
After lunch some of us went back
to the line to work some more, and
about 4: p.m. word was sent over
that each squadron was to get
its' 18 ships completely ready to go
by monday. So we rushed around
getting the rest of the men to work.
I helped Perry of the Armament section
load some ships with 50 cal. belts, and
others loaded 30 cal. wing guns.
It looks as if we may get out
about Tues. or Wed. at least.
Shilling came back from
Kunming via C.N.A.C. tonite and
reports that all is ready up there +
that it is much better than here, altho
the bombing season is Commencing.

Everybody up at 6:00 a.m. and back to work at the line. We got our last 2 ships bore-sighted and shot in on the range. Some of the guys still painting their ships, but should finish up today.

We will be ready to go tomorrow or whenever they want to send us.

Word via radio that Kunming was bombed yesterday.

I think that only 18 ships + pilots from each sqdn. will go up right away. The rest will probably stay here for more training and come up later on.

My ship is in A1 condition, altho I'd like to fire the guns again. The armament section "thinks" they have all the "bugs" out, but I'd like to be sure. We may see action on the way up. — I hope.

As indicated briefly in preceding pages, we attended lectures frequently, most of them given by Chennault himself but with occasional guest speakers who'd had combat experience or could speak on technical matters. All of these lectures were interesting, and helped to prepare us for what lay ahead.

Chennault showed us sketches and actual photographs of Japanese fighters and bombers that we could expect to encounter, primarily the Mitsubishi Type 97 "Sally" twin-engined bomber, the Nakajima I-97 "Nate" fighter, the Nakajima "Oscar" fighter, and the Mitsubishi Type 0, or "Zero" fighter.

We were told that the defensive armament of the Sally bomber consisted of seven flexible 7.7mm machine guns, and that the best method of attack was from the rear quarter and beneath the bomber, then to break off the attack by diving and turning sharply away.

All of the Jap fighters were said to be highly maneuverable, and that in a turning dogfight the P-40 would be at a distinct disadvantage. This was due to the much greater weight and wing-loading of the P-40 due to its armor-plate protection for the pilot, behind and under the seat, its self-sealing fuel tanks, and heavier overall construction. The Japanese had sacrificed these things in order to achieve a higher rate of climb and better maneuverability. Therefore, the old man told us, we should use hit-and-run tactics; the P-40 had a slightly higher top speed in level flight, and could easily outdive any of the Jap fighters, thus giving us a way of escape when one of them got on our tail. This proved to be sound advice, and was the key to our success in the weeks to come. However, as time went on, some of us did engage in actual dogfights, particularly on those infrequent occasions when we could square off in a one-on-one situation. We discovered that sometimes, due to an enemy pilot's lack of skill, or perhaps inexperience, he could be out-maneuvered without diving away and breaking off the combat, and so long as a couple of his buddies didn't come to his rescue we could stick around and play that game too.

Much has been written about Chennault's concept of always attacking in pairs, with the lead plane doing most of the shooting and his wingman keeping an eye out for enemy fighters approaching from above or to the rear, and then calling out a warning to his flight leader in time to break off the attack. Well, this is one of those theories that sounds good and looks good on paper, but it didn't work worth a damn in practice so far as I could ever see. The main reason, of course, was that we were nearly always outnumbered by the Jap Fighters, and the moment the combat with them started everybody scattered and it was every man for himself. For that matter, even when our overall numbers were the same, the odds would still have been two to one in their favor so long as we insisted on flying in pairs while being attacked by a single Jap fighter. Consequently most of our engagements developed into a wild rat-race in short order, and it would have taken not only a lot of will-power but one hell of a pilot to stick on my wing once the action started. I was promoted to flight leader after the first two fights over Rangoon in late December, but was McMillan's wingman at that time. We didn't even attack the bombers in pairs on those occasions; our flight was strung out and we attacked the bombers from the classic high-side initial approach, peeling off individually at regular intervals in the beginning, and after that it was every man for himself.

I have spoken before of the fact that Greene and I had had no aerial gunnery experience, and as things turned out that was the case with at least fifty percent of the pilots who were finally signed up for the AVG. The ground gunnery we had done here at Toungoo was fine for learning to shoot at a stationary ground target, and for getting the bugs out of the guns and sights, but of course didn't help a bit when it came to shooting at moving targets in the air. Deflection shooting, in those days before computing gunsights, was more of an art than a science. Imagine being equipped with a rifle and sitting on a moving Ferris wheel while trying to aim and fire at one of the moving cars on the roller-coaster next door, and you'll get the idea. However, the brain is a pretty good computer too, and after a bit of experience a guy instinctively calculates the differences in speed and attitude in order to get the proper "lead" before firing. After that, corrections can be made with the help of the tracer bullets, every fifth round in each ammo belt being one of these highly visible streaks of orange fire.

Most of us learned very quickly that the surest way to success was to eliminate the matter of deflection entirely, or nearly so, and bore right on in to close range right on the enemy's tail. The problem with this method, in the case of bombers, was that it also made things a lot easier for their gunners to score hits. In other words, there's no such thing as a free lunch! It boiled down to how far you were willing to push your luck in order to score a kill, and as might be expected some pilots often decided that prudence was the better part of valor. Inevitably, there were a few, a very few, who decided early on in their first combat that they were simply not cut out for such work and steered clear of the fighting. To their credit, most of them had guts enough to admit it and were removed from combat status and placed in administrative roles.

DECEMBER 1941

Monday 1
(335-30)

Up at 5:30 and over to the line after breakfast. Final flight assignments were made the other day. I am in "B" flight, led by McMillan. Others in our flight are Mangleburg, Smith, C.E., Haywood & Jernstedt.

Our flight made an altitude test flight today. Went to 26,000 ft. and our oxygen equipment & the masks and everything worked fine.

At lunch word was passed to pack all our baggage & only keep what we'll carry up in the ships. Only sixteen out of the 18 in our Sqdn. are going. We are supposed to be ready tomorrow morning to leave on an hours notice. I am ready.

Hope we go tomorrow but we may not leave for 2 or 3 days yet.

Tuesday 2
(336-29)

Went to the line at the usual time, but nothing much doing. We had a meeting of Sqdn. pilots & Olson went over more notes on fighter tactics —mostly those used by the R.A.F. and Luftwaffe. Our ships are ready to go and we are just waiting for the word. After lunch Ed Overend & I went in to town and took some pictures. Went thru the bazaar, saw the sights and smelled the smells. We have each given Cris a roll of films to mail to the folks when he gets to the States.

It was about this time that Chennault decided to do something about our lack of reconnaissance capability by converting a P-40 into a photo ship. Erik Shilling, one of our most skilled pilots who also had considerable engineering ability, was named to head the project. He selected a plane from the 2nd squadron and supervised the installation of an aerial camera borrowed from the RAF in the small baggage compartment in the aft fuselage area. A hole large enough to permit an unobstructed view for the camera lens was cut in the bottom of the fuselage, and remote controls for operating the camera were installed in the cockpit. The four wing guns were removed, the holes for the barrels taped over, and the plane waxed and cleaned up to reduce drag in every way possible. The result was an increase of about 20 mph in top speed. The plane was used as a photo ship only three or four times, and was later returned to its combat configuration.

Wednesday 3 ☺
(337-28)

This morning the 18 men going up to Kunming flew in a Sqdn. formation for an hour. It was the most ships our Sqdn. has ever had in the air at one time. All 18 got off and back without any trouble. We have organized the Sqdn. into a twelve-ship day-time unit, and a 4 ship night flight, with two or 3 reserves. I am in the assault flight along with Mac, Maybury, & C. E. Smith.

We tried out our various formations this a.m. for the first time as a sqdn. Didn't look too hot but will be OK. in another hour or two. Still no word as to when we will leave — dammit!

Thursday 4
(338-27)

Our 12 ship daytime Sqdn.
flew again this a.m.
I was designated to be the "weaver"
or lookout, and flew detatched, —
about 2,000 ft. above the Sqdn.
We ran into Sqdn. 1 doing
the same maneuvers etc. We tangled
with them 3 times, and I never
saw such a rat race before in my
life. About 25 ships in all, diving &
zooming all over in combats etc. I
took on the "weavers" and others of the
other Sqdn. Lots of good practice,
but too many close calls for
comfort. One guy whizzed right
in front of me while I was in a
turn. He passed within about 30 ft.
& I didn't see him till he went by.
Still no word as to moving.

Friday 5
(339-26)

Not much doing as far as Sqdn.
operations go this a. m.
Bronk, Haywood, + I took our
ships up and went to the range for
ground gunnery to check our guns
again. Mine didn't work so hot
last time. But today they, all six,
worked practically perfect. I fired
500 rounds in each wing gun and
50 rounds in each 50 cal. synchronized gun.
My sight was still right in the groove,
+ I was pretty hot. Got 657 hits on
the target, over 130 in the bullseye.
Total score was 2125 – a new
record for that number of rounds.
Several nice comments on it from
the gang. Now I have to buy a
round of beer for the armament men
after telling them I would if my
guns all fired right.

Saturday 6
(340-25)

Everybody was late this morning
getting up. We didn't get to breakfast
until 6:30 Went to the line, after
that, and spent the morning checking
my ship. Warmed it up and she's
still ticking 'em off like a sewing machine.
Helped the armorers install my guns
after cleaning, and re-loading.
Then Cruickshank & I pulled the
prop + inspected the thrust bearing.
We found a little rust but not bad.

Spent the afternoon reading a "late"
issue of time — Oct. 6. Ha!

If the Wizards of Washington
ever make up their minds what to do
about the Japs maybe we'll know
when the hell we go to China. I
guess that's what's holding us
up. Anyway the Convoy picked up
all our excess baggage to go up
the road, so now we have no
clothes or anything.

Same old thing — spent the day reading and writing a couple of letters.
Went to town this morning and took a few pictures. Nothing new to report and no prospects even.

It might be of interest to note the contrast between the apprehension we felt in Burma and the relaxed atmosphere that prevailed in Hawaii on the day before Pearl Harbor was attacked. Bear in mind that, due to the International Dateline, the 7th of December in Burma was only the 6th in the USA. The following are excerpts from a letter I wrote to my parents on this date:

Dear Mom and Dad:

Your last letter received over a week ago, and of course I was delighted with the notes from all the Nebraska folks as well as your own.

I've been holding off in writing to you as I thought surely we'd be in China by now. We've been under instructions to be ready to leave on an hour's notice for about ten days. All I can say is that we—half of us, at least—are ready. There will be sixteen from my squadron flying up when we go, and about the same from the others. Naturally we're all anxious to get going, and irked at the delay.

There is no news to report here, except that the Englanders are reinforcing their borders. Things are getting tenser and tenser, but nobody knows what'll happen, or when. The Japs have been reported several times as having crossed the Thai border, but all these rumors have been denied. Of course if Thailand is invaded openly we will probably swing into action from here and never get to China. Makes no difference, just so we get to doing something!

On a lighter note, Paul and I have had a lot of fun showing up a few wiseguys who used to make nasty cracks about instructor-pilots. We don't hear any of that crap any more, and both know we can hold our own with anybody when it comes to flying these ships. We've each got about forty hours in them, and by now my P-40 feels as comfortable as an old pair of shoes. My plane is No. 77, I've got a hell of a crew-chief, and we're ready!

Sure hope you have a swell Christmas—I guess this will be the screwiest one I will ever see. Please tell everybody to write; you can't realize how much a letter means to somebody over here.   All my love to all,

Bob

Monday 8
(342-23)

Boy, did all hell break loose today?!
We all went over to the line after
breakfast, and about 7 o'clock
somebody ran in to the ready-room
and said the U.S. was now at
war with Japan. We could hardly
believe it even tho it was confirmed
on the radio. Everybody stood around
laughing + kidding about it, altho it
was easy to see there was really plenty
of tension. Here we are in the middle
of the works now — with the Japs
pounding Hawaii, Manila, Singapore
and Thailand — 60 miles away.
We all went on a constant alert
for enemy ships, but none sighted.
Plans were made for our Sqdn. to
go to Rangoon, as they need
more support for the R.A.F. there.
They expect an air raid any
time now. If they don't bomb
our field here before we get away,
we'll be lucky.

Tuesday 9
(343-22)

Well, no alarms or raids last nite.
We are now getting up at 4:30 a.m.
and standing by all day until 6:00 p.m.
We started patrol over the mountains
toward the Thailand border today.
About 4:00 p.m. an observation ship
was sighted at about 20,000 ft.
One flight from each of the 1st & 2nd
Sqdns. took off to go after it, but
never saw it again. Our Sqdn. stood
by in our ships, warming them up etc.,
ready to go if bombers followed up.
An hour later tho all clear siren
sounded and we dispersed the ships.
Nothing more happened.
We in our Sqdn., the 18 of us ready to go,
have orders to be packed & ready to leave
on 10 min. notice, altho were not going
to Rangoon as previously planned.
Six men to stand by tonite on alert.
We are expecting a raid tonite – full
moon & good weather – just made to
order for those little yellow Japs.

Wednesday 10

Quite a thrill last nite - or early this a.m. rather. At 3:00 a.m. the air-raid siren sounded + we all piled out and into our trenches by the barracks. The six men on night alert took off to find the bombers. They all said they heard a bunch of them, but they didn't drop any bombs and nobody could see them.

An hour after the alarm the all-clear sounded. We went back to bed + the guys came in + landed. Tex Hill landed way too long and washed out his airplane completely at the end of runway. He wasn't hurt. Our Sqdn. has nite alert tonite - Six of us volunteered for it — McMillan, Mangleburg, Haywood, Jernstedt, Reed + myself. Hope they come over tonite!

Thursday 11 ☾
(345-20)

Stood by on alert all last nite but nothing happened. No signs or sounds of any enemy.

Once more the R.A.F. has called for help as they expect trouble in Rangoon. Our sqdn. is definitely slated to go down there tomorrow. Our Regular 18 men will go plus Shilling, Merritt, Dean, Hoffman, and Hoskee.

Word comes up that the Japs have bombed an airdrome within 200 miles of Rangoon.

We are slated to leave at 9:00 in the morning.

Shortly before going into production of the P-40, Curtiss-Wright had designed and built a few lightweight interceptor planes called the CW-21. This was a low-wing monoplane with a radial engine, somewhat similar to the Japanese Zero, and supposedly with even better performance when it came to rate-of-climb and maneuverability. The Air Corps had failed to place an order for this plane, but Bill Pawley, head of CAMCO, had landed a contract with the Chinese to build fifty of them, under a licensing agreement, at his little factory in Loiwing, China. Three of those built by Curtiss, to be used as prototypes, had been delivered and assembled in Rangoon, but after the Japs attacked Pearl Harbor it was decided to turn these planes over to the AVG. When fully ready, they were to be delivered to AVG headquarters Kunming. Eric Shilling and Ken Merritt of the 2nd squadron, plus Lacy Mangleburg, were named to fly them up to Toungoo, then on to China a few days later.

Friday 12
(346-19)

Left toungoo, 18 ships, at
9:30 and got into Rangoon
a little past 10.
After landing + dispersing our
ships, we went to our quarters
in the Officers barracks.
Nice quarters + good mess. A
better setup than Toungoo
Two men per room — Greene +
myself in one.
Shilling flew a camera ship
over Bangkok yesterday + took
pictures of the airdrome. Counted
over 90 ships parked on the field.
Mac, Mangle, + Myself want to go
over + strafe the field + put some
ships out of commission.
Yesterday a Jap observation ship flew
over here, and the R.A.F. thinks they
will raid Rangoon tomorrow or
next day. Our flight is on alert
tomorrow, so if they come we'll be
the first in action — I hope

Saturday 13
(347-18)

Up at 5:30 and over to the line where our ships are. Sixteen of us on alert all day.

About 9:30 we had a raid siren warning and stood by our ships for about an hour. Nothing developed. Again at 12:30 p.m. a report that 27 enemy bombers were headed this way & would arrive in 15 minutes. The R.A.F. Brewsters took off first and then our 16 Tomahawks. Our flight went to 16,000 ft. + patrolled over the river, town, and gulf. The others went elsewhere. After an hour and a half we came back down. Nobody ever sighted the bombers and they never appeared anywhere near Rangoon, so guess they turned back. They did bomb Mergui tho, about 150 miles from here.

. We all thought sure we'd see action today.

Back on alert after breakfast this
morning. We were all turned out
at 9:30 last nite when a raid
warning was sounded. Some
airplanes were heard within
fifteen miles of Rangoon — in fact
we heard a distant drone ourselves.
We all went out to the trenches
near the barracks, with our
tin hats and gas masks. All clear
sounded in about an hour.
Those little yellow so & so's will
catch hell for disturbing our sleep if
we ever get close to them.

The day so far (5:00 p.m.) has been
very uneventful. We got word
this p.m. that we will probably pull
out of here for Toungoo tomorrow a.m.
Then the whole group will go to
Kunming I think. Col. Chennault
called Olson to that effect this morning.

Monday 15
(349-16)

The R.A.F. issued us our passes last
nite & most of us went to town:
Greene, Bartelt, Bishop & myself
ganged up and had a little party
at various joints in town.
Quite a time was had by all.
We got home at 4:30 a.m. and I
had to get up at 5:30 to go on
dawn alert. After breakfast at 8:00
tho I came back to quarters & slept
until noon. Then back on alert till
dark. No alarms - all quiet.

Thought we'd be going back to Toungoo
today as reported yesterday, but we
received no orders so here we sit.

I wish somebody would make
up their mind what the hell they
want to do with us & then do it.
This is the damnedest war I
ever saw.

Word came down from Toungoo
that Laughlin had a forced landing
wheels up on the river bank. Motor
conked out in formation. He's o.k.

Tuesday 16
(350-15)

Went on morning alert — breakfast
until 1:00 p.m. today. We are
alternating shifts now — one flight
on 5 min. readiness while the other
is on 30 min. call at barracks etc.
Nothing new or exciting.
Got a 30 min. hop and did a
few acrobatics.
Spent the afternoon listening to
the phonograph and sleeping.
Olson flew to Toungoo this p.m.
to see in person what the score is
I hope he comes back with
something definite.
This clothing situation is getting
serious. None of us have
more than a couple of shirts +
I only have one pair of slacks.
We make quite a sight — I
imagine the R. A. F. gets a kick
out of this screwball outfit.

It was about this time that we learned of the fall of Hong Kong, and that
Joe Alsop was now a prisoner of war. Joe had gone to H.K. in search of
much-needed supplies just before the Japanese attacked many major objec-
tives in southeast Asia at the time of Pearl Harbor, including that British
colonial outpost on the China coast. Joe was unable to escape, but being a
civilian he was later repatriated in a diplomatic exchange.

Wednesday 17
(351-14)

On the afternoon alert today.
Nothing of importance happened
until about 4:00 p.m., when in
from the West came a B24, 4 engine
Consolidated Bomber, with U.S. Army
insignia. It sure looked good.
It landed and we learned it was
Major Gen. Brett & staff. He is Chief of
the Air Corps, and one of his staff is
Maj. E. H. Alexander, my old C.O. of
Primary School. Also aboard was a
medico named Crane who told some of
the boys he knew Greene & me at Randolph
   Col. Chennault is coming down
tonite on a Blenheim the R.A.F. sent up.
The B24 came in from India today.
spent the evening with Capt. Davis,
the pilot. We went over to the ship &
he showed me all over it. Some ship!
They expect to be here a day or two.
I am going to try to see Maj. Alexander
tonite if he's around.

Thursday 18

(352-13)

Our flight went on dawn patrol this a.m. — 5:30-7:30. Thought we might find some Japs but no soap. The other flight did a patrol this p.m. We all rather expected a raid today. Wish they'd come and give us some action.

Looks like we're to be the Lost Squadron, as the others are moving out of Toungoo & on to Kunming. Overend & Gunvordahl came down by train today & reported that Bartelt was shipped up to Toungoo yesterday for insubordination etc.

The General's gang still in Rangoon, but the B24 pulled out today. Nobody knows where they went, but rumor has it that they went back to India so the ship wouldn't be damaged in case of a raid here. Haven't seen Maj. Alex. yet.

Standing by on alert duty each day, and flying long hours on patrol without ever seeing the enemy, were nerve-wracking as hell. Someone once described the life of a fighter pilot as being filled with endless hours of boredom, occasionally interrupted by brief periods of stark terror. I always thought that summed it up very well.

Friday 19
(353-12)

Our flight released after early
alert. We were off from breakfast
until 1:00 p.m.

Went to the line at 1:00, but due
to an upset stomach was relieved
by Olson at 2:00. Went to Hospital
and was given some medicine by
R.A.F. flight Surgeon, + came back
to quarters + went to bed. Shortly after
going to bed some Brewsters and our
flight of Tomahawks took off. I
was cursing myself for being sick
because it looked like the Japs
were coming. Two enemy ships
were reported heading this way, but
they didn't come on in + nobody
saw them.

They say the other 2 squadrons have
gone to Kunming now, + it was bombed
3 hours before they got there.
Bergard's engine conked on take-off +
he plowed into the trees at end of runway.
Ship demolished but he was unhurt

Saturday 20
(354-11)

Stayed in bed most of the day.
I'm feeling better now, after
having cramps all night.
Several of the others complaining
of the same thing. "Something
we et, no doubt."
Got up and shaved & showered at
4:00 p.m. & feel pretty good now.
The General's B-24 still gone. Am
going to see if Lt. Crane or Capt.
Davis will take some letters
back for me & mail in the States.
All mail service has been
suspended, but they will be
back home in a month or less
I think.

By now we had gotten acquainted with some of the RAF pilots at Mingaladon, mostly by talking with them at the pilots mess which we shared. There were a few from England, but most of them were from Australia and New Zealand, and we hit it off with them much better than with the more reserved Britishers who often seemed quite snobbish. The RAF had a squadron of about 20 Brewster Buffalo fighters, and a squadron of a dozen or so Blenheim light bombers. Their ground crewmen, also a mixture of British with Aussies and New Zealanders, seemed much more relaxed about the precarious situation we were all in than seemed warranted. Every day at mid-morning and mid-afternoon they took their tea break no matter what, while our guys continued working their tails off in the hot sun. This somewhat lackadaisical attitude prevailed even after the shooting started, and in time led to some marked differences of opinion, often expressed verbally, and was the beginning of considerable friction between the AVG and the British.

Damn! We got a telegram last nite from Kunming which said the first pursuit Squadron had intercepted 10 Jap bombers and shot down three for sure, and 2 or 3 more thought to have gone down. That was damn good work, but we're all mad because they got into action before we did.

Stayed on alert duty all day but nothing happened, as usual.

Maj. Alexander came out this evening and we spent about 4 hours together talking over old days at Santa Maria etc. He is still the same swell guy.

He is going to say hello to Ross W. when he gets back to Washington.

We later learned that flights from both the 1st and 2nd squadrons had been invlolved in the action in China, and that four Jap bombers had been shot down for certain, plus several "probables." This, the first action of the AVG, had been something of a comedy of errors in some respects, but served as a baptism of fire that provided some valuable lessons for the future. Fourteen pilots shared in the 4 kills.

Mitsubishi Type 97 "Sally" bomber

Mitsubishi model "0" Zero fighter

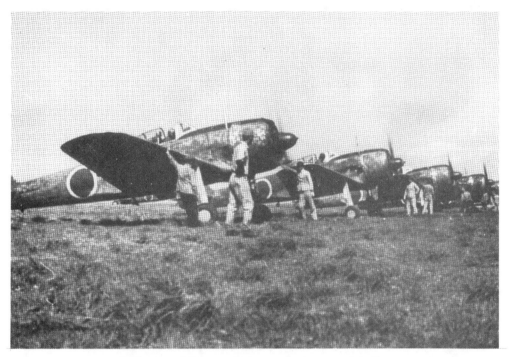

Nakajima "Oscar" fighters ready for takeoff.

Nakajima I-97 "Nate" fighter

Monday 22
(356-9)

*All day on alert again.
Not much excitement.
Four of the ships in DuPuoys
section went off to find an
unidentified ship reported, about 30
miles east. Nobody sighted it tho.
Brouk & I went up and did a
little formation around the field, &
I rolled around him while he
slow rolled. Lots of fun but
pretty sloppy, I'm afraid.
Then I went off & checked my
ship for various things.
Crookshank, my crew chief, &
Schram, another one, worked on it
all morning getting it in good
shape. My gas selector valve was
leaking & some other thing needed
fixing. She's 100% now tho.*

A couple of the other guys and I drove into Rangoon to do some shopping late in the afternoon. Everything seemed as usual, nobody seemed terribly concerned about the war situation. I stopped by the jewelry shop where I'd ordered the ring two or three weeks earlier, and was delighted with what they'd done. It was beautifully hand-crafted of 22K yellow gold, an almost exact duplicate, with a flat signet top displaying my initial "S" in fancy Old English engraving. I started to pay for it, but the British manager of the store said not to bother, they'd be happy to bill me at the end of the month. Little did either of us know that before that time the store would be in ruins and the city evacuated. I still owe somebody for that ring, which I wear to this day.

Rangoon
Burma

Boy, it all came today! We got a report
at 10:00 a.m. that large numbers of bombers were on the way.
14 ships from our Sqdn. + 10 Buffaloes from RAF took off.
We intercepted them at 12,000 ft. 15 mi. east of Rangoon.
Two waves of bombers, 27 in each wave, + about 40
fighter escorts. We started making runs on them and
shooting like hell. After bit I couldn't see any of
our fellows up there. Found a bomber away from
the formation, made about 3 passes, and on the
last one went in to about 50 yds., firing all 6 guns,
and he blew up right in front of me + down in flames.
Went after another, + McMillan + I together put out his
right engine + smoke trailed out. He was losing alt.
last time I looked, but about that time I was jumped
by 3 Jap fighters. Shot at one + dove away.
Went back up + fired at more bombers till ammo out.
Greene was shot down by fighters, bailed out, +
they strafed him going down. Wasn't hit. Landed OK.
Martin + Gilbert both shot down + killed.
My ship had a few holes in it. Several killed at
the field here, + about 1000 in Rangoon. Fires all
over + smoke very thick. After the raid, refueled
+ went on patrol. A busy day. Let em come.
We got about 15 ships to their 3.

In the *INTRODUCTION* to this book I told of my first impressions upon sighting the enemy and going into action. I can only add that the thought flashed through my mind that I would probably be killed on this fine sunny day, and yet despite being scared half to death there was never any thought of turning tail and running. And so, although this wasn't quite what I'd had in mind, I went to work at the profession I had so eagerly chosen, simply determined to kill as many of the enemy as I could before they killed me. I'd never had much use for the Japanese, particularly after reading about the countless atrocities and ruthless slaughter they had inflicted upon the Chinese people, and the AVG had offered a way to come to the aid of the underdog and strike back at the bully. But now, after their sneak attack at Pearl Harbor and their avowed plan to conquer all of Asia, I hated them with a passion.

I learned after only a few passes at the enemy bombers that deflection shooting was for the experts; I was sure I was scoring some hits, but the results were not at all satisfactory. And so I picked out this one bomber, got directly behind him and just under his prop-wash, and opened fire at about 200 yards. I could see my tracers converging on the fuselage and wing roots as I rapidly overtook him but kept firing until he blew up right in my face. His gas tanks exploded in a huge ball of flame, the concussion tossing my plane upward like a leaf. I fought for control, flying through the debris, felt a thud as something hit my left wing, let out a shout of triumph into my oxygen mask and thought *By God, I got one of the bastards no matter what happens from now on!* I was thinking strictly in terms of "one" plane, not the six or seven members of its crew; they were faceless individuals, seen only as shadow-figures if at all. I was elated beyond words, but there was little time for self-congratulation. With one victory in hand, I wanted more, and God knows there were plenty left. And so I went back to work, my attacks on the bombers now interrupted all too often by their fighters which were every bit as maneuverable as Chennault had said. Outnumbering us as they did, it was hard to get a shot at one before another was on my tail and I was forced to do a half-roll and dive away

For those who have never flown a fighter plane in combat it may be difficult to imagine just how incredibly busy the pilot is. Of course the flying itself, the movement of stick and rudder pedals and the many other things involved are done without conscious thought, but both hands and feet are constantly busy making adjustments. In addition to controlling the throttle, the left hand must be used for making changes in rudder and elevator trim tabs required with changes in speed and power settings. The right hand grasps the pistol-grip atop the control stick, index finger poised on the trigger, a squeeze of which will fire all six machine guns. Sometimes a gun jams and has to be cleared manually by pulling one of the six charging handles located in the cockpit and connected by cables to the individual guns. And all this time, if the pilot is to live, his head is constantly turning in every direction to locate the position of enemy planes, trying to make sure that one or more of them haven't swung in behind him, ready for the kill. *"Okay, Gibson, give me a few lazy-eights now...and get your head out of your ass! We're not alone up here, remember?"* Well, there's no way of knowing, but I'd bet that the majority of fighter pilots who were killed by enemy fighters never saw the plane that shot them down, never knew what hit them.

I finally ran out of ammunition after chasing the bombers about fifty miles out over the gulf of Martaban, sending another Sally down in a lazy spiral with his right engine and wing ablaze. During all this time—probably no more than forty minutes—I'd seen very few other P-40s, but now as I headed back toward Rangoon another one closed in on my wing: it was Haywood, grinning and giving me the thumbs-up sign. I saw him press his throat-mike and his mouth was moving, but could hear nothing on my radio. It dawned on me then that I hadn't heard anything on the radio since the fight first began; later a Jap bullet was found in the receiver.

Tom and I saw lots of smoke billowing above Rangoon, mostly from fires in the dock area, and more smoke from burning aircraft and buildings at Mingaladon. We buzzed the field, did victory rolls, and managed to dodge the bomb craters on the runway, landing safely. As we taxied to our dispersal area I saw that several of our planes had already returned.

Jesse Crookshanks, my crew-chief, jumped up on the wing the moment I cut the engine and slid back the canopy. God, I was tired and thirsty, but felt jubilant about the day's work. This feeling vanished immediately when Jesse told me that three of our planes had been shot down. "Who were they, Jesse, do you know?" I asked him.

"Yeah," he replied, "Martin and Gilbert and...Greene."

"Oh God, no!" I groaned, and there was a fleeting thought of a kiss on the cheek and whispered words, *"You take good care of Paul over there, R.T., hear?"*

But Paul was lucky; he'd been shot out of control, bailed out, then was strafed by enemy fighters while hanging from his 'chute but wasn't hit. He showed up a few hours later with a sprained neck, but otherwise O.K. Unfortunately, Neil Martin and Hank Gilbert were killed. They were buried the following day in the RAF's Airmen's Cemetery.

Neil Martin

161

Wednesday 24

(358-7)

Rangoon

12:00 p.m.

Two of our ships put out of commission on ground by fighters strafing field yesterday during raid. Reed hit a hole in runway & nosed up —— leaves us with 12 ships able to fly. Mine OK.

Spent 5 hours on patrol today with Mac & Haywood & others. Nothing sighted.

9 enemy ships reported heading this way but didn't come on in. Bangkok radio broadcast by Japs says they're coming over & give us some Xmas presents tomorrow. So we'll have to be ready for them.

Five of the RAF Brewsters destroyed on the ground yest. That leaves them about 15 ships.

Shell holes all over the runways & field. All buildings riddled by m-g. bullets by the fighters that strafed the field.

Went into town tonite & it is like a ghost town. Everybody has evacuated & only 2 or 3 joints open. Some of us ganged up with a bunch of seamen from the freighter Tulsa, in port here. They took us aboard & fed us & gave us Amer. cigarettes etc. A swell bunch.

There was still another "casualty" from the battle on the 23rd. Curtis Smith, the former Marine who was several years older than the rest of us, decided very early in the fight that this sort of thing was not for him. He returned early with nearly a full load of ammunition and was removed from combat status. Chennault then transferred him to his Kunming headquarters and named him Group Adjutant.

About 11:00 a.m. we got word the Japs were on the way
in again, so both flights took off, 6 in one + 7 in Mac's.
I was on Mac's wing. Went to 16,000 ft. and patrolled near
Rangoon. They came in from N.W. at 19,000 ft. Three
waves of bombers, 27 in each, and about 30 fighters.
Mac took our flight into one bomber formation + we
started making passes at the left flank. On the third
pass I got the last man, he started smoking badly
+ dove out heading for the ground. Turned around +
saw a fighter coming towards me. Turned at him
+ opened fire at about 400 yds. head on + held it.
They poured into him and he passed about 10 ft. below
me. Turned again + he was in flames + went down
in the gulf. Went back + shot more bombers. Several
fell out of formation + crashed all over. Mac, + myself +
Hedman on left flank. Older, Haywood, + Overend on Rt.
Mac + Overend both shot down + made belly landings,
but we didn't know it till they finally got home late.
Had given them up for dead. Other flt. got about 8 fighters.
All told we got about 14 bombers + 12 fighters.
My ship shot full of holes — 24 in all — five by cockpit.
Rangoon had a number of fires from bombs, + the field hit
runways but not much damage. A strange Xmas.

Just as advertised, the Japs showed up with more than enough presents to go around on Christmas day. This time they approached from a different direction and at a higher altitude, hoping to surprise us, but again we were ready for them. Our cast of characters had changed somewhat, of course, due to the tragic loss of Martin and Gilbert; their places were taken by Fred Hodges and Ralph Gunvordahl. Curtis Smith was replaced by Lew Bishop. Greene was unable to fly due to his neck injury, but since only thirteen planes were available anyway, that didn't matter. Originally the schedule had called for Reed, Overend, and myself to have this day off, but we were convinced the Japs would come as promised and raised such a stink with Olson that he put us back on the duty roster. We argued that we were veterans now and had established seniority rights, and Oley finally bought the idea. So there were ten of us on alert that morning who'd seen action on the 23rd: Brouk, Dupouy, Haywood, Hedman, Jernstedt, McMillan, Older, Overend, Reed, and myself; four ex-Marines and six from the Air Corps. The lessons we'd learned two days earlier were about to pay big dividends, once again proving that experience is indeed the best teacher. We had much more confidence now, both in our planes and in our own ability, a hungry handful of pilots in the right place at the right time. What more could anyone ask?

Duke Hedman, our piano-playing buddy from South Dakota, was destined to be the star of the show. He'd been skunked on the 23rd, but this was another day and by the time old Duke had exhausted his ammunition and was nearly out of fuel he'd shot down four bombers and a fighter, a record seldom surpassed in the annals of aerial combat.

Chuck Older and I each brought down two bombers and a fighter, and McMillan added three more bombers to the total. The rest of the guys each scored one or two victories except for Hodges and Bishop, each of whom claimed a probable or two.

A number of accounts have been written about how many enemy planes were shot down by the 3rd squadron in these two big air battles, most of them highly exaggerated. Now, while I don't pretend to be the final authority on the subject, as near as I can determine from the records available we were officially credited with 12 victories on the 23rd and another 23 on Christmas day, plus about a dozen probables for the two days. Of the 35 confirmed, 10 were fighters and 25 were bombers. Our losses amounted to five planes and two pilots. So much for the *invincible* Imperial Japanese Air Force.

Of course, the best present of all was the fact that we didn't lose a single pilot on Christmas day. There were some close calls, however; McMillan and Overend sustained hits in their coolant systems late in the fight, but instead of bailing out when their engines failed they elected to make belly landings in the rice paddies and escaped without serious injury. The rest of us didn't know this at the time, and when they failed to return to Mingaladon we assumed they'd been killed. But during the evening, an hour or two apart, they both showed up, a bit the worse for wear but in good spirits, precipitating a wild celebration that lasted far into the night.

Parker Dupouy was another who had his full share of luck on this day, surviving a mid-air collision with a Jap fighter; his right wing-tip sliced through the middle of the Jap's wing, sending the Oscar spinning to the ground. Dupouy was still able to control his plane with considerable difficulty despite having lost three feet of wing-tip and aileron. Somehow he managed to bring his P-40 down safely at Mingaladon, making a very hot landing with only marginal aileron control on a bomb-damaged runway. A tremendous bit of flying.

I was plenty lucky myself, coming within inches of a mid-air collision with a Jap Zero. We turned into each other in a head-on pass, both of us opening fire at about 400 yards. With a combined closing speed of nearly 600 mph things happend fast, allowing for less than two seconds of firing time. I could see my tracers converging on his engine, and his blazing directly at me, but neither of us took any noticeable evasive action and he passed directly beneath me, probably with about a foot of clearance between our prop-tips. I turned hard to the left, fighting his propwash and nearly blacking out from the "G" force, hoping for another shot; but it was unnecessary —his plane was burning like a torch, rolled slowly over and dove straight down toward the gulf. It struck me that head-on passes could be strictly non habit-forming

Later, many of the others had equally hair-raising experiences to describe, and hands were flying all over the place demonstrating the action. But our morale was higher than a kite now, and it was evident that suddenly the "Hell's Angels" squadron had come of age; in a matter of forty-eight hours we had progressed from an unknown quantity to a battle-tested unit, a dozen or so who could now lay legitimate claim to being fighter pilots. The necessary ingredients were all there: flying ability, courage, determination, desire, opportunity, and luck, all of them necessary for success and survival. And of all of these qualities, perhaps the most important is the one that is most difficult to define — luck! How else could we explain the deaths of Martin and Gilbert, while the rest of us survived? As Black Mac McGarry might have put it, think about it, friends.

I have spoken very little about the activities of the RAF during this period only because we saw them infrequently both during and after the action. They scrambled fifteen or so of their Brewsters each day, but judging from their sketchy reports they didn't fare very well. The Jap fighters were their equal when it came to speed and armament, and superior in climb and maneuverability. Unlike the P-40, the Buffalo could not out-dive the enemy, a disadvantage that often proved fatal. Even so, the RAF pilots were game and did the best they could under the circumstances. I believe they shot down a dozen or so of the enemy while losing the same number of planes and nearly as many pilots. In any event, the friction that had existed between us earlier was now largely replaced by a feeling of mutual respect.

Duke Hedman   Chuck Older

Paul Greene and Oley Olson outside our Alert tent. Rangoon

Parker Dupouy's plane after mid-air collision with Jap fighter

RTS beside battle-scarred –77 after Christmas day fight over
Rangoon.

Cruickshanks got my ship patched up & I was all set to test it when we got a raid warning at 10:00 a.m. We could only get 7 tommies in the air & the R.A.F. had about 7 Brewsters. They lost about 5 out of 12 yest. 3 killed.

We went to 22,000 ft. & patrolled for 2 hrs. but never saw a sign of any enemy ships. They didn't come in at all, which was ok with us. We have a lot of work to do to get more ships in shape. Got 2 more down from Toungoo yest. after the raid. They brought word that the 3 CW 21's, Shilling, Mangleburg, & Merritt, were lost en route to Kunming. One killed, one injured, & one ok., I guess. No names known.

It's getting hot as hell around here. The way the enemy has been coming, we're outnumbered about 7 or 8 to one. We heard today that they have said they were going to come tonite & take Rangoon with parachute troops. I think they'll get a warm reception again if they try it. God how we need more ships & men. Greene went up to Kunming this a.m. with Bill Pawley to see about reinforcements. Food situation is bad & our ammunition low. Some fun.

Saturday 27
(361-4)

We all expected another raid today, as this is an odd day & they have been coming every other day. We had an alarm at about 10:00 a.m., just the usual time, and ran to our ships. We were all on the runway just ready to take off when they said it was a mistake. No other activity so far as a raid goes.

The B24 came back today. Talked to Capt. Davis a while.

The Gov. of Burma & Gen. Brett came out today to our alert tent — both gave nice speeches congratulating us on our work. Still no definite word as to reinforcements.

Gunner, Overend & I went into town & had a good meal at the Silver Grill. Saw the boys from the Tulsa. I took one of them a souvenir — an instrument from a Jap bomber.

Several Jap planes had been shot down in the vicinity of the airfield, and some of our ground crewmen went out to have a look when they were off duty. One of them gave me an altimeter from a Sally bomber, which I in turn gave to a crew member from the *City of Tulsa* that night. They were a great bunch of guys, and due to leave in two or three days for Calcutta, India. Strangely, it never occurred to me to keep such a souvenir. On second thought, maybe it wasn't so strange after all.

Stood by on alert all day but nothing happened.

Good news finally got here - along with bad news. First, Rector, Wright, + Hurst blew in on CNAC. They are the advance guard of the 2nd Sqdn, which gets to toungoo this p.m. en route here for reinforcements. They should be on down here in a day or two. There is some talk that we may fly our shot-up ships to Loi Wing for repair + rest a few days ourselves! The guys brought the report of the 3 CW 21's. Got lost on way to Kunming + ran low on gas + all tried forced landings. Mangleburg was killed, Merritt injured, + Shilling OK. but all ships a washout. It really hurts to hear that kind of news — especially about Lacy M.

Erik Shilling led the flight of three CW-21s from Toungoo with Kunming, China, their destination. He was the only one who'd been over the route before, and had the only copy of a crude mimeographed map of the area. After flying for a couple of hours and being right on course, Shilling's engine suddenly conked out. He spotted a clearing on a small mountain plateau and made a wheels-up landing. There were no radios in any of the planes, so Erik was unable to tell Merritt and Mangleburg that they'd been on the corrct heading and Kunming was less than fifty miles distant. They had plenty of fuel, and to this day Shilling doesn't know why they didn't continue on course instead of trying to land, one in the rice paddies and one on the sandy bank of a river. Mangleburg's plane flipped over and burned, but Merritt was only slightly injured. He and Shilling eventually made their way to Kunming many days later, aided by Chinese tribesmen who spoke no English.

Monday 29
(363-2)

Stood by on alert again today.
This p.m. Newkirk & Bacon flew
in from Hetb. They said the rest of
the 2nd Sqdn. would be down in
the morning to replace ours.
We will leave for toungoo when
they get here!
A bunch of us went into Rangoon
tonite. Had dinner at the Silver
Grill & saw the boys from the
Tulsa again. They gave us
a pound of Amer. coffee, some
peanut butter, preserves, etc. which
we will eat for breakfast. I haven't
had a cup of Java in 3 days.
. Our diet consists of bread + beer.

The *City of Tulsa* sailed the following day bound for Calcutta. Weeks later we learned that it had been torpedoed and sunk by a Jap sub in the Bay of Bengal just a couple of days out of Rangoon. The reports indicated that there might have been only a handful of survivors. To my way of thinking there were a number of occupations more hazardous than my own, and being a merchant seaman during WW II was definitely one of them. Flying bombers was another!

Rangoon to
Toungoo

Tuesday 30
(364-1)

15 more ships from the 2nd Sqdn.
flew in about 10:30 this a.m.
We, ten ships + pilots, took off
about half an hour later.
Mac had engine trouble on take-off.
Stayed over here + will leave
for Kunming tomorrow,
Gunner + I + Keller had a
little party at the mess after
dinner. After shooting out
some of the lights, went to bed.
Olson, Reed, Greene, Adkins,
Loughlin, + Mac stayed in Rangoon.
They will come up in 3 or 4
days — soon as some of the
other ships are patched up a bit.

Our little base at Kyedaw was almost like a ghost town by this time, with only a few mechanics left to try to repair some of the damaged P-40s, at least to the extent that they could be flown on up to Kunming. "Point A," as it was now called, was in the charge of Ed Goyette, another of the older pilots who had asked to be taken off combat status and placed in an administrative job by Chennault.

Only one mess hall was now in operation, and following a lousy dinner that evening Ralph Gunvordahl and Danny Keller, one of our crew-chiefs, and I lingered on, sharing a bottle of scotch after the others had turned in. We were all wearing our side-arms, of course, and began to argue over who was the best shot, and laying bets. The lights were fine targets and we were having a wonderful time until Goyette showed up, mad as hell, and ordered us to cease and desist. We laughed and threated to shoot him, but were only kidding of course.

Toungoo to
Kunming.

Wednesday 31
(365)

We took off about 10:30 for Lashio.
Flew over Mandalay + then cut over,
landing at Lashio about 12:00.
Refueled + had lunch, + took off for
Kunming at 2:00 p.m. My ship
acted up all the way — prestone trouble
+ I was plenty worried. This is the
roughest damn country I ever
flew over, bar none.
We got into Kunming at 3:30 +
received quite an ovation from
the rest of the Group.
Drew winter flying equipment +
then came out to our Hostel, about 8
miles from the field. We have individual
rooms, hot water etc. It's really nice
Weather is quite cold here now.
The food is very good + plenty of it,
+ after Rangoon we're eating like hogs.

A helluva place to spend
New Years Eve. Ha!

MEMORANDA

In case of my death, this diary
and the one (for) 1942 are to be
sent to my parents, Mr. & Mrs. E.W.
Smith, 5853 La Cresta Court,
Hollywood, Calif.
                    R.T.S.
    New address — Febr. 4, 1942

          E.W. Smith
          1915 Oak St.
            Los Angeles, Calif.

Also, in event I pile up, I want the
following articles sent to my parents:
  1. Complete Air Corps dress uniform, ie:
     Blouse, cap, slacks, & shirt, Sam Browne, etc.
  2. All articles of clothing bought in
     Burma or China, such as women's woolen
     jacket, wool scarf, etc. Also silk &
     linen bedspreads, table-cloths, etc.
     Also the silk scarf given by Generalissimo
     Chiang Kai Shek, and silk embroidered
     bedspread from Gen. Mow, Chief of Chinese A.C.
  3. All curios, jewels, & souvenirs
     collected in various places.
  4. My Leica camera, No. 240597,
     which is to be given to Lt. B.T. Kleine,
     Randolph Field, Texas, and my
     .38 Colt Revolver, to be given to
     Jack Gellatly, Lincoln, Nebr.
     These two items to be sent on to the
     above mentioned parties by my parents.
                    R.T.S. Febr. 4, '42

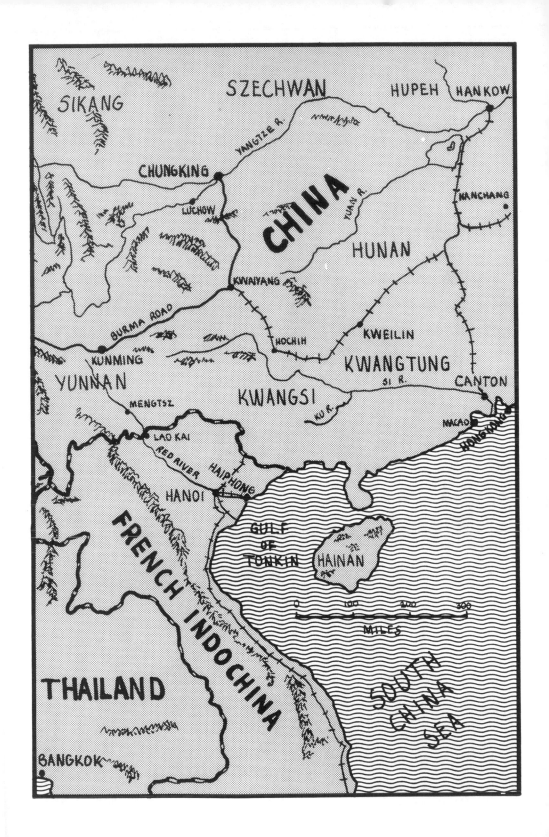

Thursday 1
(1-364)

Slept late this a.m. Up at about 7:30 + had a good breakfast. After that some of us went to town + sent radiograms to the states. Got some money changed. Rate of exchange is about 50 Chinese dollars to one U.S. I nonchalantly borrowed $500 from Bishop. Ha!

After lunch Gunner + I went out to the field with Skip Adair. He showed us all around. We looked in on my ship, + they are going over it completely. They're doing a good job of patching the holes, about 30 of them in all, + the mechs are working on the engine. She should be running sweet in a couple of days.

Compared to Toungoo and Rangoon, Hostel No. 1 in Kunming looked like the Waldorf. Each of the pilots had a large, comfortably furnished room in the dormitory building that had once been part of the University. Suddenly there was hot water for bathing and shaving, indoor toilet facilities, and a Chinese "room-boy" assigned to each of us to look after our laundry and housekeeping needs. This was where the 2nd squadron had been quartered before going to Rangoon, but the 1st squadron was located at Hostel No. 2 near the airfield so we didn't see much of them.

In another building nearby was the pilot's mess which also served as the theater where old movies were shown occasionally. Another large recreation room had a well-stocked bar, card tables, etc. Best of all, the food was both tasty and plentiful for a change, with our own experienced Bill Towery acting as Mess Supervisor.

Friday 2 ☺
(2-363)

Got up late again. This rest is really OK. After breakfast some of us got a car & went into town. Rode around looking the place over. Saw the "thieves market" etc. Quite an interesting sight. Kunming is probably the dirtiest town I've been in, and there is more poverty & squalor here than one can imagine. It's plenty chilly too, but the Chinese seem to be a hardy race & don't mind it.

I spent part of the afternoon in bed trying to get warm, but only partially succeeded.

After dinner played "Red Dog" with some of the boys — lost about $400 Chinese, which is about $8. gold.

Kunming was an ancient walled city of some 300,000, the capital of Yunnan province, located on a plateau some 6,000 feet above sea level. We arrived in mid-winter, and it was cold and damp. The airfield was a huge pastureland with wood-frame stucco buildings surrounded by revetments for bomb-protection. Several hundred Chinese coolies were hard at work building a wide runway of crushed rock which they carried by the basketful, laying a two-foot foundation which would some day be covered with asphalt and capable of handling heavy bombers. Meanwhile, we were limited to the sod areas which were dusty when the weather was dry and muddy when it rained. The runway wasn't completed until after we'd left, but it was a remarkable feat of engineering considering that it was built without the aid of any modern machinery or equipment.

Saturday 3
(3-362)

Olson got in last nite on CNAC from Rangoon via Calcutta. He says Pan Amer. is now operating a clipper run from New York to Calcutta, so maybe we'll have some Air Mail service again. I haven't had a letter in several weeks.

Got word this p.m. that the rest of our men were coming in this p.m. from Rangoon. McMillan, Greene, Reed, + Adkins all flew P40's up, so now our squadron is complete again. They report that the 2nd Sqdn. is raising merry hell about conditions in Rangoon — especially the food. They have also washed out two ships since they got there. Olson + I drove out to the field + met the guys when they came in.

Spent the rest of the p.m. talking to Mac + Greene.

Home + to bed early after dinner.

We had finally received some area maps printed in Chinese that were only slightly better than the crude mimeographed copies we'd been using. There was very little detail shown, few identifiable roads, lakes, rivers or airfields, and only a couple of railways. Add to this the fact that the many villages, mountain ranges, and valleys between looked distressingly alike, plus the complete lack of navigational aids; getting lost was no trick at all, we did it all the time.

After another late breakfast, Shilling, Mac, Greene, Foshee, + myself got a car and drove into town. Tried to find J. B. Foster, one of the fellows who was on our boat who is here in Kunming. We found where he lived but he wasn't home.

Came back to the Hostel, had lunch, + sit around listening to the phonograph and shooting the bull.

About 4:00 p.m. We all went back to town to try to do some shopping. Didn't get much done but had a lot of fun seeing the sights etc. Paul + I each bought a big wall-map of the world for our rooms. Couldn't find any rugs for the floor.

After dinner we had a movie here — College Holliday — about 4 yrs. old.

Six of the boys go on night alert at the field tonite.

I don't know exactly when it started, but at some point in their reporting of our activities the Chinese newspapers began to refer to the AVG as the *Flying Tigers*. We thought this was pretty amusing, especially a few weeks later when we received a bunch of large decals meant to be applied to the sides of our planes. They depicted a caricature of a winged tiger and were designed by the Walt Disney studios.

Monday 5
(5-360)

Not much in the way of excitement today. I am to be on night alert tonite. Went out to the field this afternoon and tested old "77". She's all patched and tuned up now, and running like a million bucks. Flew around for 45 min. looking over the country etc.

Older, Greene, Jernstett, Bishop, Overend, & myself went on night duty at 6:00 p.m. Spent the evening playing poker. I lost about $500 Chinese — or $10 gold. Went to bed about midnite on cots in the alert shack.

Nothing happened after that.

Some of us learned on this day that Marion Baugh, one of the instructor-pilots at the Chinese flight school in Yunnanyi, had been killed in the crash of his little Ryan primary trainer. With him, as a passenger, was Julian Terry, one of our administrative clerks. Terry was pinned in the wreckage and seriously injured, but made a complete recovery after spending several weeks in the French hospital at Kunming. Baugh was killed instantly, and buried in the Kunming cemetery.

3rd squadron ground personnel: Kneeling, l to r: Francisco, Perry, Hoyle, Stiles, Baisden, R.A. Smith, Loomis, Engel, Regis, Clouthier, Losonsky, Riffer. Standing, l to r: Osborne, Gallagher, Christensen, Poshefko, Blaylock, Stolet, Van Timmeren, Schramm, H.L. Olson, Crookshanks, Seiple, Fauth.

Got up late & spent most of the day reading a mystery book.

Word from Rangoon that the Japs sent over about 40 fighters and 6? bombers. Squadron 2, there now, intercepted them and shot down 4 or 5 — but 3 of our boys were shot down too — all got down safely. Bright, Christman, & Paxton were the three. Haven't heard any particulars. Now they know what we went thru down there. Ha! — Only they didn't come close to our record of shooting down the damn Japs.

After dinner some of us had a black-jack game & I dropped a few hundred bucks again.

Bright, Paxton, and Christman all wound up in the Rangoon hospital according to later reports. Their wounds were not serious, but all three were lucky (that word again) to be alive. Bright crash-landed his crippled plane in the rice paddies, escaped just before it burst into flames. Paxton, his windshield shot away and suffering from wounds caused by shrapnel and glass splinters, made it back to Mingaladon. Christman bailed out safely after being shot out of control, a bullet crease along his lower jaw. Incidentally, Christman was the fifth AVG pilot whose life had been saved by a Chinese parachute and we no longer questioned their reliability. Burt Hooker and Charley Leighty, our parachute riggers who packed and inspected them periodically, deserve much of the credit. Our lives were literally in their hands.

Wednesday 7
(7-358)

Went into town this a.m. + sent Cablegrams to the folks + to Tedder. After lunch stayed up in the rec. room + read till 4:30. At that time Alder, Haywood, Jernstedt, Overend, Hodges, + myself went to the field for night alert duty. Spent most of the night playing poker + blackjack — my luck finally turned + I won about $800 Chinese.

We turned in about 1:30 but none of us slept much due to a couple of Coolies making noise in our shack all night. No excitement - solid overcast.

Ben Foshee, Lew Bishop, and Oley Olson outside our quarters in Hostel No. 1, Kunming.

Thursday 8
(8-357)

Got off alert at 6:00 a.m. + came back to our quarters. I turned in + slept till noon. Spent another afternoon reading. Our Sqdn. goes on daytime alert along with Sqdn. 1 starting Sunday.

Reports from Rangoon say the Japs are bombing at night now. The 2nd Sqdn. is on night alert there now.

Ken Merritt was killed at Rangoon last night. Some ship landing at night ran off runway + into a car in which Merritt was sleeping. That makes 7 pilots killed so far.

Played a little more poker last nite + picked up about $500.

Greene, Bronk, + Sawyer went to Yunnany for a couple of days hunting.

Ken Merritt was killed in a freak accident, asleep in a car near the edge of the runway. Jim Howard, Gil Bright, and Pete Wright of the 2nd squadron had taken off at 3:00 a.m. in an effort to intercept Jap bombers in the bright moonlight. They failed to make contact and returned to land. When Pete lowered his landing gear a hydraulic line in his cockpit ruptured, spraying Pete and the entire cockpit with hydraulic fluid, nearly blinding him. He managed to set the plane down on the runway where several cars had been parked alongside with their headlights on to help guide the pilots. His plane veered off to one side and Pete, half-blinded, tried to steer it between cars. The lights on Merritt's car were not on; Wright's P-40 crashed into it, the propeller chewing it to bits and killing Ken instantly.

Friday 9
(9-356)

Spent the day in loafing, mostly, altho I flew an hour this p.m. Did some acrobatics & buzzed some of the gang out on the lake in a boat. All of us who fought at Rangoon received copies of recommendations for citations, from Olson to Col. Chennault. Word from Rangoon that some of the 2nd Sqdn. went over to a Jap field in Thailand & strafed planes & stuff on the ground. Charley Mott was shot down by ground fire & was seen to land right next to the field. If he wasn't killed in the crash he is either a prisoner of war or else has been "eliminated" by the little yellow —.

Charley Mott, along with Moose Moss, Gil Bright, and Percy Bartelt made an early morning strafing attack on the Jap airfields at Meshod, Thailand. They set fire to eight Jap planes, but Mott was shot down by ground fire and made a crash landing in a clearing near the field. The other three returned safely to Rangoon without knowing Mott's fate, but a few days later some members of the squadron heard Charley on a radio broadcast from Bangkok, reporting that he was being held prisoner but was unhurt and being treated well.

2nd squadron pilots l to r: Newkirk, Geselbracht, Bartling, Howard, Layher, Rangoon, Jan. '42

Chennault with a group of pilots study a map while planning a mission at Kunming in early '42. Standing, l to r: Carl Brown, Jack Croft, Charley Bond, Ed Leibolt, Louis Hoffman, Oley Olson. Kneeling: Matt Kuykendall, Dohn Dean, Joe Rosbert, Chennault, and Sandy Sandell.

Saturday 10 ☾
(10-355)

Went hunting this afternoon with Skip Adair. Drove out about 15 mile & found a nice little lake. Saw a big flock of geese but couldn't get close enough for a shot at them. We got three doves apiece in the surrounding woods, and some exercise.

Went on night alert duty at 6:00 p.m., played cards & listened to phonograph till pretty late.

Col. Chennault got back this p.m. from Chunking conference. No news received of any importance.

Chennault and Skip Adair, Kunming

Didn't get much sleep last nite
on alert, so went back to bed
after breakfast + slept till noon.
Played some cards + read this p.m.
Greene + Brouk + Sawyer got back
from Yunnan Yi + report good
duck hunting up there.
Our Sqdn. started holding a 12
man alert on daytime duty today.
I was off today but go on tomorrow.

Cloth patches, such as the one shown being worn by "Oley" Olson, were sewn to the backs of our flight suits and leather jackets. The Chinese characters say: *"I am an American pilot fighting for China against the Japanese. Please take me to the nearest communications agency."* Later these things became known as "blood chits," though I don't recall hearing them called that while in the AVG.

Monday 12
(12-353)

Up at 4:15 and out to the field.
Spent the whole day on alert duty.
Haywood, myself, + Shilling were
assigned a photographic mission. Shilling
flew the camera ship, + Haywood + I
were to escort him. We were to go over
the border into French Indo-China
and get pictures of Jap air bases,
troop concentrations, etc. We started
out for our objective, but about
45 minutes out we ran into a
solid overcast + had to turn back.
Maybe we'll go again tomorrow if
the weather is better.

Got off duty at 6:00 p.m., + after
dinner some of us sat around the
rec. hall shooting the bull.

I'm on again tomorrow so it's up
early again.

5 pilots + ships from the 1st Sqdn.
left today for Rangoon to go down
+ help the 2nd Sqdn.

Tuesday 13
(13-352)

Up again at 4:15 for duty.

Shilling, Haywood, & I took off again at 12:00 to get pictures across the border, but again encountered solid overcast & had to come back.

Got back over Mengtze and received radio message saying there were three enemy bombers in immediate vicinity. We hunted all over for them but never sighted them. They must have seen us as they unloaded their bombs on side of a mountain, & we later saw the smoke.

That would have been duck soup.

Got a wire from the folks this p.m. & felt better about everything. Some more of the fellows are resigning to go home, but they will be dishonorably discharged.

The rest of us will stick it out for our full year — with luck.

Among those resigning were a couple of ground types named Larry Moore and Ken Sanger, thought to be madly in love. With each other, that is. They made for Hollywood, posed as pilots who'd shot down many Jap planes, and received the hero treatment. And damned if *Republic Pictures* didn't buy their story; the result was an unmitigated abortion of a movie called *The Flying Tigers*, starring a young John Wayne and John Carroll. It was released in late '42, is still shown in re-runs on TV, and must surely rank as one of the ten worst pictures of all time.

Wednesday 14
(14-351)

Stood by on alert again all day, but no excitement.

Spent some time supervising the Chinese painters who are re-painting our ships. They are looking like new with our new paint jobs. Our "Hell's Angels" were getting a little pale.

"Gunner" Gunvordahl is the only pilot from our Sqdn. who is resigning to go home. I argued with him for 3 hours trying to change his mind, but he is still leaving.

Reports from Rangoon say that the Japs are bombing only at night now. Guess its too expensive to come in the daytime.

Ralph Gunvordahl, a big jolly guy from Burke, South Dakota, was a good friend and we hated to see him leave. I'm sure his decision was based on some personal reasons which he chose not to discuss, and all of our arguments fell on deaf ears. Shortly after his return to the "real world" he was hired by the Republic Aircraft Corp. on Long Island as a production test pilot. A year or two later he was killed in the crash of a P-47 on a routine test-hop.

Thursday 15
(15-350)

Spent the day on alert again.
A batch of photographers took pictures
of our Sqdn. today, & said some
would be sent to the states for publication.
Got a letter from Van Mullem mailed
the 13th of October.
Bill Reed & I flew an hour local
today. Did some Combat & acrobatics
& had fun in general.
The Chief of the Chinese Air Corps
is here for a few days. Reed, Bishop, &
I shot the bull with him for a
couple hours after dinner tonite.
My promotion to Flight Leader
was authorized by Col. Chennault
effective today.
I'm off tomorrow, but have night
duty tomorrow night.
Mac, who is also off, & I plan to
go hunting tomorrow.

I don't know the exact date, but it was at about this time that Paul Frillman, our Chaplain, officiated at a ceremony other than a funeral. This was a happy occasion, the wedding of one of our nurses, Emma Jane "Red" Foster, to 2nd squadron pilot John Petach. Their courtship had begun aboard the *Jaegersfontein* six months earlier enroute to Burma. The happy couple's honeymoon was to be very brief, however; Johnny had to hurry back to rejoin his squadron for the continuing battles being fought over Rangoon.

Friday 16 ●
(16-349)

Mac & I took off this morning and drove up to the mountains above the lake. Did some rifle & pistol shooting, & also got some good pictures. On the way back, for lunch, we ran into a mob of people coming from town, & trucks parked along the road under trees. They said there was an air raid warning. We hurried back to the Hostel only to find it was a false alarm. After lunch we went hunting again, out to a little lake Skip & I discovered. Mac shot a duck & we got several doves. Had a swell time all day. Drove to the field & I went on night alert duty.

For several years the Chinese had operated an air-raid warning net throughout eastern and southern China. This net consisted of scattered outposts located within a grid sector-map, each equipped with a low power radio transmitter capable of sending messages by Morse code to a central receiving station. The radios were manned by Chinese operators who reported enemy air activity in their sector, such as the number and type of planes, estimated altitude, and heading.

Chennault significantly upgraded the system by establishing additional stations with voice transmitters operated by AVG radio operators. These guys had a very lonely job, but they were dedicated and did an outstanding job, not only in giving us warning of impending attacks but in helping to guide lost pilots. An excellent account of their work can be found in the book "With Chennault in China-- A Flying Tiger's Diary," written by Robert M. Smith, who had operated one such station.

189

Saturday 17
(17-348)

Got off night duty at 5:30 a.m. & came back to Hostel to go to bed. I was awakened at 9:30 by my boy who said there was an air raid alarm. I got up & dressed & they said it was a false alarm. This happened twice more during the morning, but nothing developed here. However, three enemy bombers were reported 100 miles South East, and MacMillan, Shilling, Oller, & Haywood flew down to get them. They found them and shot down all three. I went out to the field in the afternoon and led a six plane flight down almost to the border to cover up for the photo mission to Hanoy. No enemy ships sighted tho, so we came back 2 hours later. I have been cussing plenty about not being on hand to take care of the three bombers. The guys who got them have been ragging me & telling me what fun it was. That is something we have all prayed for, & I missed it.

JANUARY 1942

Sunday 18
(18-347)

Spent a very uneventful day
on alert. Sat around + wrote a
long letter to the folks for
Gunner to take back. He and Houle,
Bernsdorf + Knapp leave via CNAC
for Calcutta tomorrow headed for home.
Spent the evening shooting the bull
with them + Van Shappard.

Staff members at Kunming, l to r: John Williams, Curtis Smith,
Skip Adair, Dr. Tom Gentry, Chennault, Dr. Everett Bruce,
Harvey Greenlaw, Ed Conant, Dr. Lewis Richards.

Monday 19
(19-346)

Another day on alert without any excitement. Flew two ground gunnery missions, as my ship was re-boresighted for 300 yds & I wanted to see how the guns fired in the air. They didn't work too well, partly due to faulty ammunition, & partly mechanical failure. I have to get them going better than they were today before I'll be satisfied.

Word from Rangoon that 4 of the boys from the 2nd ran into one Jap bomber & shot the hell out of it. Down by Tavoy or Moulmein somewhere. One of my 50 cal. guns shot the prop on my ship so its' out of commission now.

The two .50 caliber machine guns mounted above the engine were synchronized to fire through the prop blades, or rather between them. Occasionally the synchronizing mechanism would malfunction, or a faulty round of ammunition might result in a split-second hangfire, and result in a neat half-inch hole in one of the prop-blades. Since the hole was drilled in the "meaty" part of the blade, near the hub, the prop would continue to function okay and there was surprisingly little vibration due to the weight imbalance. Fortunately, this sort of thing didn't happen often, although this was the second such experience I'd had, the first being during one of the fights at Rangoon.

Tuesday 20
(20-345)

Up at 4:15 a.m. again and out
to the field. We had an alarm
at 10:00, got in our ships +
warmed them up, but it proved
to be a false alarm + nothing more
was heard about it.

Played black-jack all afternoon
and won about a thousand dollars.

"Crook" got a new prop on
my ship + reports she's ready
to go.

I'm supposed to be off tomorrow
but traded it for Thursday with
Du Puoy, who's feeling low.

A wire from Rangoon today said
that 6 P-40's escorted 6 Blenheim's
of the R.A.F. on a raid in Thailand.
All got back OK. with the exception
of Moss, who was last seen in
a dogfight with an I 96 jap fighter.

Wednesday 21
(21-344)

Older & I flew an hour with Donnovan & Raines today, trying to show them some formation flying. They were pretty lousy, but maybe they'll catch on sooner or later—probably later.

Our Sqdn. is supposed to escort about 30 Russian-built bombers to Hanoy or some place in Indo-China on Friday. That should be very interesting.

Another wire from Rangoon today saying Moss had turned up in Moulmein safe. Hot damn!

Tomorrow is my day off, & Mac's too. We plan to do some more hunting

Moose, the "acrobat," performed an unexpected tumbling act on the previous day, bailing out after being shot down by Jap fighters. This happened during a strafing raid on the Tak-Meshod area of Thailand near the Burma border. Moose was only slightly injured, and with the help of friendly natives made his way back the next day to Moulmein, Burma, and later returned to Rangoon. He was doubly lucky on this occasion, as many of the Burmese were anti-British and pro-Japanese, and might just as easily have turned him over to the enemy.

Thursday 22
(22-343)

Spent the day off, but didn't do much Mac & I were going hunting, but couldn't find a car not in use, so called it off.
There was supposed to be an execution this afternoon, and we thought we might take that in, but it was postponed or something. Somebody was supposed to be shot, against the wall of the East gate of the city, which is only a couple of blocks from here.
Mac, Shilling, & I spent the evening shooting the bull etc.

Friends, I simply can't believe that I wrote the lines appearing above concerning an execution, or that I was the "callow youth" that the words imply. In retrospect, I can only say that by this time many of us had become more or less casual about the thought of death. and were fatalistic about the chances of our own survival. As for the Chinese, life was one of the cheapest commodities imagineable. The man who was supposed to be executed had been found guilty of stealing about two hundred feet of copper telephone wire. There was no trial or jury involved, of course; he was sentenced to die by a Chinese magistrate, the usual penalty for a crime of this magnitude. Mac and I learned that the execution had indeed taken place a couple of days later, with the kneeling culprit shot in the back of the head with a revolver in the hand of a policeman. We agreed that we were lucky it had been postponed and that we had missed it, although such occurrences were fairly common and always drew a big crowd of Chinese who seemed to thoroughly enjoy the show.

Friday 23
(23-342)

Up at 4:15 for alert duty again.
Bad weather caused postponement
of the bombing raid to Hanoy, but
we'll probably go tomorrow.
Flew 45 min. today — Brouk & I
did some combat & acrobatics.
Radio from Rangoon tonite said
they had two air raids today, &
that R.A.F. & A.V.G. planes shot
down twenty Jap ships, & two
of ours were missing. Don't
know whether they meant A.V.G. or
R.A.F, or who the two are.
Skip & Chuck Older & I spent
the evening talking over old times.
Got a wire from the folks
today, an old one forwarded
from Rangoon.

The two missing pilots turned out to be Bill Bartling of the 1st squadron, and Bert Christman of the 2nd. Bartling's controls were damaged but he was still able to make a crash landing in the rice paddies and escaped serious injury. Bert Christman was not so fortunate (lucky?) he was jumped by three I-97 fighters, his engine and cockpit shot up badly, and for the third time in as many weeks tried to bail out. Apparently he was fatally hit as he went over the side; his bullet-ridden body was later recovered, and the ripcord of his chute had never been pulled. Bert Christman, talented artist and wonderful guy, was the second of the "Bloom bunch" to die.

"Hell's Angels," l to r: McMillan, Greene, Hedman, Bishop, Donovan, Reed, Brouk, Laughlin, Groh, Raine. My plane is in background.

Saturday 24 ☽
(24-341)

Our Sqdn. was given the job of escorting the 18 Chinese bombers on a raid to Hanoi today. Olson, Reed, Older, Jernstedt, Mac, Haywood + myself went, plus Dean + Hoffman in the photo ship + it escort. We flew to Mengtze, refueled, took off + joined the bombers there over Mengtze. When we took off, we all felt as if it was our last flight — going 150 miles into enemy territory + expecting to encounter Jap fighters 4 or 5 to one is no picnic. Possibility of being forced down + held prisoner etc., or shot, was what worried us most. But, it was overcast all the way + we all got back without meeting any trouble. We were in the air 3 hrs. + 15 min., + all landed with only 10 gal. of gas. Mighty low grade!

In the raid on Rangoon yest., Christman and Bartling were shot down — Chris was killed + Bart made crash landing unhurt. 12 more ships + pilots from 1st Sqdn. went to Rangoon today. Report from R- says they had another raid today.

Spent a quiet day on alert — nothing much happened. As reported for yesterday, 12 ships from 1st went to Rangoon to help out the 2nd.

In the raid today we heard the boys shot down about twenty more but don't know the details.

Rumor running around again about the Army taking over our group.

Mac + I are off tomorrow & plan to go hunting if possible.

Nine E 15's, Russian built pursuit ships of the Chinese air force, flew in + landed late this afternoon. Don't know whether they are to stay or not.

Rumors about the future of our little group abounded. One had it that we would be disbanded and sent home within a matter of weeks. Another said that the Army Air Corps would soon take over and all of us would be inducted whether we wanted to or not. Nobody seemed to quite know what would happen, and the rumors were to continue for months. Meanwhile, all we wanted was to be left alone and allowed to continue the fight under the terms of our original agreement, though we knew that this could not continue indefinitely.

The Russian-built E-15s were obsolete biplanes armed with two .30 caliber machine guns, built about the time of the Civil War in Spain in the mid-thirties. They were no match for the Jap fighters, although to their credit the Chinese pilots never hesitated to attack. A few days later most of them returned to their home base at Chungking.

Monday 26
(26-339)

Mac & I were off today, so we went hunting this afternoon with Col. Sutherland of the McGruder Commission and Skip Adair. Went out to some lakes about 20 miles from here, but didn't have much luck. Skip & Mac each got two doves, but all I could do was wing three, & they all got away.

Wire from Rangoon saying there had been a raid today. Our gang shot down three or four, but "Cokey" Hoffman was shot down & killed. We all feel bad about that. He was the oldest pilot in the Group, & left a wife & 2 children.

They had a phony air raid alarm here today, but nothing developed.

Louis "Cokey" Hoffman, of San Diego, was the oldest pilot of our group at forty-three, and the only enlisted pilot; but unlike some of the older pilots he looked forward to getting a crack at the Japs. An ex-navy pilot, Cokey arrived in Rangoon in mid-January with Bob Neale and a handful of other 1st squadron pilots sent to augment the 2nd squadron. On the second scramble of the day he and Bob Prescott were jumped by five I-97 fighters: Cokey was shot down and killed, but Prescott escaped.

Both squadrons in Rangoon were doing a terrific job against formidable odds. Jack Newkirk, leader of the 2nd squadron, was racking up quite a score, as were Tex Hill, Frank Lawlor, Gil Bright, Ed Rector, Frank Schiel and others. And the 1st squadron, newly arrived, was chalking up its share; Sandy Sandell, Bob Neale, George Burgard, Charley Bond, Bob Little, Moose Moss, Black Mac McGarry, Dick Rossi, Greg Boyington, all were among those taking a terrible toll of the Jap fighters.

Tuesday 27
(27-338)

Spent the day on alert. Nothing happened until Older & I took Raines & Donovan up for some training on formation & attacks. We had been up for about 30 min. when they said to come in & land over the radio. Older led us back to field & I saw about 8 ships taxiing out to take off. I knew there must be an alarm on, so when the others landed I stayed up & joined the ships taking off. There had been a report of 6 Bombers over Mengtz & we headed that way. Got about halfway & were told to return, as the bombers had hightailed for the border. So we all came back. If it hadn't been for a "tie-up" in operations we would have got there in time — dammit anyway. That would have been easy pickins!

3rd "Hell's Angels" squadron pilots: Standing, l to r: Greene, Dupouy, Groh, Adkins, Raine, McMillan, Olson, Smith, Jernstedt, Brouk, Shilling, Hodges. Kneeling: Reed, Laughlin, Overend, Haywood, Older, Bishop, Foshee, Hedman, Donovan, Cavanah. Kunming, China, January 1942

Wednesday 28
(28-337)

About ten o'clock this morning we had an alarm & warmed up our ships ready to go. Got word that 6 enemy bombers were headed for Mergiz again, & six of us took off & went down there looking for them. Never got sight of them, & guess they must have headed back for the border before we got there - dammit!

The rest of the day was quiet.

We had Squadron Group pictures taken yesterday, & saw them today. They turned out fine.

Message from Rangoon this p.m. said 40 Jap fighters came over Rangoon this morning. Our gang shot down 10 & the R.A.F. got 7, making a total of 17, & we never lost a single ship.

Maj. Alexander stopped in for a few minutes from Chungking to Calcutta via C.N.A.C. Hedman & I had a good talk with him.

Thursday 29
(29-336)

Col. Chennault wanted some pictures of
bases in French Indo-China & called for
volunteers to make the flight. Olson led,
with Shilling in the photo ship, + I led
the 2nd element with Laughlin on wing.
Went to Mengtz & landed to refuel.
While refueling we had an air-raid alarm.
Oley & Laughlin took off immediately, but
Shilling couldn't get started + took cover. My
battery was dead & I had to get some Chinese
to crank my engine by hand. I finally got
it started + took off, expecting to get shot in
the back any second. Climbed to 22,000 +
joined the others. Nothing developed + we
landed soon after + refueled. Took off for
Son La, about 100 miles across the border in
Indo-China. Got pictures there, + at Lao Kai
on return. No enemy ships sighted.
Returned to Kunming without stopping.
They say they had another raid in
Rangoon today + 16 Japs were shot down
+ we lost none.

Friday 30
(30-335)

Spent a quiet day on alert.
This p.m., Paxton & Petach flew
in from Rangoon. They tell some
very interesting stories of the action
down there.
An R. A. F. Blenheim flew in with
a lot of rank aboard, & brought
official confirmation of our claims
down there.
Van Shappard flew in from
Yunnan Yi today in a Ryan trainer.
Telegram received about dinner time
from Rangoon says Tommy Cole was
killed in a crash there today.
Don't know the details.
Received a radiogram from
Mom today. She's keeping a
scrapbook of clippings concerning
the A. V. G.

Tom Cole, an ex-navy pilot from Clayton, Missouri, was strafing enemy troop positions near Meshod, Thailand, when he crashed. Others from the 2nd squadron who were on the mission couldn't be sure wether he'd been hit by ground fire or simply failed to pull out of his diving attack in time. This was a common hazard called "target fixation," wherein a pilot becomes so intent upon shooting a ground target that he keeps right on firing until it is too late to pull up safely and his plane mushes into the ground at high speed. The usual result is a cartwheeling ball of flames followed by a column of black smoke; not a very pretty sight.

I came frighteningly close to a similar fate a few months later while strafing a train locomotive in Indo-China.

Saturday 31
(31-334)

Another day on alert, with no excitement.
Killed some time by shooting pistol
& rifles on our private range at the
alert shack.

The Beechcraft came in from Rangoon
this p.m. Wright, Moss & a couple
of mechanics came up to rest a while.
Wright is recovering from an
appendectomy & Moss needs some
work done on his teeth, some of
which were chipped when he
bailed out after being shot down.

They say Cole crashed while on
a strafing mission. Was either
hit or didn't pull up in time, &
crashed into some trees.

I wish they'd send us back
down to Rangoon to relieve the 2nd Sqdn.

All combat pilots here were presented
with a pair of Gold wings of the Chinese
Air Force by some ranking Chinese guy
today. Quite a speech & ceremony
connected with it.

Same old grind again today.
Flew an hour this p.m.
Took Raines out for some formation,
Combat, & acrobatics. Had a lot
of fun, but he wasn't too tough
in combat.
After dinner went to an old 1937
picture show here, & talked to a
guy down from Chungking. He has
a Leica camera that he said he
might sell me, & if the price is
right I may buy it.
I may sell overend my movie
camera too while I'm at it.
Tomorrow is my day off, but
haven't made any plans.
No raids the past 2 days in Rangoon.

After the movie Ben Foshee stopped by my room to chew the fat for a while, saying, "I swear, Tadpole, that 'ol movie really stunk up the place." I agreed, laughing at his use of the nickname that Tex Hill had given me. That had come about one night when somebody asked me what the "T" in my initials stood for, and Tex promptly said, "T stands for Tadpole, what else?" From that point on I answered to that as well as to R.T. Actually, the T stands for Tharp, my mother's maiden name, and while I'm proud of it I must admit that Tadpole sounds a bit more distinctive.

Speaking of surnames, we had some real beauties; how about Geselbracht, Losonsky, Misenheimer, and Mihalko for starters? Or Rodewald, Uebele, Janski, and Daube? Believe it or not, none of them played football for Notre Dame.

Today was my day off, & spent most of the day just loafing. However, this afternoon they held a mass meeting of A.V.G. personnel & Chinese Air Force, soldiers, etc. A lot of Chinese dignitaries were there & a couple gave speeches. It was designed to boost everybody's morale & pay honors etc.

About eight of us got gifts. They are beautiful silk bedspreads with a lot of fancy embroidery on them. They were gifts of Gen. Mow, the Chinese Chief of the Air Corps.

After all this, Olsen was told to get five other men & put on a 6-ship formation review etc. I was in it, and they said I was to do some acrobatics after we were thru & they started to land. Did a few rolls etc., & then came in. Col. Chennault came over later & paid me a nice compliment.

Tuesday 3
(34-331)

Back on alert again today.
All quiet & a dull day was
had by all.

No raids in Rangoon lately.

Met Mr. Taylor at the rec. room
at dinnertime. I had met him a
couple of nights ago & expressed an
interest in a Leica Camera
which he is thinking of selling.
It is really a little beauty,
with an F 2 lens & 1/1000 second speed.
I am to keep it a couple of
days & shoot some film & see
how it works, & then buy it
if the price is OK.

Our nurses, Emma Jane "Red" Foster and Jo Stewart.

Wednesday 4
(35-330)

Another day on alert, + no excitement. Spent some time shooting a roll of films with the Leica. Turned them in to the Photo section this p.m. + can see the results tomorrow.

Bacon & Swartz of 2nd Sqdn. came in from Rangoon today. They say Toungoo was bombed 3 times in past 24 hrs.

The latest rumor is that a Bombardment Group of the U.S. Air Corps is on the way here. I hope its true

Thursday 5
(36-329)

Today was my day off, so got to sleep late this a.m. Nothing much doing. After lunch Overend, Hoslee, Pete Wright, & myself went into town. Sent a radiogram to the folks. We all had our cameras and took a lot of interesting shots. Some of the bombed section of town + some of the poor beggars wandering about.

Pietsker of the photo section says the roll I took yesterday was very good, so think I'll buy the Leica if it isn't too high. I think I'll draw the line at $150.00

Conant, the Group transportation officer, has arranged to get a BT-14 to fly, & has Greenlaw's permission for me to go along as his instructor. It will be a good break in the monotony around here to fly in it for an hour or so a day.

Ed Conant, it will be remembered, was the former navy PB-Y pilot who had wrecked a few P-40s at Toungoo; we kidded him about being a Jap Ace. So I agreed to become a part-time instructor| again, but it was almost a lost cause. Conant, like a few others in the outfit, simply wasn't cut out to be a fighter pilot.

Friday 6
(37-328)

Some break in the monotony on alert today. They are having 7 Chinese fighter pilots check out in P-40's starting today. Five of them checked out today & did a pretty fair job of it, except for the 5th one. He came in & the cross-wind got him & he ground-looped. Wiped off the landing gear, & ruined the engine & wing tips.

Shot some more pictures with my new camera, and after dinner Mac & I went into town to see the guy who owns it. I bought it from him for $135.00 gold — a steal.

Word from Rangoon that they had another raid, the first for a week or so. 1st Sqdn. shot down 7 and R.A.F. got 3.

This little Leica was a beautiful piece of German craftsmanship; it was the latest model, a G as I recall, with an F2 Summar lens and shutter speed up to 1/1000th second. Included in the price were three rolls of 35 mm Kodachrome color film, impossible to find in Kunming. Later I got hold of two or three more rolls, and wound up getting some excellent color pictures, both on the ground and in flight. One of these has become rather well known to aviation enthusiasts; a photo of five "Hell's Angels" P-40s in echelon formation, much like the posters I'd seen outside those post-offices when I was a kid. So far as I know, I was the only one in the entire AVG fortunate enough to get any good color photos of this type.

Saturday 7
(38-327)

On alert duty again today. Flew an hour with Cavanah, Overend, & Donovan, practicing gunnery runs & combat. Also flew an hour in the BT with Conant. Tried a few acrobatics, which were lousy, & Conant got sick & we came in. Tomorrow we start in earnest.

I'm off tomorrow, but go on nite alert for the coming week, starting tomorrow nite — with Oller, Groh, & Adkins.

Bad news from Rangoon today — Sandell, 1st Squadron Leader, was testing his ship, which had a new tail assembly after a Jap dove into the old one. He spun in & was killed

Got my pictures today from the photo section, & they all turned out damn good.

Sandy's plane had been damaged while parked in Rangoon by a crippled Jap fighter whose pilot tried to destroy it in a Kamikaze dive. He succeeded in smashing the tail assembly, but it was replaced by that of another damaged P-40. It was while testing his plane after the repairs had been made that Sandy apparently overstressed it and the new tail assembly failed. Too low to bail out, Sandy was killed. His deputy, Bob Neale, was named to replace him as leader of the 1st squadron, a very popular choice.

I was off duty today, as I go on night duty all this week, starting tonite.

Overend, Hodge, Reed, + myself went out to the photo lab. after lunch, + spent the afternoon developing + printing pictures. Also enlarged some from some 35mm. rolls, mine included.

. Went on night duty at 5:30 with the other 3, + spent a quiet evening listening to the radio etc

1st "Adam & Eve" squadron pilots, l to r: Neale, Burgard, Little, Bond, Blackburn, McGarry. Kunming.

Monday 9
(40-325)

Off all day, but went out to the photo section with Overend, Hodges, Reed, & Older. We printed & enlarged some pictures from various negatives. & got those from yesterday. Flew an hour with Conant in the BT, going over elementary stuff. Back on night duty at 5:30

News Bulletin: It was reliably reported that Robert B. "Buster" Keeton of the Panda Bears squadron shot down a Jap bomber over Toungoo yesterday. Bus hails from Manzanola, Colorado, (pop. 534), famed Watermelon Capital of the World. His daring feat was witnessed by his best buddy, Bob Layher, from Otis, a somewhat smaller town in eastern Colorado. Both are former navy PB-Y pilots.

2nd "Panda Bears" squadron pilots: Standing, l to r; Keeton, Lawlor, Ricketts, Layher, Geselbracht, Jones, Schiel. Kneeling; Rector, Paxton, Wright, Newkirk, Hill, Bright, Conant. Kunming, February, '42.

Tuesday 10
(41-324)

Older + myself stood by on day alert today, as they planned a photo mission, but it fell thru.

Crew Chief Olson got back from Calcutta. He sold his movies of the action at Rangoon to some Newsreel outfit for a good price.

Flew again with Conant. He's coming along pretty well considering everything.

Tex Hill, Howard, + some of the others from the 2nd got in today. Others on the way up the road in a convoy.

Another quiet evening on nite alert.

Henry Olson, sometimes called "Little Oley" to distinguish him from our squadron leader, was Greene's crew-chief. During the attacks on Rangoon in late December, Little Oley took cover in a slit trench but not before grabbing his little movie camera. He shot several hundred feet of film that caught some of the action above the field, flaming planes falling from the sky, Jap fighters strafing Mingaladon, bombs exploding on the field, the works. I never saw this film but was later told that some of it was quite spectacular. Olson got a few days leave and took it to Calcutta for processing, then sold it to an American newsreel company that had offices in Calcutta; I've no idea what they paid for it.

Wednesday 11
(42-323)

Another day off, & nothing new. Flew with Conant, & then took my P-40 out & combatted with Cavanah, & flew formation & just fooled around for an hour.

Most of the 2nd Sqdn. is back up here now, & the rest on the way.

Got a radiogram from the folks this evening saying Criz had stopped in to see them.

Olson got back from Chungking this morning, & says he has some hot news, but can't put out any dope on it yet. I have a suspicion as to what it is tho. There has been a rumor that some of us may get to go to Calcutta, or possibly on to Africa to ferry back some new ships. Boy, what a trip that would be.

For weeks Chennault had been trying desperately to get some new planes. By this time we probably had fewer than fifty flyable P-40s and they were becoming worn out, with spare parts unobtainable. Curtiss-Wright was now building a later and much improved model called the P-40E, and it was this plane that we were all hoping might be made available to beef up our puny little air force. Obviously we couldn't go on much longer without replacements, and time was growing short.

Thursday 12
(43-322)

Off again today, but went out to the field at noon. Hooker, our chief parachute man, made a test jump shortly after I got out there. Greene took him up in the BT + he bailed out over the field at 5,000 ft. Delayed opening until about 2,000 ft, + lit on the field. Chute shook him up some, + one shoe was knocked off his foot.

Flew again with Conant, same old stuff

Went on duty at 5:30 p.m.

Newkirk, 2nd Sqdn. Leader, came in on CNAC tonite.

3rd Squadron Ground Personnel, left to right standing,, Sweeney, Losonsky, McHenery. Kneeling, Perry, R.A. Smith, and Colquette.

Friday 13
(44-321)

Got by this day with no
bad luck noticed.
Rumors are flying thick &
fast about everything in general.
One good one is that a couple
of Sqdns. of B17's from the State
are supposed to be here within
10 days. Sure would like to
see them come in.
Olson let out a little dope on
the ferry trip to some of the boys.
We're all sweating that one out now.
Flew again with Conant,
practicing landings & take-offs.
He did a pretty good job of it.
Another quiet night on alert.

Oley told us that Chennault had received word to the effect that some new P-40Es would definitely be made available to the AVG very soon, but didn't know exactly where they were located. He said the old man had a hunch they might be in Cairo, Egypt, and it would probably be up to the AVG to send some pilots there to ferry them back to China. Naturally, every pilot in the outfit wanted to be tabbed for such a trip, and Oley seemed certain that the 3rd squadron would be named to go after the first few planes.

Saturday 14
(45-320)

Off duty today, but go on day alert tomorrow, as the 2nd Sqdn. is taking over nite alert starting tonite.
Went to the field after lunch, but Conant didn't show up so didn't fly.

If the present plan goes thru, some of us are liable to go all the way to the Gold Coast of Africa for our new ships. What a trip we would have if that comes true.

Greene & I went into town after dinner & fooled around. We each bought a fancy dagger at one of the shops.

3rd Squadron pilots, left to right, P.J. Greene, Tommy Havwood, Link Laughlin, Catfish Raine, Ken Jernstedt and Chuck Older.

Hot damn! McMillan broke the news to the Sqdn. this morning that 6 of us are to go to Cairo, Egypt, to ferry back the 1st 6 new ships. McMillan, Laughlin, Older, Haywood, Greene, + myself are the six to go. There will be more ready later + some of the other guys get to go then, but were all glad were the first bunch. We are supposed to leave for Calcutta tomorrow morning on CNAC, + then board a U.S. Bomber of the Ferry Command + go on to Cairo. Dont know how long it will take but it should be ten days at least — we hope. We're all packed + rarin' to go.

After the boredom of the past few weeks, the six of us picked for the ferry trip were overjoyed. Here was an unbelievable opportunity to see more of the world's exotic and mysterious places, and the promise for adventure that otherwise we might never know. Mac was to be in charge, which pleased us all, and hereafter he was referred to as "our Fearless Leader." We were all good friends by now, having gone through the rough times in Rangoon together; only Link Laughlin, through no fault of his own, had missed the action in late December.

FEBRUARY 1942

Monday 16
(47-318)

Got up before dawn & out to the field to await CNAC's arrival. They got in about noon & we left after lunch. Stopped in Lashio for a half hour & then on to Calcutta. The weather was sort of nasty & very bumpy, & all of us were rather uncomfortable. Got to Calcutta after 7 hours flying time. Had dinner at our hotel, the Great Eastern, & then went out to some night clubs. Mac & I were together & had a big time. Later ran into the others at one of the local joints.

Got home at dawn & went to bed. Mac had to get up soon after, as Commander De Wolf had told him we might have to leave on a British Overseas Airways flying boat in the morning.

British Overseas Airways' route stretched from London to Calcutta. They operated the commercial version of the British Short-Sunderland flying boat used by the Royal Navy for long-range patrol and anti-submarine work. This was a 4-engine monster with a built-in headwind that cruised at about 140 mph, quite similar to the Boeing Clippers flown by Pan American on their trans-pacific route.

Tuesday 17
(48-317)

Mac came in & got us all up at 10:00 & said we were leaving immediately on the B.O.A. plane. So, we all packed up and went out to the river base & got aboard. They started up the four engines & were all set to take off, when the right inboard engine started backfiring & loading up, so we taxied back & they said we would layover until tomorrow. So back we went to the hotel. We all went to Jirpo's Cafe for dinner, & most of us ate two huge steaks with lots of French fries. after that we went out to the "300" Club, & got acquainted with some people there. McDonald & Scott, CNAC pilots, were there & introduced us to some English gals, & we all had a big time. Had to be back to the hotel by 4:30 to go out to the river again.

We got aboard the flying boat
again at 5:30 & took off before dawn.
There are twenty passengers aboard.
They have stripped the ship of its
decorations & soundproofing & heating
system, so it is noisy & cold.
We landed on a lake at Gwalior,
in about the center of India, after
five hours flying. Re-fueled & headed
on west for Karachi. Got to
Karachi after six more hours, &
landed in the harbor. After taking
care of Customs they brought us in to
the Killarney Hotel to put up for the night.
Found out about dinner time that
we are not priority passengers, & that
only four seats are available for our
bunch in the morning. Mac doesn't
want to split up the gang, so we're
going to wait till next plane. Looks
like a good town. Camels all over the
place, pulling carts & wagons. After
dinner we all went out to some of the
local English Clubs.

Thursday 19
(50-315)

All of us went in to the American Consulate today, & saw the Consul, Mr. Macey. He arranged getting some checks cashed & getting us priority on British Airlines, so we can get out on next plane. Greene & I stayed downtown & looked around & took pictures, while the rest went out to the field to see Major Necrason of the Ferry Command. They saw him & he said there may be an I.C. ship thru here in a few days & we may take it to Cairo. He & some others are coming in to dinner tonite. We found out Blankenhorn, a classmate of Greene's & mine, is pilot on a B17 laid up here for repairs. Maj. Necrason, "Nick" to us, & Blankenhorn & other officers in his crew, came in to dinner, & then we went out — all over town to all the clubs. We had a hell of a big time all nite.

If you are getting the impression that we were fast catching up on social activities, something decidedly lacking in Kunming, you are absolutely right. In addition to visiting what passed for night clubs open to anyone, we soon learned that the private British clubs, while not exactly welcoming us with enthusiasm, would allow us to purchase temporary memberships and spend our money freely. Admittedly, we often had more dollars than sense.

Friday 20
(51-314)

Went back to the Consulate this
morning, & Mr. Macey had gotten
our checks cashed, so now we've
got money. He also had official
word from Delhi that we now
have triple A priority for air passage.
We're invited to his house for
dinner this evening.

We fooled around town most of the
day & all bought souvenirs & curios.
Came back to Hotel about 4:00 p.m.,
& Nick & a couple others were here.
Ed Goyette's brother was one. He flew
in a Ferry Command DC 3 last nite.
He's with Pan Am., & leaves in the
morning for Columbo, Ceylon. Nick's
going with him, & they'll be back
Sunday. If we don't get out before then,
we can go back to Cairo with him on
Monday. They left about 7 & we
all got cleaned up & went to dinner
at Mr. Macey's. Had a very nice
time, & came home & to bed about
ten o'clock.

Saturday 21
(52-313)

After breakfast we all went out
to the airdrome & saw a bunch of
the guys who are here on B17's
headed for points further east.

P. J. Wright, a west-pointer in
our class at Randolph, is here & we
had a good visit with him. There are
4 B17's here now, awaiting further
orders & getting some repairs made.

We were notified this morning that
another B.O.A. flying boat would be
in tomorrow, so we leave at 6:00 a.m.
tomorrow on it.

Went to a show this afternoon —
"Kiss the Boys Goodbye" — pretty good.

After dinner some of the gang went
to another show, but I stayed
home to pack & go to bed.

Quadragesima
1st in Lent **Sunday 22**
(53-312)

Left at 6:00 a.m. on B.O.A.C.
flying boat. Made two or three
stops before arriving at Basrah.
These damn boats have all the
soundproofing and heating systems
removed + are cold as the devil, flying
at 10,000 ft. or so. I have had a
hell of a cold since leaving Calcutta.

We arrived at Basrah about 4:00 p.m.
and put up at the airdrome hotel.
It is the nicest terminal I've seen
for a long time. Very modern and
comfortable. The country around here
is covered with date palms, + looks
very nice from the air.

After dinner we all went into a
club in town, + were amused by the
old Arabs sitting around, turbans etc.

Ran into some fellows from American
military Mission. They took us to their
camp + gave us Amer. beer + cigarettes

We leave for Cairo early in the
morning.

Monday 23 ☾
(54-311)

Off again at about six this morning. Stopped at some place in the middle of some God-awful desert. We've seen a lot of desert since leaving Calcutta. A few lakes to land in though. Landed at lunchtime on the Sea of Galilee, praise the Lord, & it was very beautiful. It's about ten or 15 miles across & surrounded by hilly country. Left after lunch & flew on over Palestine & a piece of the Mediterranean, over the Suez Canal, and landed on the Nile at Cairo at 4:00 p.m. Went into town & put up at the Grand Hotel, & went out & wandered around the streets to have a look.

After dinner the rest of the gang went around & took in some of the local joints, but I went to bed as I've been feeling lousy all day. This cold is getting no better fast.

Oh, yes, today was my birthday (24) too. Ha!

While none of us were overly religious, landing on the Sea of Galilee was still a memorable experience. We had lunch in the quiet little city of Tiberius where, we were told, Christ had once lived.

Tuesday 24
(55-310)

Mac went over this morning to the Ferry. Command office to get the word on our ships. He came back + said they were in Takeradi or Accra, on the Gold Coast, + that we leave on Pan American tomorrow for there. Of course we're all tickled over the news!

We spent the day looking around town, and went out this afternoon + saw the Pyramids + Sphinx. It was very interesting, but we didn't have much time + didn't explore much. Got some good pictures tho, I hope.

After dinner some of the guys went to a show, but I stayed home + went to bed early again.

The lack of an adequate military air transport system had been apparent even before Pearl Harbor, and now with the U.S. at war on a global basis steps had been taken to improve the situation. Pan American Airlines had been given a contract, administered by the U.S. Ferry Command, to establish facilities and air routes throughout many out-of-the-way parts of the world in order to facilitate the movement of men and supplies. A number of Air Corps pilots had been allowed to resign and join Pan Am, and many Douglas C-47s and C-53s had been allocated to the airline in order to make up for the deficiency in record time. Pan Am and all concerned did a tremendous job under very difficult circumstances!

FEBRUARY 1942

Wednesday 25
(56-309)

Up early this morning and out to the airport. Got aboard an Army C53 troop transport, being used by Pan Am, & were all set to leave, when up the aisle walks Ross Herman, an old friend who was in 40A whom I knew in Lincoln when he was in Primary. He was released by the army with a bunch of others to come over & fly here for Pan Am. He was Captain of our ship today, & soon after taking off he sent his co-pilot back & I went up to the control cabin. We batted the breeze a while, & he turned the ship over to me & went back in the cabin. Greene came up & we flew for the better part of 5 hrs — or rather kept the automatic pilot trimmed up. Landed at Khartoum & are staying overnite here. Damned if we didn't run into Tiller, 40-C, and Blakely from 40 B. Tiller cracked up a B17 in Accra, & Blakely with pan am. After dinner we all went in to see the night life of Khartoum. This is the country where the British used to fight the Fuzzy Wuzzies, & they still have troubles

The C-53 was a military version of the Douglas DC-3, equipped with un-padded metal bench-type seats along each side of the cabin.

Thursday 26
(57-308)

Left Khartoum this morning about 7:00. We made four or five stops enroute and got into Kano about 4:00 p.m. The Pan am boys brought us out to their base + we got rooms. Then all enjoyed a Coca Cola, as we had yest. at Khartoum — the first Cokes we had tasted since September.

Then one of the P.A.A. guys took us to the native village nearby + I got a bunch of good pictures of native life in the raw. Ha.

We then bought a bunch of souvenirs + stuff from some natives near the camp here. I got an old knife, a python skin, + some ivory carvings. Some of the boys really loaded up.

We should get into Accra tomorrow.

The Pan Am men had warned us that the native traders tried to charge outrageous prices for their artifacts, so we haggled and argued just as we'd learned to do in Burma and China. When I had finally agreed to a price of $40.00 in U.S. money for my purchase and dug out my billfold I discovered that I also had some Chinese twenty-dollar bills. Just for the hell of it I handed two of these to the trader. He looked them over, frowning, then saw the picture of Sun Yat Sen, the revered former Chinese premier, and asked, "Who dis mon?" I assured him it was President Roosevelt, and he was delighted. I quietly passed the word to the others; they pulled the same stunt and we got the hell out of there. Terribly unethical, granted, but funny.

Friday 27
(58-307)

Left here about 7:30. Stopped at
Lagos, on the coast, for an hour &
left again about 11:00. We arrived
in Accra, on the Gold Coast, shortly
after noon. Our new ships are
here on the field, ready to go.
They look pretty good to us too
    I found two or three more
guys I knew in the States, which
is only about 5,000 miles from here (ha),
and they are working for Pan am here.
One is Wayne Eveland, an upperclassman at Santa Maria. Then there
is Halley, a former student of mine
at Randolph, and Lanning, the
fellow who married Helen Cook.
Two or three others I knew slightly.
They have quite a camp here, good
food, etc! We're supposed to go
to the field tomorrow & try out
our new ships.

231

Saturday 28
(59-306)

Got up at 7:30 & went to the field. We all got lined up on our ships eventually, & each flew about an hour. I was lucky & got the 1st one, & was first in the air. Greene's & my ship had no belly tanks installed, & we put on a little show for the Pan Am boys. The ships are quite a little nicer than the Tomahawks. These are called Kittyhawks, & have better cockpit arrangement, 6 50 cal. M.G's., more power, speed, etc.

Spent the afternoon at camp loafing & chewing the fat with some of the boys here. Also went into town & sent a cablegram to the folks.

We are supposed to head back for Cairo Monday. Some of the rest of our gang from Kunming are there on their way for more ships.

2nd in
Lent

Sunday 1

(60-305)

St. David's
Day

We all went out again this morning and flew again, this time with belly tanks installed on all ships. They will give us a range of about 4 hours — one hour more than without them. They slow us down about 30 m.p.h.

We got our gear together to leave tomorrow, including tools, emergency rations, water flask, etc.

We get new U.S. parachutes with the ships, + that tickles us all to hell too. They are much more comfortable + reliable. Our bags won't fit in the baggage compartment tho, as they are smaller than on the Tomahawks. So we're stuffing some of our clothes in parachute bags + taking what we can. The rest has to be sent back to China on the next transport plane to go East.

So at last, two weeks after leaving Kunming, we were ready to head back; little dreaming that it would be another three weeks before we'd see China again. Our proposed route of some 7,500 miles was roughly the equivalent of a flight from New Orleans to the South Pole. All of us were to experience problems, but in my case Murphy's law seemed to be working overtime.

MARCH 1942

Monday 2
(61-304)

Well, the six of us got started this morning, led by an RAF Blenheim. It seems that all fighter convoys have to follow a Blenheim as far as Cairo. Suits us O.K. as the navigation is pretty rough, but it's too slow.

We landed for refueling + lunch at Oshogbo, Nigeria. When we got ready to leave, discovered a "blister" on one of Aldie's tires, + Haywood's plane was running rough + cutting out, so they stayed there for repairs + we pushed on. They'll come up to Cairo in a few days we hope.

We went on to Kano + spent the night. Admiral Hart, CinC of the Far Eastern Naval forces was here. He's on his way to States via Pan Am. We sat at same table for dinner + talked to him. Also, McDonald, CNAC pilot, on his way back for 2 mos. vacation.

Native traders here still screaming about getting "taken in" on the Chinese money all the Pan Am boys very happy about that.

I'm sure it goes without saying that we didn't go shopping in the little native village this time around.

234

Tuesday 3 ☺
(62-303)

Took off at 7:30 & landed at Ft. Lamy, Free French Territory, at 10:30   It was blowing about a 30 mile wind, dust & sand all over. Took an hour & a half to refuel. Went on to El Geneina, & too late to refuel & go on. There are two Pan Am men here, & they put us up. Saw the native village, & a Giraffe wandering around. Took pictures of it, as its pretty tame.
Went to bed after a good dinner.

RTS with new Kittyhawk in Accra

RTS and Laughlin, standing. McMillan is the jockey. El Geneina, Sudan.

Wednesday 4
(63-302)

Up + off again at 7:30. Landed at El Fasher + refueled an hour later. Then found a leak in one of Laughlin's gas tanks. Couldn't fix it, so went on to Khartoum. Landed at 1:25 p.m., + they wouldn't let us go on after 2:00. So, we put up at Pan Am's base here — a good place. Had Coca Colas, a swell dinner, + went to town, 20 miles away, for fresh milk and malts. Then to G.B. Club.

El Fasher, on the west side of the Anglo-Egyptian Sudan, was typical of the many little airfields that served as refueling stops along the way. Some were operated by Pan Am, some by the RAF, with only a handful of people including the natives to do the work. It was at El Fasher, an RAF stop, that we were lounging in the little building that served as an operations office when in through the door bounded what at first glance appeared to be a full-grown lion. The four of us scattered as if a live grenade had been tossed among us, much to the amusement of the two RAF men in the room. They assured us that the big cat would not harm us, that it had been raised as a pet from the time it was a tiny cub. By now, however, the damn thing must have weighed two hundred pounds and had fangs a couple of inches long, so we didn't hang around long enough to get acquainted.

Since leaving Accra we'd flown over jungles and rain forests, then arid, mountainous country, and now we were back to endless miles of desert. Occasionally we had dropped down to low altitude, buzzing native villages and herds of game animals before climbing back up to join the lumbering old Blenheim that led the way.

MARCH 1942

Thursday 5
(64-301)

We were all set to leave at 6:00 a.m,
but the Blenheim hadn't been serviced, so
we didn't get off until 7:30.
We were supposed to go to Wadi Halfa to
refuel, but they were having a terrific
sandstorm, & we sat down in the
desert at a little place called Station No. 6.
Waited there a couple of hours & they
reported the storm still on & visibility
only 50 yards. We then headed for Atbara,
on the Nile. My prop control went out
on full low pitch. Then all my instruments
& everything electrical went haywire.
I dropped behind the convoy as my engine
was heating pretty bad. Lost sight of them
finally. Kept on the heading, over desert, &
then hit the Nile river. Flew down it &
landed at Atbara. Another convoy here
because of sandstorms up the way. The
storm hit here about 8:30, & it is sure
hell. High wind & sand all over.
Looks like we're stuck here awhile.

I confess to feeling pretty damned lonely as I watched the Blenheim and
the others disappear into the murky sky up ahead. I couldn't call them on
the radio to advise them of my problem, and they didn't even miss me until
they were out of sight. So I sat there cursing them and Curtiss-Wright, indicating about 110 mph, and with **practically** nothing working the way it
should, visiblity about two miles and no place to land. Of course my
magnetic compass still worked, and I knew I'd eventually find the Nile.

237

Friday 6

Sandstorm going full blast when
we got up at 8:00 o'clock.

After lunch I got a mechanic from
the RAF & we went out to try to
find out what ails my ship.
We checked over the wiring, replaced
fuses, etc., but couldn't get it
fixed so she'd run at all.
So now I've had them wire Port
Sudan for an electrician to be
flown down in the morning.
Should hear late tonite whether or
not they'll do it. If not, Mac &
the others will probably go on to Cairo
& I'll have to wait until I can get
my ship fixed.

The sandstorm is letting up some
now, & visibility is about 1 mile.

Saturday 7
(66-299)

Got up at 5:00 a.m. & out to the field at 7:00. Mac, Greene, & Laughlin & the Blenheim pushed on for Cairo as I still hadn't heard when an electrician would get here. I phoned Khartoum & they didn't seem to know much of the situation. Then about 3:00 p.m. we got a wire that an electrician was to come down on Monday's train — and I about blew a fuse at that news. So I phoned Pan Am Ferry Command at Khartoum & told them the story. They called back an hour or so later & said they'd fly a mech. over & he'd be here at 8:00 in the morning. So maybe I'll get out of here tomorrow. The damned stupid British tied things up as usual. I get sicker of them every day — no wonder the tea-drinking stoops get hell kicked out of them in every battle.

My, my, it seems I was in a bit of a snit at this point, perhaps with some justification. The RAF people often seemed determined to take their own sweet time about geting things done; their attitude was sometimes expressed by "what's the bloody 'urry, Yank?" In fairness it should be remembered that the war was new to us and with typical American impatience we wanted to win it in a hurry and go home. The British, of course, had been at it for over two years and seemed resigned to the fact that it would go on indefinitely

Two of Pan Am's men from Khartoum
got here about 9:00 a.m. They were
Crooks and Lundy. They worked my
electrical system over + got it fixed
except the voltage regulator. Then my
hydraulic system went haywire. They
worked it over + I went up to test
it. One wheel wouldn't retract or
come all way down, + I finally
had to resort to my emergency
system. It worked OK + I landed.
There wasn't much more they
could do about it so I decided to
fly over to Port Sudan tomorrow,
wheels down, + get my whole ship
worked on. They have a lot of
Kittyhawks + experienced mechs
there.

   Crooks, "Mac" Lundy, + I had dinner
+ some American beer which we
found at a place in town.

The emergency landing-gear system, powered by a small manually operated
hydraulic pump in the cockpit, was strictly a one-way affair; it could be
used to extend the gear to the down and locked position, but would not
work in reverse to retract it.

Monday 9 ☾
(68-297)

Went out to the field at 7:00 and pushed off for Port Sudan about 8:00 a.m. After flying for two hours over desert and mountains, I saw the Red Sea & then got in to Port Sudan.

Told the R.A.F. mechs my troubles & they went to work.

I met two americans from the Glenn Martin Aircraft Co. here. Names were Cy Lake and Jim Dalton. Had lunch with them & they got a room at the Hotel where they live.

Had a good dinner & then a bull session with some men from an American boat in port here.

Had a call from the field tonite & they said they have my ship all fixed now, so I can leave in the morning.

Port Sudan was about 250 miles from Atbara, but it took a full two hours due to the drag of the landing gear and belly tank, and the danger of overheating the engine if more power was applied. It was strictly dead-reckoning over the worst terrain imagineable, desert and barren, jagged mountains creating what I imagined a moonscape might look like. The entire area looked uninhabited, no villages, no roads or rivers, nothing. A forced landing was out of the question, and you can bet that I listened very attentively to that big Allison up front; fortunately, it kept grinding away without missing a beat!

Enroute from Atbara to Port Sudan

Tom Haywood and friends, Bahrein, Saudi Arabia

Tuesday 10
(69-296)

Out to the field at 7:00 a.m. to test my ship. Went up & the wheels came up fine & everything seemed perfect. So I did a slow roll, and a hydraulic fitting in the cockpit cut loose & sprayed all over. Lowered my gear & landed immediately. They went to work on that, & I was feeling so lousy I went to the Doc's but he was out. Felt weak & dizzy. They got my ship fixed about 11:00 o'clock, so I loaded up & took off. She was OK. that time, so went back to Atbara & refueled. Then on to Wadi Halfa Spent the night here at Wadi Halfa. Which is just another dump on the Nile. Heard on radio that Rangoon has fallen. — Don't know how that may affect the future so far as we're concerned. With luck I should get to Cairo tomorrow.

My hydraulic problem was the same that had caused Pete Wright's accident in Rangoon. An elbow-joint in the high-pressure line down at the left corner of the seat had ruptured, filling the cockpit with a fine spray. The hairy part was that I was inverted at the time, about a hundred feet above the runway, halfway through a slow-roll for the benefit of the mechanics

242

Wadi Halfa to Cairo, Egypt
MARCH 1942

Wednesday 11
(70-295)

Took off at 8:30 a.m. and got to Luxor to refuel at 10:00. Left there at 10:30 & got to Cairo, Heliopolis aerodrome, at noon. Some Lt. from the Ferry Command met me + had a car waiting, with a good looking English gal driver, + I got a ride right into town. Went to the Grand Hotel + the rest of the gang is here. Got a room, + spent the afternoon doing nothing. After dinner some of us went out to see what was going on, which wasn't much.

Tomorrow I have to fly my ship over to Ismailia aerodrome, on the Suez, where the other ships are.

Wadi Halfa to Cairo was roughly 600 miles, with a stop at Luxor, about the halfway point. What a relief it was to be back in civilization; I was able to follow the Nile for the most part, or at least keep it in sight, and often flew low over the primitive sailboats plying the river, or the villages along its banks. While being refueled at Luxor I was sorry there was no time for exploring nearby Thebes and the Valley of the Kings. Instead, after taking off for Cairo, I had to content myself with circling these ruins and burial sites of Pharoahs dating back four or five thousand years in the past.

Thursday 12
(71-294)

Slept late this a.m., and went out to the field about noon. Flew my ship over to Ismalia aerodrome, on the Suez, and turned it over to the mechs there for a check etc.
Rode back to Cairo in an R.A.F. Blenheim. Met a Sgt. of the Ferry Command at the field, Bob Reed, + we came into town together.
Bought a bunch of film for my camera, then cleaned up + we went to his place for dinner + then out to see the bright lights, which are dim as hell in this black-out.

Anyone interested in "navel maneuvers" was bound to love the night life of Cairo. Nightclubs and bars and dives of every description were plentiful, and each of them featured an intrigueing assortment of belly-dancers. This was pretty wild stuff to us, of course, not the sort of thing you were apt to see even in Omaha. Mac, however, put the whole scene in perspective one night, saying, "as far as I'm concerned, if you've seen one belly-button you've seen 'em all!" Sage words from our fearless leader.

Friday 13
(72-293)

Stayed around the hotel till after lunch. Then I went out and bought a Mido watch, self-winding, waterproof, etc., for seven pounds. Went to see "Philadelphia Story" which I enjoyed as much as the first time.

Bought a German Luger automatic from a soldier on leave from the Libyan campaign. It had been taken from a prisoner up there. I gave five pounds for it, with 90 rounds of ammo. It sure is a honey of a gun.

I guess we're to go to Ismalia tomorrow + leave there Sun. morning Haywood came in on a convoy with a couple of Pan Am pilots. Their ships are at Is. now, + will go on with us.

MARCH 1942

Saturday 14
₍₇₃₋₂₉₂₎

We all got "briefed", or checked out on the route, + then got a ride to Ismalia on an RAF "Lodestar".

Spent the afternoon checking our ships. Mine was running sweet, + I tested it for 25 min. + it was OK. A couple of the others are having trouble with plugs — cutting out etc

They say only four ships will be ready to leave in the morning, so Macs, Greene, Laughlin + myself will go on with our four ships.

After dinner we went to a show in town — Lousy!

Over the Nile Delta

4th in Lent **Sunday 15**
(74-291)

We finally got all our ships running and took off at 9:30.

Landed at 10:40 at Lydda Aerodrome, about 12 miles from Tel Aviv.

We intended to refuel & go on to Habaneyia, but Laughlins reserve gasoline tank started leaking, so we decided to stay here while it was repaired.

Went into town after lunch & shopped for cameras etc., but they were pretty high & the boys didn't buy any. Went to a show, "Argentine Nights", had dinner at a nice place, & came back out to the field at 11:00 p.m.

This place is only 40 miles from Jerusalem, & 50 miles from Bethlehem. Hallelujah! Ha!

We're all set to leave early in the morning for Basrah, Iraq.

We were on our own now, no longer having to follow the slow old Blenheim. The Mediterranean Sea was beautiful, but we stuck pretty close to the shoreline just in case; we had no dinghies or even Mae West life preservers, and the thought of having to ditch was unsettling to say the least.

Link Laughlin was wearing a constant scowl by now; he'd been plagued with leaking gas tanks ever since we'd left Accra, and he saw no humor whatever in our remarks to the effect that his problems were no doubt caused by his lack of ability as a pilot, which of course they weren't. To add to his misery, the fumes were so strong that he was afraid to light a cigarette for fear of incinerating himself.

Monday 16 ●
(75-290)

Left about 7:30 a.m. & landed at
Habbaniya at 9:00. We got
"briefed" again and took off for
Shaiba about 10:30 after refueling.
Got there about 12:00 & had lunch
while the R.A.F. refueled our ships.
We decided to go on to Bahrein to
spend the night, so skipped Busrah.
Laughlin's gas tank is leaking again
so that's another worry.
We got to Bahrein about 4:30 &
went to the Imperial Airways Hotel
to spend the night. Could have stayed
at the RAF Camp, but we're all
getting so we can't speak to the
damn Limeys with a civil tongue, so
were glad to get away from them.
After dinner we drew up our maps
for the trip tomorrow. We're going on
into Karachi to have our guns
cleaned, sighted, & loaded.

Soon after taking off and heading east from Tel Aviv we passed just north of Amman, capital of Jordan, and on over the seemingly endless desert. In due time we saw a fertile valley up ahead and found the little airfield at Habbaniya, Iraq, fifty miles west of Baghdad. After refueling we flew southeast down the wide valley of the Euphrates river to where it joined the Tigris, names I remembered from high school geography, and then on down to Bahrein.

St. Patrick's Day Tuesday 17
(76-289)

Got off about 7:30 a.m. + headed for
Karachi, India. Made refueling stops
at RAF fields in cities in Oman +
Persia, + got into Karachi about 4:00 p.m.
My generator went out again on the way +
some of the others have things wrong with
their ships. So we left them in the hands
of the RAF, + some American Armament men
are going to fix our guns.
There are seven B17E's here + 2 B24's.
They are forming a bombardment group which
may come over our way — we hope.
Also two pursuit groups here, 3,000 men,
+ they're assembling P40E's for them here.
Ran into Earl Pack, an upperclassman,
who has been thru the fighting in the
Phillipines + Java. Got some interesting
dope from him.
We all went into town to see
"Navy Blues" tonite.

From Bahrein, on the west side of the Persian Gulf, we followed the lower curve of the shoreline up to its tip at Sharjah. The next leg took us across the Strait of Hormuz, about 50 miles of shark infested water; we all breathed easier when we got back to dry land.

"Navy Blues," a Warner Brothers picture, featured six gorgeous starlets called the "Sex-tet." One of them was a beautiful former model named Georgia Carroll. Six months later, after the AVG was disbanded, I met Georgia in Los Angeles and we dated a couple of times before I went off to do a bit more fighting. She later married bandleader Kay Kayser and they lived happily ever after.

Wednesday 18
(77-288)

Spent the day at the field checking on the progress of work on our ships. They'll be ready to test fire in the morning, but they're not getting far with fixing my generator.

Some of the boys flying the B17's were over in Burma a few days ago. They were flying troops in from India & taking Refugees back. One ship had 65 civilians & crew of 7 aboard. They say our Squadron has just relieved the 1st at Magwe, the new base.

Bob Horning & Andy ——, two Curtiss men, are working on our ships too. They're good boys.

After dinner we went to town & saw "the Little Foxes" — pretty good.

When we learned that our squadron had been sent back to Magwe, Burma, some three hundred miles north of Rangoon on the Irrawaddy river, we were more anxious than ever to get back. They were bound to see plenty of action now, and this ferry trip had gone on long enough. We figured they could use our help, and certainly the new planes would add a good deal of much-needed firepower.

They got my ship ready to fly at 9:00 a.m., so I took it up to test it & fire the guns. Got out over the sea when I discovered oil running in a stream back from the engine on the floorboards. I fired my guns a few bursts anyway, & they worked fine. My generator worked for a while & then went haywire again. I came back & landed, & as I suspected, some stupid Limey hadn't put the oil filler cap on tight, & the oil overflowed into the cockpit.

They discovered this afternoon that my generator was burned out, so they're getting one from an American P-40 that is damaged.

Went to town again tonite & saw "Sergeant York." We're really getting caught up on shows.

Friday 20
(79-286)

Well, it looks as if all our ships will be ready to go in the morning. Guentis & mine are running rough as the devil, but they can't seem to get them fixed right. They say they'll have my new generator on tonite sometime.
Bill Bowden, another upperclassman friend, came in today from Delhi. We had a good talk this p.m.
Nick Necrason, the Major, also came in - He says some of our boys made a daybreak raid on the field at Moulmein & destroyed 15 ships there on the ground.
We're all rarin' to go in the morning.

We were to learn in a couple of days that it was Bill Reed and Ken Jernstedt who made the early morning raid on the Jap airfield at Moulmein, each making four of five passes despite lots of ground-fire, setting fire to fifteen planes and damaging several more. They caught them completely by surprise, not the first time it had been done and certainly not the last. It constantly amazed us that those who had so spectacularly pulled off the surprise attack at Pearl Harbor were repeatedly caught with their own pants down. Anyway, old Bill and Ken had themselves quite a morning!

MARCH 1942

Saturday 21
(80-285)

We got away at 8:00 a.m. + set out for Asansol, which is a base about 100 mi. from Calcutta. Stopped at Jodhpur for fuel, + met the best bunch of Limey's of the whole trip. Flew right over an immense palace belonging to the Maharajah of Jodhpur. Took seven years to build + cost four million dollars. Some shack! Flew on to Allahabad + refueled again, then on to Asansol. Spent the evening in town, which is really a lousy dump.

During our brief visit to town, which was unusually dirty and smelly, Greene said, "Hell, I've heard of this place—the Asansol of Creation!"

Palace of the Maharajah of Jodhpur

MARCH 1942

Left at 8:00 a.m. & arrived in
Chittagong, Burma at 9:30.
Refueled & pushed on to Yunnanyi,
China & arrived there at two p.m.
Saw Loane, Shamblin & some mech's
there. They fed us & we had a good
bull session. Left for Kunming
then, & after wandering about thru
rain squalls etc., arrived in
Kunming — Everybody full of all
kinds of questions about the trip &
the new ships. We also asked a few.
We learned that Ed Leibolt has been
missing for 3 or 4 weeks after going up
on a raid at Rangoon. Magwe was
bombed three times yesterday. The boys had
no warning & only 5 of our ships got up.
Fauth, one of our crew chiefs killed by a
bomb, & Swartz, 2nd Sqdn. pilot very
gravely injured — 50-50 chance of recovery.
Ten ships lost up here while we were gone.
Had dinner with Tex Hill & Skip adair,
& a good gossip after that.

Our joy in getting "home" with our hides and planes intact was dampened
considerably by the sad news of Fauth's death. Swartz died a few days later,
and neither Leibolt nor his plane were ever found. Ed was the third pilot
from the "Bloom bunch" to die.

Monday 23
(82-283)

I've felt lousy all day after a typhoid + cholera shot last nite.

Went out to the field this afternoon with Mac, + we spent an hour talking to Col. Chennault.

Also went to my ship + found the men working on it + getting it all fixed up.

Ten ships left here yesterday to go to Burma, where they are to refuel + then go on a strafing raid at a couple of Jap airdromes in Thailand in the morning. Five men from the 1st + 5 from the 2nd Sqdns. on the party.

Spent the evening with Skip + some of the others in the bar + had dinner late.

I was somewhat disappointed, though not surprised, to learn that my old faithful, No. 77, was now in Magwe with the other 3rd squadron planes. A guy sometimes develops a feeling of loyalty and affection for his personal plane, and while I liked the E model I'd flown from Africa, I wasn't keen on the idea of making it a permanent switch.

But it was great to be back with the guys. Our flight from Accra to Kunming was probably the longest ferry trip ever undertaken by prop-driven fighters. There had been plenty of anxious moments, but it had been great fun—the sort of thing you wouldn't trade for a million dollars, but wouldn't do again if *paid* a million.

Tuesday 24
(83-282)

Slept till 9:00 this morning &
then, after breakfast, went to the
Hospital & Doc Bruce cleaned my teeth.
After lunch all pilots went to the
field for a meeting to determine
what range we wanted to
boresight our guns in the future.
We finally decided on 300 yds.
While we were in the meeting we
got word of the results of the raid
our boys went on in Thailand.
They destroyed about 10 Jap planes on
the ground. Jack Newkirk, 2nd
Sqdn. Leader, was shot down & crashed,
& Mac McGarry had to bail out
on the border. He should get back
OK in a few days with a little luck,
but Jack was killed. Such news is
pretty hard to take, but we're all
getting more or less used to it &
expect it by now.
Fred Hodges came in from Loi Wing
this p.m. but I haven't had a
chance to talk to him.

Spent the day around the Hostel, cleaning up my room. & sorting clothes etc. I've collected a lot of things which I'll have to throw away, I guess.

Ernstedt got in yesterday from Magwe. Has one eye bandaged up, but its about OK now. He had his windshield shot out by a bomber down there, + got a little glass in his eye.

After dinner I had an interesting talk with a Canadian Naval Officer who escaped from a Jap prison in Hong Kong! + got away OK. Took him 51 days to get here from H.K.

The raid of the day before on the airfield at Chiang Mai had been successful from a military viewpoint, but terribly costly in more personal terms. The ten P-40s from the 1st and 2nd squadron had destroyed fifteen or twenty Jap planes on the ground, but two of our pilots and planes were lost in the process. Newkirk crashed while strafing a tank or armored vehicle, whether as a result of ground fire or something else nobody could say; he never pulled out of his dive and his plane burst into flames upon impact. Jack may well have been victim of "target fixation" which I spoke of earlier.

It appeared that McGarry had been hit by ground fire and his engine finally failed. He was seen to bail out and come down safely in a small jungle clearing, but after wandering for nearly a month in the jungle Black Mac was finally captured and imprisoned in Bangkok, the fourth casualty of the "Bloom bunch."

Thursday 26
(85-280)

Got word this morning that Loughlin, Greene, + myself are to fly 3 tomahawks to Loi Wing + join the rest of our Sqdn. there. Also five others are to fly 5 more ships down but they'll return via CNAC.

They told me I'd be in charge of the flight, but about noon Olson flew in from Loi Wing to see the Colonel, + he is going to lead the flight back, which is pretty OK with me.

Also, Alder + Foshee got in from Africa in their Kittyhawks.

We all left Kunming about 2:30 + got to Loi Wing at 4:00 p.m.

A nice setup here. It's good to get back with the rest of the gang.

We start going on alert in the morning.

After dinner we had quite a party at the club.

It was soon after I arrived that I learned I'd never fly old 77 again. It had gone to Magwe along with the rest of the planes and pilots of the 3rd squadron while I was on the ferry trip. There were a few 1st squadron pilots and planes there also, and less than a week earlier Dick Rossi of the 1st had cracked up "my" plane on takeoff. It seems the old girl's ignition system failed; Rossi had too little power to get airborne and too much speed to stop before crashing. He was unhurt, but I've never quite forgiven him.

Friday 27
(86-279)

Eight of us went on alert this a.m. before dawn. At noon, while half of them were at the men's mess eating lunch, we got a report of several enemy planes down near Lashio, sixty miles south. Dupuoy & Hodges; myself, Greene, & Laughlin took off & started climbing up, heading South. Went to 23,000 & to Lashio, but saw nothing. I had radio contact with the ground station, but they had no more reports. Went back to Loi Wing, & I saw two planes about 5,000 feet below us & to one side. I gave the signal, tested my guns, & dove out of the sun on them, but on getting in range saw they were 2 of our tomahawks, Hedman & Bronk, who had been at lunch & were late getting up. Went in & landed soon after that, & no more was heard. Just a false alarm I guess.

Saturday 28
(87-278)

Spent the day on alert part of morning, & off after lunch for a while. Back on duty later in afternoon in time to go up on an alarm, but nothing developed. We're sitting here with twelve planes on alert, & were plenty jumpy as the warning net is no good. Every time we take off we're expecting to get it in the neck before we get off.

Olson says we have to go to Burma & patrol over the front lines at Toungoo. We're all against it, & it seems senseless, with a good possibility of nobody coming back. This is to be just for one day, but its mighty low grade, Lord, mighty low!

Chinese army troops, and remnants of the British army of Burma, were trying to stem the Japanese advanced in the vicinity of Toungoo. It seems that Chiang Kai-Shek decided that it would boost his troops' morale if they could see our planes overhead, flying low enough to display the Chinese 12-pointed white star insignia. Toungoo was more than 300 miles from Loiwing, which meant having to stop and refuel enroute, then fly into enemy territory at low altitude with several Jap fighter bases nearby. Perhaps it's understandable that we were not terribly enthusiastic about this idea.

I was scheduled to go on the Toungoo party this a.m., but they decided to send only 8 instead of 12 ships, so he left me in charge of the alert here — with four ships. Ha! The 8 took off early, but came back about an hour later due to bad weather. Found out later it was good thing, as He Ho had been bombed + they intended refueling there.

Had report of one enemy plane while on patrol with Prescott, but couldn't find it. Weather very poor visibility here now.

Alder + Greene went up this afternoon after an observation ship, surprised it, + Alder shot it down on first pass.

I'm off tomorrow, so can sleep in.

We were to be plagued with poor visibility from now on, mostly due to smoke and haze, but with occasional showers as well; the rainy season wasn't due to start in earnest for another month. However, this was the time of year when there were numerous forest fires in Burma, and also the season when the native burned the stubble in the rice paddies. Often on an otherwise fine day the visibility due to smoke and haze would be be down to a mile or two, which of course made navigation all the more interesting. A thick layer of the stuff seemed to hang like a blanket over Burma, about like the smog in L.A. at its worst.

Monday 30
(89-276)

Got up late this. a.m.

About 10: a.m., Oley, Older, Bronk, & I went up the road about 30 miles to try to locate the plane Older shot down yesterday. One Jap bailed out + hasn't been caught yet. We couldn't get closer than about 5 miles, as it crashed in the mountains back from the road.

Came back + spent the afternoon at the club listening to the record player etc.

I expect the Japs to come in tomorrow, so maybe we'll have some excitement.

By now the planes and personnel of the three squadrons were being inter-mingled somewhat in an effort to keep the numbers balanced. Now and then a pilot or two from another squadron would be temporarily assigned to fly with our 3rd squadron. Such was the case with Prescott and Moss, for instance, who were originally from the 1st and 2nd squadrons. We also got a few planes from the 2nd squadron, and they got most of the first batch of new Kittyhawks. We no longer bothered trying to keep the fuselage numbers straight, however; we simply repainted the band around .the fuselage just back of the plane number with the proper squadron color, red.

Tuesday 31
(90-275)

This was quite a hectic day.
We had an alarm about 9:00 a.m.
that bombers were near Lashio &
headed this way. We got 8 ships up
& patrolled nearby for over an hour,
but sighted nothing.
Then while half the gang was up at
the mess having lunch, we got
word that Bombers were over Lashio
again. Olley & "Moose" Moss were
already up looking around & went
down there. Rest of us, 4, took off &
climbed to 28,000 ft. over the field.
Radio station said they were bombing
Lashio, & Olley sighted 27 bombers & 9
fighters. He was alone so didn't attack.
We went down to Lashio & joined him
but they had left. Moss landed at
Lashio, we think, but not sure.
Message from Chennault wants the
Toungoo job done still, but we're all
agin' it. Think we'll go down &
strafe Jap fields instead.
Expect a real raid here tomorrow.

Wednesday 1 ☺
(91-274)

Another day spent at the field on alert. Turned out to be quite a quiet day too, for a change.

Got word of an enemy observation ship about 60 miles from here, & I went up with Hodges to have a look for it. The visibility was so bad tho that we came back after going about 25 miles out.

Then we had an alarm this p.m. when Lashio was bombed, & eight of us took off, but nothing happened here.

Moss got in from Lashio this morning & ground-looped when he landed.

Yesterday Boyington was taking off & his motor cut out at end of runway. He just jumped a 10 foot ditch & got out OK. Both ships washed out tho.

Shilling came in from Kunming this p.m. in a Kittyhawk. He's going down into Burma on reconnaissance mission.

Weather too bad for us to go strafing. Alcon, Greene, & myself are to go to one field, & DuPuoy, Doerend & Brouk to another.

Thursday 2
(92-273)

Had quite a party last night, for no reason at all, + everybody cut loose. I had the day off today, which suited me fine.

Adkins + a Pan Am. pilot flew a couple of Kittyhawks in here today from Calcutta on way to Kunming.

No alarms at the field today they say.

I spent the day at the club just loafing + reading.

Had a wedding at the club tonite Fred Hodges + an English girl from Rangoon named Helen Anderson. Then a buffet dinner afterwards.

2nd and 3rd squadron pilots in front of alert shack at Loiwing. l to r; Tex Hill, Bill Reed, Oley Olson, Moose Moss, Parker Dupouy Bob Prescott, Cliff Groh.

Spent the day at the field on alert, & it was pretty quiet. We had an alarm about 9:30 & 8 of us took off. My engine started cutting out very badly when I got up about 1000 feet, & I had to come back in and land. The rest went on upstairs & patrolled, but nothing developed. I tested my ship this afternoon & it ran fine, so after buzzing the field & doing a few rolls I landed. No other alarms. Hennessy flew the Beechcraft in from Laslio & brought a bunch of mail. I got two letters, the first mail in months.

Bishop & 3 Pan Am pilots brought in 4 more Kittyhawks from Calcutta. Weather too bad to go on to Kunming. If it clears up we may go strafing tomorrow.

The little twin Beechcraft was kept busy constantly, sometimes carrying Chennault and others of his staff to various places, but often ferrying pilots, spare parts, and mail. John Hennessy and Einar Mickelson did most of the flying, and did an outstanding job of it.

Greene + I were spare pilots today, so didn't have to go to the field until 9:00 a.m. Spent the rest of the day at the alert shack.

Visibility is still very bad, so our strafing mission is again postponed.

The Kittyhawks all left this morning and got to Kunming O.K.

Olson went to Kunming this p.m. to see Col. Chennault + find out whats up.

There were no raids or alarms at all today probably due to the bad weather.

Got a letter tonite from Althea Seamark in Lincoln.

All this mail coming so sudden-like has given us much comfort.

Hope it keeps coming.

Easter Sunday Sunday 5
(95-270)

Another day on alert, + all quiet. Visibility still very bad, + no alarms reported around this area.

We had Easter services at the Club after dinner this evening, + a good turnout. The R.A.F. Chaplain was in charge, + it was a pretty nice affair. Hedman played the piano for the Hymns, + that alone was worth the price of admission.

After church we played pool + bet on shots made by others playing. Grob + I had a little argument & tussled a bit with minor damage to either party. Ha!

Oh yes, 8 Hurricanes + R A F pilots flew in today to be based here. I don't know how much of a help they'll be, but hope they can do some good.

Even at his most promising stage as a boy in South Dakota it's doubtful that Duke Hedman was ever considered a piano prodigy. To say that he was a bit rusty by then is to put it charitably, and having had a few belts of Scotch hadn't helped a great deal. Most of us in the congregation were shaking with ill-concealed giggles as old Duke hit one clinker after another; I doubt if he could've played *Chopsticks* right, much less *Onward Christian Soldiers*, but he was sure trying.

I was off today, & fooled around at the club most of the time, listening to records on radio-phonograph, & reading No excitement today at the field. The weather is closing in and looks like it may rain. The rainy season is supposed to start in a couple of weeks here. Olson still in Kunming.

After dinner we all went to the club & had a movie. CAMCO has a projector & a few old films here. We saw "Here Comes the Navy" — vintage of 1934. — But enjoyed it.

Hell's Angels Overend, Older, Jernstedt, Reed, Haywood

Tuesday 7
(97-268)

It rained last nite & still
raining this a.m. at 6:00.
We got to the field for alert duty
at 7:00 & spent a quiet day.
Nothing reported around here at
all today.

Worrell & Ducklow, 2 Pan Am
pilots, came in from Calcutta
in a couple of Kittyhawks en route
to Kunming.

Weather cleared up a lot
toward evening.

Still no word from Olson, but
he should be in tomorrow.

Chowtime outside pilots' quarters at Loiwing. Standing at left:
Donovan, Dupouy. Seated: Geselbracht, Hill, Olson. Standing at
right: Lawlor, Ricketts, Croft, Keeton.

Wednesday 8 ☽
(98-267)

On alert again today. Report of one obs. ship
here at 9:30, & Older & Overend went up.
They saw it & chased it, but couldn't catch it
Alson, Jernstedt, & Little came in in
3 new kittyhawks at noon. At 12:30
we had report of many ships headed this way.
We took off, 9 tomahawks, & the three others
in their kitty's. While climbing up to altitude,
radio station called & said Japs were
strafing the field. So we went down &
in to them. There were 29 Jap model "O"
fighters very low around the field, & nine
of us went into them. Then for about
15 minutes we really mixed it up, dogfighting
at very low alt. right over the field. I
shot down two model "O's", & each of
the others in it got one. We got ten of
them & all of us got back OK.
They shot up the two Kittyhawks of the
Pan am boys, on the ground, & also
an R.A.F. Blenheim. It was the most
thrilling experience I've ever had. The guys on
the ground saw it all & are still raving. They say
it looked just like a movie only better. Ha!

This was a most unusual day in a couple of ways. First, it was bright and clear for a change in our little *Shangri-La* valley, and secondly it was to be one of the few times that we'd tangle with enemy fighters on nearly even terms; I believe there were only about fifteen Zeros to our even dozen P-40s.

As usual, the warning was short, and as usual we were all airborne within a couple of minutes. I led the alert flight of Tomahawks, and Oley and his three Kittys followed moments later. Bob Little and Fritz Wolf of the 1st squadron were with us.

We headed south in the direction of Lashio, climbing "balls out," as we used to put it, and breathing easier as we reached ten thousand feet. Suddently our radio operator at Loiwing excitedly reported enemy planes strafing the field, but didn't say how many or what type. I immediately headed back, slanting down now and indicating about 300 mph. Soon the field was in sight and I could see Zeros buzzing around like flies and a column of smoke rising from a burning plane. I called the others, told them to spread out, check their gun switches, and pick out individual targets. I fired a short burst to test my guns, and saw Cliff Groh, my wingman, do the same as he eased off to the side.

What followed was the damndest rat-race imagineable; like it or not, this was to be dogfighting right on the deck, no way to escape by diving away this time. But what made the situation truly unique was that we had everything going for us for a change; speed, altitude, and surprise. Better still, we blasted four or five of them out of the picture on that initial attack, and suddenly we actually outnumbered them.

I picked a Zero that was just completing a strafing run, apparently unaware that I was behind him. I opened fire at about three hundred yards as he began to pull up, closing rapidly, all six guns working beautifully. I couldn't miss, and the Zero flipped over on its side and dove for the ground, crashing in a ball of flame. I pulled up in a chandelle, still with lots of speed, and turned back toward the field. And then saw a strange sight: a Zero chasing a P-40 that was chasing another Zero, like follow-the-leader. I cut across to intercept the last Zero, fired a wild burst at him at too great a range and too much deflection for accuracy, but it scared him off the chase and he pulled away in a steep climbing turn. I was tempted but refused to take the bait, turning away and back to the field instead.

I spotted another Zero just starting a strafing run and peeled off after him. By the time I could get within range behind him he'd completed his run and was pulling up in a shallow climb. Just as I was about to open fire he began to roll to the left; I did the same, thinking he was about to pull around in a sharp turn, but instead he kept right on rolling, still straight ahead. By then I was already committed and had to follow his maneuver, nearly inverted when I opened fire and thinking, *"This crazy bastard's doing a victory-roll."* Mine was more of a sloppy barrel-roll, and I could see my tracers flying wildly all around him, like the stream from a garden hose held by a slowly circling hand, until I kicked rudder and saw them finding their mark; smoke and flame poured from his engine, and that was that. Sayonara!

This sort of thing continued until there were no more Zeros to be seen, a few of them having scooted away safely. I believe our final tally for the day was eleven. Fritz Wolf got a couple, and Oley, Overend, Little, Hodges, Donovan, Laughlin, and Groh each chalked up one apiece.

The guys on the ground had a worm's-eye view of the whole show from their slit-trenches and enjoyed it immensely. So did we!

Thursday 9
(99-266)

Another day on duty. We had three alarms & went up three times, but saw nothing in this vicinity. And lucky we didn't. I had a kittyhawk with a dead battery & my guns wouldn't work. Then on the second alarm I had a new battery but ran out of oxygen.

We are all expecting more action soon, probably some bombers next time along with fighters. Late this p.m. Seven Kittyhawks & two tommies came in from Kunming, flown by the 2nd Sqdn. They are to operate out of here and go down around Toungoo & patrol — 3 ships at a time, about three shifts a day. It's a foolish mission with lots of risks, & not much chance to do any good. Col. Chennault came in on a CNAC plane & is to be here a while.

The additional nine planes of the 2nd squadron brought our strength at Loiwing up to about twenty planes and thirty pilots, leaving perhaps twenty flyable planes and pilots of the 1st squadron and half that many remaining from the 2nd at Kunming. Tex led the flight to Loiwing, accompanied by Rector, Lawlor, Keeton, Geselbracht, Ricketts, Croft, Wright, and Moss. Their ground crewmen arrived later on CNAC.

Friday 10
(100-265)

We were all on our way out to the field
this a.m. at about 6:00 - the sun had
just barely come up. We were about 3
miles from the field & saw 5 Jap fighters
strafing our ships on the field. Nothing we
could do about it. After they left we found
they'd only knocked 9 ships out of Commission
out of 20 on the field. Some not hit at all.
Those hit can be fixed, & none burned.
Went on alert with 8 ships & 3 went to Toungoo.
Went up on three alarms, but nothing
happened until the third one. Then five of us
ran into 9 model 0's & had another big
dogfight, twisting & turning above scattered clouds.
Bronk & I went into four of them, he got one soon, &
I hit one & saw him dive down smoking. Then
I was alone with two of them for about ten min.
Couldn't get either of them & finally had to dive out.
Saw three in the distance heading for home.
Chased them about 40 - 50 miles and got the last
one from behind. He went down & crashed on
side of a mountain. The others got 4 or 5
more. Two Hurricanes crashed, one guy bailed out
& the other OK.

So the Japs caught us with *our* pants down this time, and thereafter our dawn patrol was reinstated. We had discontinued that practice of late due to the weather conditions and the many hazards involved in trying to take off or land in the dark at Loiwing.

Several of our crew-chiefs were already on duty, inspecting and warming up our planes, when the Japs attacked. Luckily, nobody was hurt, though new records were set in elapsed time from cockpit to slit-trench.

Older, Hedman, Brouk, Keeton, and I were in the flight of five that attacked the nine Zeros. Another flight of P-40s was up, but they were too far away to join in the fun before it was over.

There were many scattered cumulus clouds in the area, and the fight turned into another rat-race around, between, and sometimes through the big puffy white clouds. At one point I had to dive into one to shake a Zero that was about to get on my tail, and when I came out on the other side there was another Zero in front of me. I got a good burst into him but only drew a thin trail of gray smoke from his engine before he disappeared into another cloud. Then, for a few minutes, I played hide-and-seek with a couple of others. I couldn't see any other P-40s, and called on the radio, something silly like, "Hey, somebody, come over and give me a hand, I've got a couple of 'em cornered about ten miles east of the field." Just the reverse was true, of course, and I soon had to dive away for reasons of health.

I pulled out just above the mountain tops, heading south. A moment later I saw three specks in the distance, considerably higher, also heading south. They had to be Zeros, and I lit out after them at full bore, staying down to make it harder for them to spot me. Two of them were close together, the third slightly off to one side and maybe 200 yards behind, "Tail-end Charlie."

After about five minutes I was almost directly beneath them. I kept looking around behind and above; this whole thing looked too easy, like I was being set up, but no other planes were in sight. I eased back on the stick, trading speed for altitude, and reached their level about two hundred yards behind "Charlie." I cut loose then with everything, and the Zero immediately jerked up abruptly, flipped over in a half-roll, and dove straight down. I knew I'd hit him a ton, but there was no fire or smoke so I had no choice but to follow and keep shooting. He dove straight into the mountain below, no doubt dead from the moment I'd opened fire.

Too late now, I saw the others continuing south, blissfully unaware of what had happened to Charlie. I kicked myself; if I had only known he was no longer a threat I could easily have slid in behind the other two and picked them both off. I should have knocked all three out of the sky in the space of thirty seconds.

It was still a good day, as each of the others in our flight had brought down a Zero earlier.

For the benefit of any reader who may be thinking that my shooting old Charlie in the back without warning was unsporting, I can only say *neither was Pearl Harbor, friend.* War may mean different things to different people, but a "Sporting Proposition" it definitely ain't.

Saturday 11
(101-264)

I was off duty today, & slept late this a.m. After breakfast at 9:30 the siren sounded an urgent warning, the P-40's took off, & a half dozen or so of us went to the top of the hill by the club to see what would happen. We heard radial engines, & I guess there was a reconnaissance ship or two upstairs, but nobody saw anything. That was the only alarm of the day. Went out to the field late in the afternoon & fooled around until quitting time. The Col. told us the deal on induction into the army etc., - looks like we'll be able to finish our contract & then go back to the States and into the army there.

We had another picture show at the club after dinner - Varsity Show 1937, & enjoyed it a lot.

Off duty again today, due to lot of
pilot and few planes.

Tex Hill, Pete Wright, & Croft went
to Toungoo on patrol today. Tex & Pete
strafed ships on Toungoo Aerdrome &
set three on fire. Then on way home, Pete
ran into a single engine bomber & shot
it down. It was his first engagement
with the Japs.

Had one alarm today — another Jap
observation ship over the field, but
nobody sighted it in the air. Several
saw it from the ground.

The dawn patrol is still in effect to
take care of Japs who might come in
and strafe the field again.

I'm on tomorrow, so will be up
if they come — I hope.

Chennault liked to mingle with his "boys" occasionally, and on this day
he spent most of the afternoon at the alert shack on the field. He was playing cribbage with Prescott, while several of the pilots lounged around inside
and a few more sat outside under the overhang of the thatched roof. Suddenly the guys outside jumped up, screaming "Zero! Zero!" and ran the few
steps to the slit-trenches nearby. There was immediate pandemonium inside, of course, with pilots racing for the single doorway while others, including the old man, fought to get out the two open windows on the other
side as a low-wing plane with a radial engine roared just over head. But it
was only Erik Shilling in a BC-1 advance trainer coming in from Kunming,
his radio not working. Chennault and everybody else chewed his ass out
royally, you can be sure, but it must have been a sight to see and the rest of
us thought it very funny.

Monday 13

Saw a twin-engine Jap observation ship over the field this morning, & Groh & I went up after it. It hightailed for home though, & had too much of a start, & we couldn't catch it or even see it.

Then an alarm at noon — many planes over Lashio headed North — our direction.. We all went up & waited for them but they didn't show up. All quiet the rest of day.

Had a nice rain last nite, & it looks as if the rainy season will soon be here to stay.

After dinner Moss, Hedman, & myself went to club & had a few. About ten o'clock the siren blew an air raid alarm & we piled in a jeep & went across the river. Stayed an hour but no planes came in, so we went home to bed.

Off duty tomorrow..

Tuesday 14
(104-261)

Spent the day at the club reading and listening to records.

We had an air raid alarm about noon, but nothing developed.

Two Pan Am C53's came in late this p.m. from Calcutta, loaded with props & spare parts etc. Lanning was pilot of one, the only one of the four I knew.

We had another show tonite at the club — "Another Dawn".

The Alert shack at Loiwing

Up at 4;30 and out to the field.
Four ships went up on dawn patrol.
Then myself + Grok patrolled for
two hours at noon in hopes of
finding an observation ship. — No luck.
Olson, Laughlin + I went down
to Laskis, refueled, + on down to
Pyawbwe to cover up for a 3 ship
flight from 2nd Sqda. They took
off for a reconnaissance hop to
Rangoon while we circled upstairs.
Had word from the ground that
enemy ships were approaching from
the south but saw none.
We got back here after 3 hours in
the air, + I'm really tired out.

Some of the P-40s damaged by the strafing attack on the morning of the 10th had been damaged more extensively than was at first thought, and had been removed to the little CAMCO factory for repair. Others had been patched up by our ground crewmen with inadequate materials but a lot of ingenuity. Despite the load of stuff brought in by Pan Am, we were still desperately short of tires, solenoids, spark plugs, and radio parts. At best we now had only about fifteen planes that were considered flyable, and usually two or three of them would be out of commission for one reason or another on a given day.

Thursday 16
(106-259)

Another day off - spent mostly at
the club. Listened to phonograph,
played acey-ducey, & pool with
Reed, Prescott, & Greene.
One alarm this morning but
nothing happened.
Petach got lost on a recon. mission
and landed in a dry river bed
below Pyawbwe - nosed up &
ruined the prop. but not hurt.
A mission was planned this p.m.
for tomorrow morning — & is it a
stinker. 4 tomahawks & 4 Kittyhawks
to escort 6 R.A.F. Blenheims on a
raid to Cheng Mai. After the Blenheims
dropped their bombs the Tommies are to
strafe the field. It bristles with anti-aircraft
& is about 160 miles inside enemy territory.
Volunteers were scarce as hen's teeth, but
finally some of the boys who haven't seen
much action decided to go.
They went to Lashio this p.m. & are to
leave there at daybreak with the Blenheims.
We figure two or three may get back.

Friday 17
(107-258)

On alert today, & it was pretty quiet — only one alarm.

Luckily, the mission to ChengMai was called off due to the Blenheims getting lost & delayed too long.

Word from Kunming that things are in a bad state there. Several more men quitting to go home.

Adair, in charge there, got in touch with the Col. down here & told him he'd better get back up there as soon as possible.

To top matters off, the Chinese army, & of course the British, are being pushed back in Burma. Now they intend to hold the line & want us to give them air support.

Our twelve ships against the whole damn Jap air force. It seems mighty futile to all of us & we're wondering what's taking the U.S. so damn long to get something over here. At this rate, our morale won't be very good fast! Phooey!

Off duty today, + all hell broke loose.
First, Prescott + Bronk shot down a Jap
observation plane over the field.

Then this evening Col. Chennault called a
meeting. It was to tell us that we were
expected to go on any missions assigned or
else resign. Some of these missions planned
we consider pretty bad — suicide in fact.
Col. Chennault said he was now a Brig.
Gen., U.S. Army + taking orders from
Gen. Stilwell. We all got a load off
our chest as to how we felt. — About not
getting any reinforcements + being expected
to fight the whole Jap air force etc.

So, all pilots here got together, had a
meeting, + voted to resign in protest.
Twenty-eight of us out of 34 signed the
sheet, + it is to be given to the Col. tomorrow.

So, either we'll get some concessions
or be going home soon. We all want
to stay + fight back, but we can't go on
an offensive with twelve airplanes,
especially ones in their condition. Motor
failures are becoming frequent, + plenty other troubles

Chennault's announcement that he had been re-commissioned as a Brigadier General in the Air Corps and now had to take orders from old "Vinegar Joe" Stilwell, a ground-pounder in the U.S. Army and ranking officer in the CBI, came as quite a shock to all of us, since he still wore no such uniform or insignia. But it helped to explain some of the crazy missions being dreamed up of late, mostly by Stilwell and Chiang Kai-Shek apparently over Chennault's protests, but of course the old man didn't come right out and say that. Instead, he simply said we'd go on whatever missions were assigned, or he'd accept our resignations and we'd be given dishonorable discharges.

Naturally, this brought on some rather heated discussion. A couple of the guys wanted to know how we could get dishonorable discharges from a civilian company, pointing out that we were under contract to CAMCO, not the Air Corps. Chennault was hard put for an answer to that one, and another pilot or two got up and told him how most of us felt about some of the missions we were asked to perform. Chennault, both adamant and angry, finally said something to the effect that any of us who wanted to show the "white feather" should resign and clear out.

For many reasons this seemed completely uncalled for, and I stood up to offer my two-bits worth. I merely told the old man that there was a hell of a big difference between common sense and cowardice, and that after all we'd been through I couldn't believe he was now calling us cowards. There was a murmur of assent from the rest of the guys, and Chennault quickly said that's not what he really meant, and came as close to apologizing as he could without actually putting it in so many words.

There was a lot more discussion at our pilot's meeting later that same night; it was almost like a union meeting, lots of arguments back and forth, leading up to a strike vote. Tex Hill said he understood how everybody felt, and that he didn't like some of these missions any better than the rest, but that he wasn't about to resign in protest and would fly when and where he was told, regardless. Four or five others of the thirty-two pilots present agreed with Tex, but all the rest, myself included, voted to call the old man's bluff. We were damned certain he wouldn't allow half of his little air force to go home.

A letter of resignation was drawn up which simply said: *We, the undersigned, pilots of the American Volunteer Group, hereby desire to terminate our contracts with the Central Aircraft Mfg. Co. and our services with the AVG.* It was signed by twenty-six rather than the twenty-eight mentioned in my dairy, and presented to Chennault the following morning. We didn't expect him to accept it, and few if any of us wanted to leave, but we did hope that some good might come of our protest.

This little episode became known as "The Pilots Revolt," or "The Loiwing Rebellion," and served to demonstrate that both mentally and physically we were nearing the breaking point. Those months in Toungoo and Rangoon and Magwe and now Loiwing had taken their toll, and the signs of stress were apparent in gaunt faces, and bodies that had lost many pounds. And yet, despite the hardships, we continued to get along well with each other and even managed to retain a semblance of a sense of humor.

I was off duty again today & spent it loafing as usual.

The resignation paper was given to the Col. this a.m., & he promptly called a meeting for 8:00 p.m. tonite. At the meeting he said he couldn't accept our resignations and anyone leaving would be guilty of desertion etc. We all expected that, but at least we showed him what we thought of some of the missions + tactics employed. So, he, and all of us are forgetting the whole affair + carrying on as usual.

We are still carrying on patrols over the lines, + reconnaissance missions etc.

No alarms here today.

Hedman + Rector shot down a Jap Observation ship while on patrol over the lines today.

While we agreed to carry on with the patrols and recon missions, we were never again ordered to escort the RAF Blenheim bombers deep into enemy territory at comparatively low altitude, which was the thing we were bitching about the most. Whether or not our stand in the meetings with Chennault was responsible we had no way of knowing, but I have always had the feeling that the old man somehow got the message across to Stilwell to "knock it off."

Monday 20
(110-255)

Spent the day at the field on alert.
All quiet + no alarms.
Nothing much to report.
We all had a big time kidding
Tom Jones all day about various
things.
"Went to a show after dinner —
Romance + Rhythm."
Am off tomorrow. Most of our
ships will be on patrol over lines
all day.
Hennessy + Mickelson came in on
the Beechcraft today + went back to
Kunming. They say 8 or 9 of the
ground personnel have quit + left.

According to Hennessy, Greg Boyington had been threatening to resign too, and in fact did so a day or two later. "Pappy" had had his share of problems, hitting the bottle much too much, often becoming belligerent when he had a snootful and picking fights with anyone close at hand. There were few who dared challenge him, for he was built like a bulldog and had been an intercollegiate wrestler. For whatever his reasons, Boyington felt that the Generalissimo and Madame Chiang Kai-Shek were more interested in maintaining power and in lining their pockets than in prosecuting the war against Japan, and that Chennault was their willing stooge. Chennault considered Boyington a chronic troublemaker, a pilot who'd led a flight of five P-40s that got lost and all forced to make belly landings, and was often insubordinate. The upshot of the whole thing was that Chennault supposedly told Greg to clear out, that he was being dishonorably discharged. Boyington insists that he told Chennault he was resigning, and suggested that the old man stick his dishonorable discharge "where the sun don't shine." There being two sides to every argument, perhaps the truth lies somewhere in-between.

Tuesday 21
(111-254)

Off duty again today & nothing new. We had two alarms here this a.m., but nothing happened.

Some of the boys were down on patrol today & plenty happened.

Brouk was taxiing his plane at Nam San to take off when a bunch of model "O"s started strafing the field. Brouk was hit by six slugs, mostly in the legs, but will be o.k. they say. His plane burned up.

Then four of the 2nd Sqdn on patrol ran into 18 Jap fighters, but didn't engage them, altho Jones made a couple of passes at one flight of them

The Japs are still running the Chinese & British back, & it looks pretty bad.

Schilling & Hoskee flew in from Kunming today & are to stay here now.

There is some talk about us going on a "sweep" somewhere tomorrow.

Wednesday 22
(112-253)

Went up at 5:30 on dawn patrol but no trouble encountered. Then we had an alarm about 10:00 and circled above the field, but still no excitement.

I was detailed to go to Shwebo, 160 miles S.W., taking Laughlin along, to see about field conditions there with a view to using it as a base. We got out about 80 miles and the visibility was so bad that I decided to come back here. We got back O.K., with luck, but I sure felt relieved. Groh went to Kunming today — or rather started, + is now unreported, so he must have gotten lost + had to set down somewhere.

Went to show at Club after dinner.

I don't recall why Cliff Groh was flying a lone P-40 to Kunming; it may have been to ferry the plane there for repairs or an engine change. Whatever the reason, he encountered bad weather enroute, got lost, and finally had to crash-land in an isolated valley, only slightly injured. He showed up in Kunming several weeks later with a full growth of beard and about twenty pounds lighter. We were all delighted to see him, of course, after having given him up for dead. Later, just kidding, we accused him of malingering, going to such lengths to avoid flying combat missions, and he laughed as hard as the rest.

St. George's Day   **Thursday 23** ☽
(113-252)

Slept in this a.m., as it's another day off. Visibility still very bad. The Beechcraft came in from Lashio with Bronk aboard. His wounds are mostly in the legs and Doc says he'll be OK, altho they have to dig out some shrapnel.

Wayne Cveland brought a Pan Am DC in today. We had dinner & a talk together tonite.

Col. Chennault called another meeting tonite & told us there were a few regular army commissions being given out here pretty soon, & all desiring same were to apply.

We also hashed over the tactics & prospects of the war etc.

Not many of us were terribly interested in regular army commissions at this point, although we knew that soon we'd have to decide what to do when the AVG was disbanded. Our main concern these days was simply survival from day to day, each of us hoping his number wouldn't come up before it was time to head back for the good old U.S. of A. To use that word once again, we prayed that our *luck* would continue.

Friday 24
(114-251)

On duty today again. We had about 3 alarms & went up but no Japs appeared.

This afternoon six of us went down behind the lines on a fighter sweep, looking for Jap planes, and observing troop movements on the roads.

Didn't run into any trouble and all got back O.K.

Weather pretty bad nowadays. Visibility very poor & rainstorms quite frequent.

Nakajima Ki-51 "Sonia" recon/observation plane

Saturday 25
(115-250)

I was off duty today, supposedly, but Reed came after me after lunch & said they wanted us at the field. We went out & they were planning another fighter sweep over the lines. The second Sqdn., with 6 Kittyhawks with bombs were to bomb & strafe truck convoys on roads, & two more flights, one of tomahawks, & one of Kittyhawks to act as middle & top cover. I was in Kitty - middle cover, - & after we got down behind the lines we spotted two Jap observation ships. Our flight went after them. I got the first one on the first pass. He caught fire, crashed, & exploded. Made a couple of passes at the other, but so did about 8 others, & somebody else got him The others bombed & strafed trucks, & then we came back. We had 17 planes on the mission - The most in one mission of the war A mission this morning also shot down two Obs. ships & bombed & strafed. The Japs are now only 40 miles from Lashio — or 100 miles from here.

The two Jap observation planes were at very low altitude, single-engine low-wing monoplanes with tandem 2-place cockpits; they resembled the old Air Corps A-17 attack planes. In the mad scramble to shoot down the second one I nearly collided with another P-40 and got the hell out of there.

3rd after Easter **Sunday 26**
(116-249)

On duty again today. We had three alarms & went up, but no Japs appeared.

Four of our gang started on a mission to the lines this morning. They were jumped by 12 Jap fighters, broke up, & returned here safely.

The weather closed in this afternoon & it's been clouded over solid & raining off & on since noon. The Japs are reported in Lashio now, 60 miles away by air — too damn close! Sooo — our Sqdn is moving up to Meng Shih with 13 ships tomorrow, & the 2nd sqdn., with 10 ships, is staying here. We're all steamed up now because the Col. won't move us all out & farther away. There will be no warning from Lashio now on air raids, & a good chance the Japs may cut us off at the road above Meng Shih. Some fun! If we all get out of this spot, it'll be a miracle.

Monday 27
(117-248)

Another day – same old story.
We had a couple of alarms + took
off, but no enemy planes were
encountered.

According to the latest reports, the
Chinese troops are still fighting the
Japs south of Lashio, so the
situation isn't as bad as we thought
yesterday. However we are (our Sqdn.) to
go to Meng Shih tomorrow. The men
left today to get things set up there.

Hubbard flew a Pan Am DC3 in
today. He told us about his forced
landing in India in one a couple
of weeks ago. Sounded like a good job.

Tuesday 28
(118-247)

Our plans for today called for a fighter
sweep over the front in Burma, and
then our Sqdn. proceed to Meng Shih.
We took off, 15 ships, & got about 30
miles S.W. of Lashio, & Tex Hill saw
a formation of 27 bombers + 15 fighters
headed for Loi Wing. Everybody chased
them except myself + Greene, who was
with me. I saw a bunch of
fighters circling about 3 miles to our left,
so we went over there. Turned out to
be seven model "O"s. We went at it
with them, and each shot one down.
Finally we both had to dive out + leave
because of a couple on our tails.
The others engaged the other formation, +
we shot down a total of 13.
I ran out of gas on way to Meng Shih +
made a crash landing on the side of a
mountain. Washed my plane out but
didn't hurt me any. Plenty lucky!
Rode a truck up the road to Meng Shih. Our
setup here is pretty rugged.
The Japs bombed our field at Loi Wing — little damage.

Tex was leading the fighter sweep, along with six others from the 2nd squadron. Chuck Older led a flight of six from the 3rd, while Greene and I had been designated to fly as weavers, higher than the others and weaving back and forth to act as lookouts. I called Tex when I spotted the circling Zeros and he said to go have a look.

As we drew closer I counted seven of them, at least a thousand feet below us, and for some unknown reason they were flying in a big Lufberry circle. Paul moved off to the side as we dove down and each picked a target, then opened fire at about three hundred yards. Unbelievably, they seemed not to have seen us until the shooting started.

Neither Greene nor I scored on that first pass, but we had lots of speed and were able to pull up high above them before turning back down for another attack. This time we were successful, and a couple of them burst into flames at almost the same moment. We went on dogfighting for a few minutes, but our excess speed had been used up and soon we had to dive away. We'd been separated since the fight began, but eventually we spotted each other and joined back up.

By now the others were long since out of sight, so we headed northeast in the direction of Mangshih, a place neither of us had ever seen about eighty miles on up the Burma Road from Loiwing. The visibility was bad and getting worse, and as we flew on and on I began to be concerned about my fuel supply. One of my tanks had been only half full at take-off, and we'd used up a lot of extra fuel while flying as weavers and in the combat with the Zeros. I called Paul and told him of my situation, and he replied that he wasn't real thrilled with what his own fuel gauges were reading. There was nothing to do but continue on the heading that I guessed would lead us to Mangshih. Nothing looked familiar, but at last we found a valley where there was a village we thought must be Mangshih. We looked all over but there was no sign of an airfield, so I got on the radio, giving the proper callsign, and asked the operator where the field was located with respect to the village. He replied that it was four miles due east, and asked if there were two of us. I replied in the affirmative, and headed east. A minute or so later he called back and said "you're right over the field now." I banked over and looked down; nothing but rice paddies, no sign of an airfield. And it was then that it dawned on both of us that we were in the wrong valley; the radio operator had seen two other P-40s circling Mangshih.

By now I had run two tanks dry and the needle on the gauge for the third was hovering on empty. I knew there wasn't enough fuel to climb back up and fly another twenty or thirty miles over the next mountain range, so I called Paul and told him I was going to try to land on a pasture-like area on the side of a low mountain near the road. I was naive enough to think I could save the airplane, and that later it could be flown out.

Paul circled as I landed; I set her down as slowly as possible and was rolling nicely, but then ahead appeared a swale and I was momentarily airborne again before smashing down on the other side. The gear was wiped out immediately, the plane began to spin around, and suddenly all my guns were firing; I'd forgotten to turn off the switches, and squeezed the trigger on the stick. Dust and rocks and pieces of airplane were flying all over, but finally we came to a stop. I was relatively unhurt, climbed out and waved at Paul, and he headed out toward Mangshih.

I stumbled down to the road, hailed a Chinese army truck full of wounded soldiers headed north, and a couple of hours later arrived in Mangshih and joined the rest of the gang. Lucky? You know it, friends.

Wednesday 29
(110-246)

The weather closed in today, & it has been raining almost constantly. The field is very sloppy, as is everything else, & we aren't even maintaining an alert crew. Spent the day in writing a couple of letters and loafing at the alert shack.

Olson flew down to Loi 'Wing to see what goes on, & will be back tomorrow.

(continued from April 28)

Green had been lucky, too. He had climbed back up to altitude, crossed that next mountain range, and finally found the right valley and the little airfield. The others had already returned when he landed, and after turning around at the end of the muddy strip his engine began to sputter and then died before he could taxi all the way back.

The rest of the gang had done very well in their battle; Tex and Bishop and Older had each shot down a couple, with single victories going to Jones, Overend, Adkins, Haywood, and Jernstedt. We had suffered no casualties, and only one plane was lost. Mine, dammit!

Thursday 30 ☺
(120-245)

Another rainy day — solid overcast. Olson came back about noon & said the latest news is that the Japs now have Lashio. All the radio net reporting stations are out now, so the Col. has ordered everyone out of Roi Wing. This afternoon Rector led 9 ships of the 2nd Sqdn. in, and said all the ground personnel were packing up & coming up by road. They are supposed to go on to Kunming tomorrow, weather permitting, & we are to bring what ships we have left up in 3 or 4 days. It will be mighty good to get back to Kunming for a few days. Then I suppose we will go to Chungking for the summer bombing season there.

Word from Kunming that Blackburn was killed yest. in a crash there. Another damn good boy gone.

John Blackburn was from Amarillo, Texas, a member of the 1st squadron. He was flying a Kittyhawk, practicing gunnery runs on a floating target in Kunming; apparently he failed to pull up in time and mushed into the water. It may well have been another case of "target fixation."

Friday 1
(121-244)

Things were looking so bad that we all got orders to pull out for Kunming today. The Japs are well above Lashio and should be to Loi Wing in a couple of days. We took all the ships from both Sqdns., 30 in all, and took off at 2:00 p.m. Flew thru several rainstorms etc., but got into Kunming OK.

It sure is good to get back where we can relax a little, & have hot baths etc.

Spent the evening with Reed, Skip, Baumler, Shamblin, etc., celebrating our return.

The "Baumler" mentioned above was Ajax Baumler, now a captain in the Air Corps who had recently arrived in Kunming. Ajax was a former soldier-of-fortune pilot who flew with the Loyalists during the Spanish Civil War and reportedly had shot down several enemy planes. He had signed up late for the AVG in the fall of '41 and was enroute to Burma when Pearl Harbor was attacked. Unable to complete his trip as planned, Ajax was forced to return to the States where he accepted a commission in the Air Corps, and finally he'd managed to get orders sending him to China. When we were disbanded he stayed on with our successor, the 23rd fighter group, and shot down several Jap planes in the months to follow.

Saturday 2
(122-243)

Slept late this morning. After lunch Ricketts & I went to town & sent some radiograms.

I guess we're going to start on alert duty again in a day or so. Plans now call for moving to Chungking in a couple of weeks.

The first Sqdn. was sent to Pao Shan today to see if they can do any good down that way.

MacMillan went up to Chengtu yesterday for his operation.

There's a bit of a mystery here about McMillan. I can't remember what his operation was for, or why he went to Chengtu, about 350 miles north of Kunming, to have it done. He was back on duty before very long, so apparently it wasn't anything very serious. There was a French hospital in Kunming that was occasionally utilized for treating serious illness or injury in cases where our own facilities were inadequate.

Went back on alert today, and all was very quiet.

The Col. lectured to us this p.m. about night fighting. He seems to think we may have a night raid pretty soon.

Jonls went on a photo mission to Hanoi today, and flew over the airport there at 1000 ft. Saw 40 model "O"s on the field, but no activity at all.

So, 4 guys from the 2nd, in E's, are going bombing & strafing there tomorrow.

Neale's outfit shot down a Jap observation ship near Mengshih today.

It's up at 4:00 a.m. again tomorrow for alert.

Monday 4
(124-241)

We had an air raid alarm after
lunch and patrolled for an hour + a half,
but nothing came on in.
The 1st Sqdn. was raided at noon
at Pao Shan by about 50 bombers
and ten fighters. The bombers bombed
Pao Shan but not the field. Only
Little + Bond got off the ground, as
they had no warning there. A bunch
of Zero's strafed the other ships on
the field, ruining about three or 4.
Bond got shot down while slow -
rolling over the field, but bailed out ok,
except for some burns.
Ben Foshee was very seriously
injured in the bombing in town.
They are going after those 2 in a
DC tomorrow + bring them back.
Four pilots of the 1st flew in here
this p.m. with the ships that would fly.
Plans for tomorrow are for a sweep
down that way, but I'm off duty.
Got a letter from the folks today
1st in a long time.

In the letter from home my folks advised that a deposit of $2500 had
recently been made to my account in the bank of Fort Sam Houston. I soon
learned that it was the first of two bonus checks, and represented the five
planes I'd shot down over Rangoon in December.

Tuesday 5
(125-240)

I was off duty today + just loafed.
The guys on alert went on a sweep
down around Pao Shan. The 2nd Sqdn.
saw 27 bombers escorted by 20 zeros, +
another formation of 96's. They hit the
latter + shot down 8 of them. Schiel
is missing, but may have landed at
Pao Shan. Our guys, 3rd Sqdn., were
close to Pao Shan but were called back
here as there was an alarm here at
the time. Nothing happened here tho.
Benny Foshee died of his wounds
at Pao Shan last nite. He was one
of our Sqdn. pilots, + a good friend.
Plans for tomorrow call for
another sweep around Pao Shan.
I hope we can hit them good
down there this time if they come.

We went on a sweep to Pao Shan with 16 ships today, but found no Japs. On the ground they are moving right up the road.

Probst had a forced landing at YunnanYi due to engine trouble today. Still no word as to what happened to Schiel.

Funeral services for Ben Foshee held today at Airmans' Cemetery.

I'm a little worried because Greene hasn't gotten in yet. All the rest of the guys who came up the road in convoys are here now, but he may just be staying over at Yunnan Yi or something.

Our Padre, Paul Frillman, conducts funeral services for Ben Foshee, Kunming.

Thursday 7 ☾
(127-238)

Another day of the same old grind. No alarms + no excitement.

Olson + Alder both off tomorrow, + I'm to be in charge — which isn't exactly to my liking.

Reed + I + a few others had a little party after dinner which lasted pretty late.

Ed Rector, Jim Howard, Bob Neale, Oley Olson, and Curtis Smith. Kunming, May, '42.

Friday 8
(128-237)

Col. Chennault called a meeting this morning of Sqdn. ldrs. or their representatives, so Neale, Rector, & myself went. He got word that Schiel had gotten to Yunnanyi after being forced down several days ago. Hastey is still missing.

He proposed a mission of 4 Kittys from 2nd, & our 8 tomahawks to go to the Salween river & bomb & strafe Jap truck convoys. We went this p.m., a 2 hr. & 40 min. hop, and found a batch of trucks on the road. Jones & his gang did the dirty work while we stayed on top. They blasted about 50 trucks.

I'm off tomorrow, but turning in early anyway as I'm about dead tired.

Our Tomahawks were unable to carry bombs of any type, nor even belly tanks for that matter, but the Kittyhawks were built to accommodate bomb racks. I never flew one of those with bombs, but I believe the wing racks could each carry three small fragmentation bombs, and the belly rack could take up to a 500 pound demolition bomb. Most of the Kittys had been turned over to the 2nd squadron which had several pilots who'd had experience in dive-bombers in the navy, but due to the excessive speed picked up by the P-40 in a dive it was far from being satisfactory in that role.

Saturday 9
(129-236)

Spent the day doing nothing.
Had an alarm this morning,
and those of us off duty took to
the hills. The alert gang went up
& the 1st Sqdn. shot down a Jap
observation ship.

Paxton wired from India that
Swartz died of his wounds, from
the Magwe bombing, a few days ago.
Latest reports were that he was
getting along fine, but acute
encephilitis developed unsuspectedly.

Mc Allester, crew chief in our
Sqdn., was caught on the other side
of the Salween after the bridge was blown
up while coming up the road. He's
either a prisoner or trying to get up by
foot some way. Still no word
from Greene & Regis. They were
down that way, but may still be
OK. and on the way here by truck.

Six "E's from the 2nd, & 6 of our Tomahawks went on a sweep to Mang Shih today. The E's bombed & strafed truck convoys and burned a Jap obs. ship on the field there. We stayed up for top cover but met no opposition.

It seems the Chinese are driving the Japs back down the road now. Hope it continues that direction.

Landed at Yunnan Yi on way back & saw Greene & Regis.

Hasty came in there on a burro this morning — he ran out of gas the other day & bailed out 40 mile from there.

McAlhister also came in today after coming thru Jap territory & getting across the river + up the road. All good news.

It was at about this time that the Chinese Air Force decided to discontinue their flight school at Yunnanyi and send future classes of flying cadets to the U.S. for pilot training. This meant that the American instructors who'd come over in late '41 were now surplus. They were given the option of returning to the States or joining the AVG. All of them decided to stay, checked out in the P-40 without difficulty, and were soon flying combat missions with the rest of us. They were: Al Wright and Bus Loane, former classmates of Greene and mine, and Les Hall, Harry Bolster, and "Red" Shamblin.

Monday 11
(131-234)

Another day off with nothing happening. We had one alarm, but again no Jap planes showed up.

Spent part of the day packing + getting ready for the move to Chungking.

The Chinese have pushed the Japs back down the road a little more, + perhaps they can hold them, for a while at least.

Chennault with Madame and Generalissimo Chiang Kai-Shek.

Tuesday 12
(132-233)

Went on alert again at 5:00 this a.m. Spent a very quiet day, with no alarms whatever.

Went to town with Skip after dinner, rode around, + stopped in some shops to look at silk + embroidery work.

We found out later about the strafing mission to Hanoi.

Jones took a flight of six from the second Sqdn. + hit the field there at about 5:30 this p.m. They set fire to about 15 ships on the field, but Donovan was shot down, — It wasn't worth it.

As it turned out there were only five on the Hanoi mission led by Tom Jones, and two of the pilots, Link Laughlin and John Donovan, were from the 3rd squadron. The other two from the 2nd were Frank Schiel, and Lew Bishop who had recently been reassigned from the 3rd.

Donovan, another good friend from Alabama (Montgomery), crashed after being hit by anti-aircraft fire while strafing. We were unaware of it, but obviously he had a strong premonition of his death; he left the following message to be sent by cable to his mother in the event he didn't return from the mission:

Dear Folks: You must not feel badly about my death. The small part that I have played in the war, though it has cost me my life, I am glad to give that. Life has meant much to me, but not so much that I am distressed at leaving, and neither must you be. I had only a few things planned for the future, one of the most important was a nice home for Momma. It will please me much if she will live in a more comfortable home with many flowers and trees. I am happy, and so must she be. Love to all, John Junior

Wednesday 13
(133-232)

Spent the day on alert. Weather pretty bad — overcast + rainy. Nothing happened all day.

No news as to when we're to move to Chungking, but it may be a couple of weeks yet.

Skip + I went into town + fooled around after dinner. Then Oley, Reed, Sesel, myself, + a couple others killed a few hours in the rec. room + our roomshere. I'm off duty tomorrow, but go on nite alert at 6:00 p.m. for a few days.

John Donovan

Spent the day loafing around the Hostel.
Went to the field at six to go on nite alert.
Nothing happened & we had a good sleep.

RTS in the cockpit

Same old stuff — nothing to
do + I did it all day.
Saw Bob Scott this p.m., the
same one I knew back in Santa
Maria as a check pilot. He was
a 1st Lt. then and is now a
full Colonel. We talked over old
times, + he is going to take my
trunk full of souvenirs back to
India with him, + ship it
home on the Ferry Command.
All the gang that went to
Hanoi on the strafing mission
got promotions of one grade, +
we are all rather sore about
that now. The Col. says it
was an order from the Generalissimo,
but there is some doubt about that
in some people's minds.
Went on nite alert duty at six,
+ spent the evening talking about
getting home with the rest of the boys

Robert L. Scott had given me a couple of check rides when I was a flying
cadet in primary. As a check-pilot he was a mean s.o.b., washing out as
many cadets as he passed, but now that we were on more or less equal
footing he was as affable as could be. Later he was my wingman on what I
believe was his first combat mission in China.

Saturday 16
(136-229)

Another day of loafing. Tonite is my last nite of nite alert duty, for which I am thankful.

Some of us were having a bull session this p.m. before going on duty, and Rector brought in the news that Jones had crashed + was killed. He was making dive-bombing tests with an "E" and apparently blacked out in a pullout and went in. That's mighty rough news, as he was married + had a baby he'd never even seen. He led the Hanoi flight + was eager as hell about such things.

Spent the evening at the alert shack batting the breeze + sleeping.

Some of the gang strafed a train today about 30 miles below the border south-east of Lao Kay in Fr. Indo China. Blew up the engine etc.

Tom Jones, ex-navy pilot from Seattle, was one of the most likeable pilots in the 2nd squadron. He had been stricken with malaria shortly after arriving at Toungoo, had missed much of the action that took place in the first weeks of the war, and was determined to make up for lost time. He planned and led the raid on Hanoi, and was convinced that the Kittyhawk could be used as a dive-bomber; he died while trying to develop a technique that might be both effective and safe.

MAY 1942

I was on duty today as well as last nite. Reed + I went as top cover on a mission to Lao Kay with four of the boys from the 2nd Sqdn. Got down there, about 50 mile below Lao Kay + I spotted a train going up that way. Bishop, who was leading the others, in "E"s with small bombs, didn't see the train + headed back. I called him + told him about the train + he said for us to go back + strafe it, + his gang would bomb the station at Lao Kay. Reed + I went back + made 4 passes each + blew up the engine. Bishop was shot down by anti-aircraft at Lao Kay. His ship caught fire + he bailed out, landing in the town. He is now a prisoner of those damn Jap's. And he's another married man with a new baby.

Everybody else got back O-K. He was the 3rd member of the Hanoi mission to be lost in the past 5 days.

Greene got in from Chunnan Yi today.

Lew Bishop, of DeKalb Junction, N.Y., was the third AVG pilot to be captured and imprisoned by the Japanese. Like the others, he suffered untold hardships before being released at the end of the war.

Same old grind again today.
Nothing has happened, as usual.
The Jap air force doesn't seem to
be very active these days, at
least not in our territory. But
I expect they'll come one of these
days, & when they do they'll probably
be plentiful as hell.

Parker D. & I flew down to
Mengtze today to deliver some
money etc. to Richardson, the
radio operator there. I spent
most of the time on the way
down brushing up on acrobatics.
We had a lot of fun playing around.

Schramm, my crew chief now,
is busy installing a new engine
in my ship. Should be out
in a couple of days.

Evening spent as usual.
Had a talk with Gen Chennault at
dinner, & he said we would all get
to go back to the States on the 4th of July
if we didn't accept induction into Army.

Tuesday 19
(139-226)

We had a swell storm last nite — all kinds of lightning, thunder, & rain. Still bad this morning at 4:30 when we went to the field. It stayed overcast all day and we got off at 4:00 p.m. Spent the evening doing nothing.

Rumor has it that one of our convoys going up the road to Chungking was ambushed by Chinese and four Limeys + two of our men were killed. Regis and Pietoker left 9 days ago + haven't been heard from since, so we're all afraid maybe they were done in. Nothing official yet tho.

Another rumor that we may not move to Chungking at all. I hope this one is correct.

I'm off tomorrow.

As if there were not enough other problems, simply trying to drive a truck up the Burma Road could be a pretty sporty proposition. The hills were full of outlaw bands still controlled by Chinese warlords, and even armed convoys were often attacked, their cargoes looted, and there were many casualties. This was definitely no place for a Sunday drive in the country.

Wednesday 20
(140-225)

Went into town this afternoon.
Greene & I sent Ed Fox Hall a
wire trying to find out what
the car situation is back home.
Spent the rest of the day
loafing around the Hostel.
Jo Stewart had eight of us
plus the Consul & Vice Consul
to dinner this p.m. in the
private dining room. Had a
swell feed & a good time
all around.
Word from Chungking today
that Regis & Pete arrived OK., so
guess it was only rumor about
two of our guys being killed going
up the road. However, there
are some more on the way who
haven't arrived as yet.

Among the handful of people who came into the AVG late, actually hired after they'd arrived in China, was a little refugee German Jew named Gerhard Neumann. In his early twenties, he'd somehow escaped the Nazi horror and the fate suffered by many of his relatives and friends. How or why he managed to get to Kunming I don't know, but he was a skilled mechanic who volunteered his services and was hired immediately. Later he joined the Air Corps, and later still emigrated to the U.S. and in due time became a citizen. He found employment with General Electric, rose rapidly within their ranks, and ultimately became the president of G.E.'s Jet Engine Division. How's that for a success story?

Thursday 21
(141-224)

Weather still pretty bad — overcast & rainy, so we're running two shifts on alert — four on in morning + 4 others relieving them for afternoon. I was on third p.m. & nothing happened. I wrote a long letter to the folks today & got it in the mail.

Twelve of us were notified today that we were to stay here when the others move to Chungking, along with all our mechs.

We are supposed to stand alert and also train 20 new army pilots due to arrive in a few days. That is fine with us.

Gen. Chennault & Gen. Bissell had a meeting of all personnel tonite, & gave us the final dope on induction on the 4th of July, etc. It seems we'll all be able to leave then if we don't join the army.

Brig. General Clayton Bissell of the U.S. Air Corps had all the charm of a cobra. He advised us that if we had good sense we'd agree to being inducted into the Air Corps there in China, and that we'd all be drafted as buck privates the moment we reached the States if we refused.

Friday 22
(142-223)

Nothing new or exciting happened today; so far as being on the alert goes.

I flew a half hour test hop, did some acrobatics etc. over the hostel + field + came in.

Little was killed today on a mission to the lines at the Salween. Cause of the accident not certain, but some think one of his small bombs may have been faulty + blew up when he tried to release them. Anyway, someone else in the flight said a wing come off + he spun right in, in flames.

That makes Number 23.

Olson + a bunch of the others congregated in my room after dinner + we had a good bull session with light refreshments. Ha.

Before that they held an auction of Jones + Hoskee's stuff.

Bob Little, of Spokane, Washington, was one of the best fighter pilots in the business, liked and respected by all. His loss was still another debit in what had become an alarming rate of attrition. And while it wasn't discussed, I'm sure that most of us were wondering if we'd still be around six weeks later when we'd be free to go home.

Saturday 23 ☽
(143-222)

Was off duty today & loafed.
Went out to the field this afternoon
after lunch & took a bunch of
color pictures of the planes etc.
I'd like to send them home with
one of the Camco guys who is
leaving tomorrow.
A B-24 came in today, & rumor
has it that some of the B17's in
India may come up in a few
days to do a little bombing down
around Hanoi & Haiphong.
If the weather is good tomorrow,
the group, with exception of our Sqdn.,
is moving up to Chungking.
Then we're to move to the other
Hostel near the field.

It seems that Paul Greene and Bob Prescott had somehow been deprived at a very tender age of the benefits of a simple surgical procedure which young males of the Jewish faith receive automatically. Apparently they decided that now was a perfect time to rectify this oversight, the idea being that they could get it done for free by one of our flight surgeons, and it wouldn't interfere with their sex life since that was non-existent anyway.

And so these two intrepid airmen arranged for a few days leave and went under the knife, as the saying goes, of Doc Rich, who refused their pleas to use pinking shears instead of a scalpel. True to the code of doctor-patient confidentiality, Doc refused to discuss the details of these delicate operations. Both patients recovered nicely, although they walked in a strange manner for some time and were unable to fasten the crotch-straps of their parachutes without pain for a week or so.

Back on duty today. We went down to the Salween front today, four of us escorting 4 "E"s with small bombs. I don't think they did much damage tho.

Got some more good color shots of the other three in our flight in formation.

The move to Chungking was called off temporarily, + now nobody knows what the score is.

Gen. Chennault has put out a list of the pilots with the rank they would recieve if they stayed on and accepted induction. I, along with several others, was offered the rank of Major. So far only one or two pilot have signified their intentions of staying.

The idea of jumping from former 2nd Lieutenant to Major in less than a year's time, without ever having to be a 1st Lt. or Captain, had considerable appeal, to be sure. But it meant having to stay on in China for an indefinite period, and most of the dozen or so pilots who were offered this opportunity declined. By now the appeal of home and family, American girls, an up-to-date movie followed by a hamburger with shoestrings and malted milk, and the chance to relax in a clean and peaceful atmosphere, outweighed whatever inducements were being offered.

Monday 25
(145-220)

Another day + still no action.
Slept + read most of the day,
but after lunch a few of us
got hold of a Ryan trainer
belonging to the Chinese + went
riding around like kids with
a new toy. I took Stiles up
and did some acrobatics. He
really loved it - first time he'd
ever done acrobatics too.
It was quite a change from a P-40.
Paxton + Layher, with two
R.A.F. pilots, brought in 4 new
Kittyhawks this p.m.

Parked P-40s on alert readiness, Kunming.

MAY 1942

Tuesday 26
(146-219)

I was off duty today & did nothing in particular.

Overend, Lawlor, & Croft left for Karachi today on a Ferry trip.

Still no word as to when the gang moves to Chungking.

1st squadron personnel

Wednesday 27
(147-218)

Back on alert today.
No excitement.
I flew an hour + a half this
p.m. putting slow time on my
ship with new engine.
The 2nd Sqdn. bombed
Lungling today + hit pretty well.
They tell me there have been
8 or 10 Jap. bombers bombing
Pao Shan for the past 3 days in
the morning between 8 and 9.
   Sooo, we eight on alert from
our Sqdn are going to be there at
that time in the morning to
greet them if they come again.
Maybe some fun.

Among the Tomahawks that had been reassigned to the 3rd squadron was No. 47, which I had claimed as a replacement for old 77. I spent a lot of hours in the cockpit of this plane and, still with the expert help of Crookshanks, we came through unscathed.

Eight of us went to Yunnan Yi this morning at six to refuel + go to Pao Shan to meet the Japs if they came to bomb. Shilling had a leaking gas line + couldn't go on. Laughlin's engine cut out + he cracked up on the take-off. Washed out his ship but he wasn't hurt. The six of us left went to Pao Shan + patrolled for an hour but no sign of the wily Jap.

I took some formation pictures on the way home in color, + they should be plenty nice — I hope.

Older + I recieved citations + medals this p.m. for the work done in Rangoon. Quite a ceremony. More pictures.

Nothing much to report for today.
No excitement of any kind.

Hayward + I tested a couple of
ships this p.m.- + had a big time
chasing tail + doing acrobatics.

Sorenson from 40-B flew a
B-25 in today from India, He's
flying Gen. Stillwell up to Chungking.
He says they have about 20 more
B-25's in Karachi, and rumor has
it that some are coming here in a
few days. But we've heard stories
like that so often in the past months
that nobody will believe it till they
see them - Still no Army personnel
here for us to train to take over
when we leave.

MAY 1942

Saturday 30 😊
(150-215)

Today was my day off, and I
spent it as usual. Not a
damn thing to do except read
old magazines and listen to
the photograph.
After dinner we had an old
movie which was lousy.

Flight of Hell's Angels over Burma-China border, May '42

Well, we had a little excitement
today although nothing came of it.
We had an alarm this morning
and one this afternoon. The 2nd
Sqdn. took off & patrolled both time
& we warmed up our ships &
stood by. The Japs bombed and
strafed Yunnan Yi which is
only a half hours flight from here.
But they didn't come on in here
so we didn't get any action.
The W.A.S.C. threw us a big
lawn party this evening, with
Chinese chow, entertainment, etc.
It was quite an affair &
everyone enjoyed it a lot.

Monday 1
(152-213)

Another day with no excitement.
Reed & I tested two ships and
did some formation acrobatics
and chased tail for a while.
Had a lot of fun at that.
Weather closed in this afternoon —
very cloudy and slight rain.
Parker Du Puoy treated Reed,
Keller, Frillman, & myself to
a wonderful Chinese dinner at
the Cantonese restaurant tonite.
We had all the best dishes and
Champagne to boot.
Some Army pursuit pilots got in
today, & two are assigned to our
Sqdn. for training etc.
Also Rose, from 40 B, came in on
a Ferry Command DC today &
gave us news from the States.
He just left there the 11th of May.

I don't remember who first discovered the Cantonese restaurant in the
middle of the city, but it had absolutely the finest Chinese food that I have
ever tasted, before or since. Several of us became regular patrons, having
dinner there three or four times each week. The place had a seemingly inex-
haustible supply of the finest of French wines that had been brought in from
French Indo-China before it was occupied by the Japanese, and usually each
of us would order a bottle of champagne with dinner. *Moet & Chandon* and
Piper Heidsieck cost about $12.00 per bottle in U.S. money, which we
thought was quite reasonable.

Tuesday 2
(153-212)

Weather still rainy + overcast.
We had one alarm today and
some went up from the 2nd Sqdn,
while we stood by our ships.
Nothing was seen tho —
the two new Army boys are going
on alert tomorrow in our
Sqdn. so I get the day off.
Had a good talk with Col. Scott
after dinner tonite.
Still no mail. It's been
a full month since we've had
a batch of mail. No doubt
the damned limeys are holding
it up in India —

Col. Robert L. Scott was spending much of his time at our base in Kunming these days, and he would soon be named to command the 23rd Fighter Group which would take over when the AVG was disbanded. While Bob was not a Flying Tiger, he did fly a couple of missions with us in order to gain some experience, and of course he was a very capable pilot. He was later to write a fascinating account of his exploits in what became a best-seller, entitled *"God is my Co-Pilot,"* which I believe was published in 1943.

A few months later after his book came out I was talking with a friend who also knew Scott. My friend said, "I hear that Robert L. is about to have another book published." I expressed interest, and asked him if he knew what the title was to be. "I understand," he said with a perfectly straight face, "he's decided to call this one *"Christ was my Crew-chief."*

Wednesday 3
(154-211)

Off duty today and did nothing to speak of.

Spent the afternoon shooting the bull with some of the mechs in Keller's room.

Saw Col. Alexander after dinner and had a good talk with him.

Two B-25's came in this afternoon after bombing Lashio from Dinjan. Six of them bombed Lashio but only the two got here. The other four are unreported & probably lost. One of the ones that got here was attacked by 2 I 97's and the radio operator was hit & killed.

Squadron leader "Oley" Olson

331

Another long day at the field.
We had no alarms today, and I
spent some time getting my ship
cleaned & painted up pretty.

No news about the B-25's yet.
Rumor has it that a B17 headed
here yesterday got lost + had to
make a belly landing in a valley
somewhere.

Gen. Chennault went to Chungking
yesterday and came back today.
And now the word has been
spread that the long awaited move
of the other 2 Sqdns. may be
tomorrow, weather permitting.

A Chinese pilot was killed today —
his ship, a Hawk 3, exploded
while he was taxiing to take off.
They think a light bomb on it blew
up. We all ran out + saw pieces
falling down — not much left of
the plane except the pilot in the
seat + the tail assembly. Not a
very pretty sight.

Friday 5 ☾
(156-209)

Was off again today. We only
have about 8 ships in commission
in our Sqdn. now, so with
the Army boys on alert too, we
are getting off quite often.
We all thought the others were
going to Chungking today, but
the weather is still bad up there
so they are being held up some
more.
Nothing much in the way of
news around here.
Some mail came in today, +
I got 4 letters. One from the
folks, written latter part of April.

Bill Reed

Saturday 6

Spent the day on alert. We
had reports this a.m. of many Jap
planes headed this way, and our
8 on alert went up. We patrolled
locally for an hour & a half &
landed. No more reports — guess
the Japs turned around & went home.
It has been very cloudy & almost
solid overcast here the past few
days — doubt if they could find
the place if they did come on up.
   Dupuy, Fuene, Reed, Frillman,
Jernstedt, & myself went in and
had another swell Chinese feed
at the Cantonese Restaurant tonite.
We had some more Champagne at
$6.00 per bottle. Ha.

1st after
Trinity

Sunday 7
(158-207)

Was off again today, but we got word here at the Hostel about noon that 27 Jap planes were supposed to have landed at Lao Kay this morning. So I went out to the field to get a ship + go up if they came on up here. Later reports stated that the first one was false. Weather still bad in Chungking.

Jap aircrew prisoner flanked by 1st squadron pilots "Snuffy" Smith, left, and Bill Bartling. Kneeling on P-40 wing are Joe Rosbert and Dick Rossi. Kweilin, China, June '42

JUNE 1942

Monday 8
(159-206)

Bad weather here now, raining & low ceiling. Spent the day on alert but nothing happened. Came home early due to the weather. Reed & I started a little party and it carried on well into the night.

Tomahawks on the prowl, near Paoshan, China, May '42

I was supposed to be off today
but was drafted, due to
Laughlin's being sick.

Went to work late, but the
weather is still bad + no excitement.
The other 2 Sqdns. left this noon
for Chungking, + got there OK.

Alder was operated on at the
French Hospital in town for
appendicitis today. He's been
having pains for some time now.

I've been going crazy trying
to get transportation for the Sqdn., +
permits for our vehicles, due to the
new rationing system.

Dufnoy, Reed, Stillman, Baumler
+ I went to town for another
big Chinese Chow tonite. A
swell feed.

Was off today. They had an
alarm today, & all of us at the
Hostel lit out for the hills in the
cemetery across the road.
Our 8 planes on alert took off &
patrolled but no Japs were sighted.
They did bomb some joint about
100 miles from here tho. It's still
cold, rainy, & overcast here.
Keller & I spent the afternoon
trying to straighten out the
transportation situation, &
fooled around a while in town.
We had a 1933 picture show
tonite that was really a stinker.

JUNE 1942

Thursday 11
(162-203)

Another quiet day on alert.
The weather is clearing up
some now, but still pretty
cloudy.
  We move over to Hostel No. 2
tomorrow, much closer to the
field.
  I've been busy tonite getting
packed so they can haul my
stuff over, as I'm on duty
all day tomorrow.

3rd squadron pilots during refueling stop at Yunnanyi. Seated, l
to r: RTS, Jernstedt, Prescott, Laughlin, Reed. Standing: Shilling,
Olson.

Friday 12

Another dull day with nothing
doing.. We got word this morning
that the 1st Sqdn.., 8 of them, had
intercepted about 13 or 14 Jap
planes up north, and shot down
8 or 9 of them without loss to
themselves. Good stuff.
Nothing at all new here.
Some of those off duty today
moved our stuff over to Hostel No. 2
so we are set up here now.
Prescott, Greene, Haywood + myself
have a four room apartment here
that is pretty nice. Knocked
some partitions out of a couple of
middle rooms, so we have a
couple of sitting rooms besides our
bedrooms.

Prescott and Greene were spending much of their plentiful spare time these days as used-clothing merchants; they bought up all the stuff that the rest of us were about to throw or give away, paying practically nothing, and then sold it at a tremendous profit to the upper-class Chinese. They'd found quite a bonanza, and made a bundle.

Most of us who had brought guns from the States were doing the same thing; though we'd been told that selling guns to the Chinese was forbidden, nobody seemed to pay any attention and with the prices the Chinese were happy to pay we couldn't afford to keep them. I had decided to keep the Luger I'd bought in Cairo, but sold my shotgun for $250.00, my Colt revolver for $400.00, and the .22 rifle for $100.00. Finally I was offered $500.00 for the Luger and decided it was a luxury I couldn't afford to keep.

Saturday 13 ⬤
(164-201)

I was off today and just loafed as usual. Tex Hill, Hedman, Ricketts, & Hodges all flew in from India in P-43's from their ferry trip. Also some Chinese Pilots with them.

Went to town this morning and sent a couple of Cablegrams. One to Mom + Sis for their birthdays the 14th + 15th.

Spent the evening talking to Hedman + Hodges about their trip etc. They say Pan Am will hire any AVG pilots who want to work for them.

Same old grind today.
Nothing happened.
Got word today that in the
fight the 1st Sqdn. was in the
other day, they shot down nine
Japs. Charlie Bond was shot
down and bailed out — his
second such experience.
Al Wright was hit in engine +
made a forced landing, but
wasn't hurt much.

I flew a half-hour's buzz
mission this a.m. to let off
a little steam.

We got paid after work this
evening — last time over here.
After that we had a little party
which lasted pretty late.
Also shot craps for a while,
and I dropped a few Rupees.

After the crap game we were talking about Charley Bond being shot down
again, and Bill Reed broke us all up when he said, "I wonder if old Charley's
got any other hobbies?"

Monday 15
(166-199)

Spent the day on alert, but again nothing new.

Hodges + I each flew a gunnery mission and I won a bet on the score.

Our three army boys are supposed to go to Chungking on a transport tomorrow, or as soon as possible. Barnum is over-eager + thinks he'll get some action at Chungking sooner, but Butsch and Minor want to stay.

Gen. Chennault is still here but leaving in a day or two.

Got a letter from the folks today mailed Apr. 30.

Tuesday 16
(167-198)

Off today & just loafed around the Hostel.
Weather here is pretty well closed in now and not much activity.
Two more B-25's came in today and are to go on a mission or two when the weather is better. We now have 7 of them here with their Army crews.

RTS beside Chuck Older's plane.

Wednesday 17
(168-197)

Another lousy day at the field on alert.

Four of us were going to escort 4 - B-25s on a bombing mission to Meng Shih today, but the weather was too bad.

Gen. Chennault went back to Chungking today, but the army boys haven't left yet.

Harvey Greenlaw and Chennault about to light up

JUNE 1942

Thursday 18
(169-196)

Off today and did nothing. Eight more army pilots came in from India & are staying with us. They may go on to Chungking in a few days.

A Chinese pilot spun in in a P-43 this morning & was killed.

Krillman, Olson, Paxton, Hodges, & myself went to the Cantonese for Chinese chow tonite. Very good too.

Chinese Air Force   P-43

Friday 19
(170-195)

Well, we finally had a little excitement today. Got a report of many enemy planes heading this way from the South-east this morning, + eight of us on alert went up. Patrolled for an hour but nothing more was heard from them.

Spent some time in getting the new Army boys checked off in our ships. They did pretty well — not even a ground-loop.

Another Chinese pilot had engine failure and undershot the field + crashed into a native village about 100 yds. from the alert shack. He died.

A dozen or so of our pilots had decided to go to work for CNAC after the AVG was disbanded. CNAC was expanding, needed experienced pilots, and offered jobs to practically all of us. They not only offered excellent wages — considerably more than we'd been making — but were also more understanding than the Air Corps in agreeing to allow their new hires to return to the States for a couple of months before starting their new careers. I was not particularly interested, mainly because I couldn't picture myself being content to fly unarmed transport planes after flying fighters. This was close to driving a bus after competing in the Indy 500, to my way of thinking.

Olson, Mitchell, Shilling + myself
went on an escort mission with
4 B-25's this afternoon. We went to
Yunnan Yi and refueled + met them
when they came over. They were
supposed to bomb Lungling, but got lost
+ wouldn't follow us. They turned
around + came home, but Olson + I
went on down to Mang Shih +
strafed a bit. The Japs threw up a
hell of a batch of Anti Aircraft
and Oley said a couple of bursts were
only 25 yds. or so behind my tail.
We didn't get back till almost dark.
DuPuoy, Reed, R. A. Smith, Keller,
+ myself went in for Chinese chow
tonite. Very good, but I was
too tired to enjoy it much.
My day off tomorrow.

Loafed around the Hostel all day.
Nothing to do but sit around
and talk with others off duty.
Much speculation as to how
long it will take to get home, etc.
Rumor has it that the Ferry
Command will only take us as far
as Din Jan, India. If that's
true it's mighty damn cheap of
the Army + everybody concerned.
Went in for Chinese chow
again tonite with Reed, Dudwoy
Keller, + R.G. Smith.

Forgive me, friends, for departing from the handwritten diary for the next few days. In the interest of conserving space, I am having the entries from June 22 through June 30 reproduced in complete but printed form. You will note that these entries are brief, and nothing very exciting took place; by now we were simply anxious to head for home.

JUNE 22

On duty today but nothing much to report. Army boys still flying our ships on formation, gunnery, etc. We had a raid alarm & went up, but nothing happened. McMillan got in today from Chengtu.

JUNE 23

On alert again today. Flew lead ship in a 6-ship formation with Haywood, Shilling, & three of the Army boys. It looked pretty bad.

Time is getting short now, and will I be glad when the 4th gets here.

Our first bunch to leave is composed of all crew-chiefs & armorers, & some leave on the 27th—4 days away.

JUNE 24

I was off today & loafed & gossiped as usual. Weather has been pretty bad lately, & it rained most of the day.

JUNE 25

Each flight on alert today only stayed on half a day due to the rainy weather. We've had all kinds of rain and things are really muddy & sloppy.

My flight had the early shift & we were relieved at noon.

Spent the p.m. trying to get a few matters straightened up, such as paying bills, money changing, etc.

JUNE 26

Off duty today. Went to Supply with Hodges to get straightened out there.

Tomorrow the first bunch is due to start home, & they're all packed and ready. Weather good here today—hope it continues.

JUNE 27

Off again today. All the gang who were due to leave today got off OK. Nothing to report except Col Sanders with 9 Kittyhawks finally got here after being lost enroute from Dinjan. They were over an hour overdue.

JUNE 28

I was on today and went up for a half-hour buzz, thinking it was to be my last flight over here. Had to go up again a half-hour after landing tho, as an obs. ship was reported in the net about 100 kilos from here. Didn't see anything of it.

JUNE 29

Oley, Reed, Dupouy, Haywood, & I all have reservations on CNAC for Saturday, figuring on getting to Calcutta as soon as possible. CNAC flies when the Army transport won't, so if the weather's very bad we may get a jump on the others.

JUNE 30

Off again today. Weather is right on the ground. Rained all last night and most of the day.

Stayed around barracks listening to phonograph most of time. Hot Damn, only 3 more days until we can pull out.

Wednesday 1
(182-183)

Spent my last day on alert today. Have been busy getting everything squared away to leave Sat.

Some Chinese newsreel cameraman, who works for "News of the day," was at the field + took a bunch of pictures.

Tex Hill + Schiel flew in from Chungking + reports that some of the gang up there are staying an extra 2 weeks to help the army out.

He himself is staying on in the Army over here.

At the request of the Air Corps, about fifteen pilots and more than that number of ground personnel had agreed to stay on for an additional two weeks in order to help make the transition more orderly after the AVG went out of business on the 4th of July. Included in the group of pilots were Gil Bright, Tex Hill, Ed Rector, Chuck Sawyer, and Frank Schiel who had decided to accept induction into the Air Corps and were to be commissioned as Majors.

Two of the others who stayed on for the additional two weeks were to pay with their lives. One of the squadrons, based at Kweilin—about 300 miles to the east of Kunming—sent a flight of four to bomb a Japanese Army installation at Nanchang. It was heavily defended, and Arnold Shamblin, one of the former instructors at Yunnanyi, was shot down. It was thought that he had either bailed out or crash—landed safely and taken prisoner, but nothing was later heard from or about him. John Petach, who had married nurse "Red" Foster six months earlier, was also shot down and killed. Six months later a lovely daughter who would never see her father was born to Red, now back in the U.S.A.

Thursday 2
(183-182)

Went into CNAC office this p.m. + got Aleys + my ticket for Dinjan Cat. We're getting them just in case the weather is bad + no army transports leave. I am all set to go except getting signature of Group Supply + Olsons on my Clearance. Many already have their Clearances, + some have already left.
Tomorrow is last day of the old A.V.G.

And this was the last entry I made in my diary. Two days later the Flying Tigers ceased to exist except in memory. Others by the hundreds, and eventually thousands, would follow us and carry on the fight to its ultimate victorious conclusion, backed by the growing might of American industry and its military machine. Those who followed the AVG were equally dedicated and capable, and perhaps it is understandable that they would later proudly proclaim that they had been "in the Flying Tigers." Perhaps it is equally understandable that those of us who had been given this rather unique title by a grateful Chinese people would resent being lumped together with all who followed in our footsteps.

At one time or another in the intervening years most of us have been faced with a situation that often borders on the ludicrous. It can happen anywhere a number of people are gathered, perhaps at a party, where someone comes up and announces that he's just heard that you were in the Flying Tigers, and states that he also was one. In the ensuing conversation it may develop that he was a 2nd Lieutenant who served in the 14th Air Force in 1944, or a supply sergeant who arrived in Kunming in 1943. Inevitably he asks when you were there, and when he's told that it was in 1941 and '42, he says, "Oh, you were in the original Flying Tigers." With which you want to go off into a corner and throw up.

Epilogue

So there you have it, friends. It had been almost exactly a year earlier that Paul Greene and I had resigned from the Air Corps and left Randolph Field to seek adventure in faraway places. We'd found it, in spades, and had been fortunate enough to survive. When the 4th of July came and went, it was the end of a unique experiment that had succeeded beyond most people's wildest expectations. Perhaps the best epitaph for this unorthodox little band of maverick Americans was bestowed by Robert B. Hotz in his book, *"With General Chennault—the Story of the Flying Tigers,"* published in 1943. The concluding sentence of the final chapter written by this distinguished aviation writer and editor said, *"On the morning of July 5 there was nothing left of the Flying Tigers but a legend."*

So what had we accomplished during the seven months we were actually engaged in combat at the very beginning of World War II? Well, our original mission had been to defend the Burma Road in order to enable China to receive the desperately needed supplies necessary to avoid being completely overrun by the Japanese Army. We had done that, for a vital three-month period at least, allowing many hundreds of tons of Lend-Lease materials to be transported to China before the fall of Rangoon. And for another three months we had helped to stem the tide into northern Burma, aiding the meager British ground troops and the poorly equipped Chinese army which belatedly had been sent into Burma. In the process, according to the AVG's official record, we had destroyed nearly 300 Japanese planes in the air and on the ground, and several times that number of experienced air-crewmen. Dozens of trucks and light tanks, and hundreds of enemy troops had been eliminated in strafing and bombing attacks, causing critical delays in the Japanese time-table for the conquest of Burma. Where they had over-run French Indo-China, Malaya, and Thailand in record time, with vir-tually no opposition, they soon discovered that Burma was an entirely dif-ferent ballgame. And at the same time we were able to stop the Japanese Air Force's indiscriminate bombing attacks on southwest China; Kunming, their favorite target for years, was suddenly freed of the terror it had known for so long. During our stay in that ancient walled city, visited by Marco Polo in another time, no more bombs were dropped. Our greatest reward was found in the smiles and cheers of the people whenever any of us passed among them; for the first time in years they had reason to hope. All of which poses the rhetorical question: *What might have happened in Burma and China if the AVG had not been there?*

And what of the cost? Well, in terms of lives I'm sure the enemy would have thought it a terrific bargain, but to us the price was high indeed. Unlike the Japanese, who considered it a great honor and a privilege to die for their Emperor, we held life to be very dear, not something we were in-clined to sacrifice unnecessarily for Franklin D. Roosevelt or anyone else if we could help it. But of course we knew at the outset that there would be casualties, and by the luck of the draw or the roll of the dice—call it what you will—twenty-two of our pilots and one of our ground crewmen were to die. Of this number, only four were killed in air-to-air combat, the rest in strafing and bombing attacks, accidents, or by enemy bombs. Three more were shot down and imprisoned for the duration of the war.

Roughly one out of three pilots who were actually engaged in combat paid the ultimate price.

In material terms the cost was ridiculously low by present-day standards. According to most estimates the entire AVG operation from beginning to end, including the price of the 100 P-40s, cost approximately eight million dollars. This seems unbelieveable; eight million won't buy even a single fighter plane at the going price these days. So it would appear that either the AVG was a fantastic bargain or the current jet fighter plane is incredibly overpriced, or more likely, both.

I am frequently asked how many AVG pilots became Aces before the group was disbanded, and I believe the correct answer is sixteen if one is to go by the usually accepted criteria. This, at least so far as the *American Fighter Aces Association* is concerned, requires that a pilot shoot down a minimum of five enemy aircraft in air-to-air combat. According to AVG records, it appears that sixteen of us met or exceeded that number of confirmed victories. Bob Neale, commander of the 1st squadron, led the way with a total of 15½ enemy planes to his credit, including 3½ destroyed on the ground. Tex Hill was next highest with a total of 12¼, which included 2¼ on the ground. In addition to the sixteen men referred to above, ten more pilots each destroyed five or more enemy aircraft if air-to-air victories and those destroyed on the ground are combined. These figures, then, can be somewhat misleading inasmuch as most of the lists that have been published show totals credited to individual pilots but make no distinction between air-to-air and air-to-ground victories. To further complicate matters, credit for destroying some of those enemy planes was often shared by two or more pilots, thus creating the fractions that appear in the totals.

I have no intention of trying to sort all of this out now, or try to set the record straight for those who like to delve into such matters. Speaking for myself only, I am positive of having shot down ten enemy planes in air-to-air combat, and until some time after I left China thought they had all been officially confirmed. Later, however, it seems some people in the records section at headquarters decided that a couple of those victories should be shared with others who had fired at the same planes before I actually shot them down for keeps. Thus, through some rather arbitrary bookkeeping after the fact, my total was reduced to 8⅔. Later still I guess they decided to round off the number; I was awarded the Chinese Air Force 9-star medal, signifying nine victories, and was paid the bonus for that number. That left my good friend Chuck Older as top man among the Hell's Angels with a total of 10¼ confirmed, all air-to-air. In addition to those already mentioned, a list of others who had anywhere from seven to ten air-to-air kills would include such names as Bond, Burgard, Lawlor, Little, McGarry, and

Newkirk. These totals, impressive at the time no doubt, would be exceeded by dozens of others before the war came to an end.

Now, please understand that I do not mean to belittle the importance of the contributions made by those who destroyed so many enemy planes on the ground. In fact, my hat is off to all of the pilots who participated in those daring raids, for their missions were usually more dangerous than aerial combat. Strafing and bombing at tree-top level, whether the targets be airfields, truck columns, or troop concentrations, was one of those occupations that could be extremely hazardous to your health. Anti-aircraft and small-arms fire was always there to greet the attackers, sending up a tremendous hail of crossfire that was accurate and often deadly. Flying into this sort of thing and pressing home repeated attacks required the utmost in courage and determination, and nine of our pilots either died or were shot down and taken prisoner while performing such missions. So, while shooting a plane out of the sky may be more satisfying to the ego, destroying one on the ground is likely to be a much tougher job. Most of the credit for these highly successful but costly missions goes to the 1st and 2nd squadrons, for they were the ones who drew most such assignments. An outstanding exception, of course, was the raid on Moulmein by Reed and Jernstedt from the 3rd squadron during which they set fire to fifteen enemy planes neatly parked on the airstrip. Nobody can tell me that those two, and all the others, were not Aces.

I have spoken previously of the tremendous job done by our crew-chiefs and armorers, a few of which have been named, but I also want to pay tribute to the many other ground-support people who are so necessary to the success of any organization such as ours. They all contributed, all were dedicated, and all helped to make the pilots' job a good deal easier than it might otherwise have been. The AVG was a team effort in the truest sense of the word, and of course the lion's share of the credit deservedly goes to our leader, Chennault. He was not just a master tactician, capable of getting the most out of his meager allotment of outmoded equipment and supplies, but he was one of those rare individuals who was able to inspire others to do than they thought they could do. He was tough but fair, perhaps lacking in "charisma" as we think of it today, yet there were some who seemed to be convinced that he could walk on water. I'm afraid I didn't go quite that far, but then I was always a bit skeptical about Christ's having walked on the Sea of Galilee, so what do I know? I guess the point to be made is that he was in the right place at the right time, the right man for the job, and perhaps the *only* man who could have carried it off so successfully. Genius? Maybe. One of a kind? Definitely!

I would be content to end the story on this note, but I realize that at least a few readers who have stuck with it this long will want to know how we got back to the land of chili-dogs, convertibles, and round-eyed girls, not necessarily in that order. At the outset, I can say that most of us were on our own, having to travel at our own expense and by whatever means of transportation we could find. The U.S. Ferry Command, apparently under orders from on high, refused to let us fly back on their often half-empty transport planes, except for those who had stayed on an extra two weeks beyond the 4th of July. To the top brass of the Air Corps, where professional jealousy often exists, we were no longer fellow Americans who'd seen more combat than most; now we were merely unemployed soldiers of fortune, civilians trying to bum a ride home. Actually, we'd have been more than glad to pay for such transportation, but such a thing was out of the question. Later it developed that a few of our guys, through personal contacts with former friends now in the Ferry Command, were able to talk them into ignoring the rules and were allowed to hitch-hike home by air. Greene and Prescott were among the fortunate few to make it this way, via England and then over the North Atlantic. Most of us were forced to do it the hard way.

Oley Olson, Parker Dupouy, Tom Haywood, Bill Reed and I flew from Kunming to Calcutta as planned aboard a CNAC DC-3 on the 4th of July. We spent a few days there in a suite of rooms at the *Great Eastern* hotel, enjoying steak dinners at *Firpo's* every night, and the other wonders of civilization. Then we learned that an American troop transport, the *Mariposa*, once a cruise ship of the Matson Steamship company, was enroute to Karachi with some 5,000 army troops. It was due to arrive in a week or so, would spend a few days in port in Karachi, then head south virtually empty; it would stop at Bombay to pick up passengers and cargo before returning via South Africa to New York. We were told that we could book passage from Bombay for about two hundred dollars each, and would arrive in New York in early September. This sounded like the best of a very limited number of options, so the five of us decided to give it a go. The problem now was getting from Calcutta to Bombay, clear across the continent of India, a two-day journey by train.

The weather in India was oppressively hot and humid, mid-July being the height of the rainy season with its frequent downpours. It was raining when the five of us boarded the first-class compartment we'd reserved on the train that would take us to Bombay. The train itself, while a considerable improvement over the famed *Mandalay Express*, still left much to be desired. We attempted to overcome the lack of air conditioning by placing a large galvanized wash-tub filled with chunks of ice in the center of the compartment; it didn't cool the air very much, but it did keep our supply of beer and scotch cold. The train made frequent stops lasting from ten to thirty minutes, and we spent much of our time and many rupees in the quest for additional ice in station restaurants along the way. Two days and nights of this mode of travel made all of us angrier than ever at the Ferry Command.

In Bombay we rented a large suite of rooms in the *Taj Mahal* hotel; three bedrooms, big living room, and even a small kitchen. We also hired a couple of bearers who sat in the hallway outside the door during the day; they took care of our laundry, housekeeping chores, and ran errands. This whole setup cost us each about six or seven dollars per day. I tell you, friends, we were living high on the hog, and enjoying every minute of it. And over the next few days many more ex-AVGers arrived, including McMillan, all planning to return on the Mariposa.

As it turned out, we were to spend three weeks there in Bombay before our ship arrived from Karachi, where still more AVGers had already boarded her. All told, there were more than a hundred of us aboard when we finally sailed early in August.

Our accommodations were nothing to write home about; triple-tiered bunks in huge rooms below decks that had once been cargo space. But the food in the dining salon—now called the mess-hall—was great, prepared by army cooks; real honest-to-god American chow and all we could eat. In a matter of days our skinny frames began to regain the weight we'd lost over the past few months.

The Mariposa was a big ship, and seemed almost empty. Aside from our own group, there were about seventy Chinese flying cadets enroute to the States for flying training, and perhaps another seventy civilians, mostly missionaries. Our shipboard routine was much like it had been aboard the old Bloemfontein, which amounted to endless days of boredom. We stopped at Capetown, South Africa, for a couple of days to take on fuel, water, and provisions, then headed into the Atlantic for the long haul to New York. This, of course, was at a time when the German U-boats were sinking everything in sight, and now we were forced to run the gauntlet unescorted, relying on the ship's speed of 20 knots or so for safety. To many of us it seemed like just another form of Russian Roulette, and anything but a pleasure cruise. If our ship had been sunk, about half of the old AVG would have gone down with her.

Thirty days after leaving Bombay we lined the rail to savor the welcome sight of the New York City skyline, and then the heartwarming figure of the Statue of Liberty. Some of the guys spoke of parents or grandparents who had been moved to tears as immigrants upon experiencing just such a moment. It was early September, a beautiful sunny day, and at last we were "home."

Well, almost home, anyway. Bill Reed and I got a room at the *Hotel Pennsylvania* and lived it up in the big city for three days after first calling our parents to let them know we'd arrived safely. Neither of us had been to New York before, so we did some sightseeing and made the rounds of the night spots, including the *Stork Club* and the *Copacabana*. We were treated royally everywhere, met a number of well-known people, and met a few beautiful young ladies, one of whom I would marry in less than a year.

Without any priority for airline transportation, Bill and I finally headed west by train to Chicago, where we parted company temporarily. He went on by bus to his home in Iowa, and I continued on the two-day trip to Los Angeles and the joyous reunion with my parents and sister. I was truly home at last, having completed an around-the-world trip that had started nearly fourteen months earlier, now a much wiser and more thoughtful young man than when I'd left.

I spent a wonderful week with my folks, registered for the draft, and returned by train to Chicago. There I bought a 1941 Buick convertible; it was in mint condition, only 8,000 miles, and I paid $1500 in cash. Then I drove to Marion, Iowa, and spent a couple of days with Bill Reed before the two of us took off in the Buick. We drove to Nebraska, stopping for a day in Red Cloud, then on down to San Antonio, Texas. Lou and Joan Van Mullem hosted a party for us at Randolph, with many of the same friends in attendance who'd been at the going-away party for Greene and me at the Officer's Club the year before. Some of them regretted not having done what we had done; they were still stuck in the Training Command and were itching for combat assignments.

Bill and I drove to Los Angeles and rented a nice apartment on Wilshire Boulevard in Westwood, intent upon having some fun before deciding what we'd do in the future. Within a matter of days we had each been offered jobs as test pilots, Bill with North American Aviation, and I with Douglas. These were high-paying jobs that would exempt us from further military duty, and looked terribly inviting. However, representatives of the Air Force had also come calling, appealing to our patriotism and stressing the need for our combat experience, etc., and promising that if we were re-commissioned as 2nd Lieutenants we'd be promoted to Major within 30 days. I think we both knew from the beginning what our decision would be, but we stalled all the parties concerned for a few weeks before finally signing the necessary papers applying for commissions. A few weeks later we were back in uniform, and sure enough, thirty days later we were Majors. This was in early 1943, shortly after we had arrived at a P-47 gunnery school in Millville, New Jersey, our first assignment.

What happened after that is an entirely different story, of course, and this one must come to an end. I feel obliged, however, to tell of the strange but sad twist of fate that was to befall three more of the pilots from the old Bloom bunch. You may recall my saying early in this story that seven of our fifteen pilots who sailed from San Francisco would be killed before the end of the war. Four of the seven—Hammer, Christman, Leibolt, and Foshee had died while in the AVG. The three remaining had all been re-commissioned in the Air Corps, once again under the command of General Chennault. Frank Schiel was the fifth to die, late in 1943, and within the space of two weeks in January of 1944, George McMillan and Bill Reed were killed near Hengyang, China. The news of Mac's and Bill's death hit me particularly hard, for they were two of the best friends I ever had. And by another strange twist of fate, I had seen each of them only a few days before they were to die.

I was back in India for my second combat tour, now a Major in the 1st Air Commando Group. I had led a flight of a dozen P-51s from Karachi to Agra, where we were to spend the night before proceeding to an advanced base near the Burma border. As we parked our planes on the field at Agra I saw that there were eight or ten P-40Es parked nearby. A few minutes later, after getting my pilots assigned to tent-quarters, I made my way to a larger tent that served as a makeshift Officer's Club, hoping to find something cold to drink. I heard a familiar laugh, and there at the bar was Major Bill Reed, whom I hadn't seen for nearly a year. You can imagine our surprise at this chance meeting, and the celebration that followed far into the night. The next morning Bill took off, leading his flight of P-40s on to China and his death only a few day later. He will never be forgotten by any who knew him, and I'm happy to say that his name lives on; my youngest son is William Reed Smith.

A week or so later George McMillan flew into the little airfield in eastern India where I was now based. He was ferrying a P-51 from Calcutta to China, and having heard that I was at a place called Hailakandi, not far out of his way, he stopped by to say hello for an hour or so. This, too, was a joyous reunion, and the last time we would see each other; Mac was killed a week or so after his brief visit. And the war went on.

Speaking of reunions, those of us left still have one every other year, held jointly with our CNAC friends, usually at a beautiful mountain resort outside the little city of Ojai, California. Time, as well as the war, has taken a big toll of our numbers, of course; of the original gang who served throughout the life of the AVG, I believe that about 35 pilots and perhaps three times that many of the ground personnel are still living. And while there are some bald heads among us now, and paunches where flat bellies used to be, the spirit and the feeling of camaraderie that we knew during those hectic and hazardous days in Burma and China are still as strong as ever. They were, and are, one hell of a bunch pf guys! And Paul J. Greene, you'll be pleased to know, is still going strong.

And so ends my tale. As I said at the beginning, I sincerely hope that you, my friends, have found it worth the effort. I'm sure that when this has gone to press and it's too late. I will think of many incidents and dozens of people whom I have failed to mention that should have been included. Still, I trust that what does appear between the covers of this book may help to give you a better understanding of what the Flying Tigers were all about. In the final analysis, of course, you really had to be there!

R.T. Smith
Van Nuys, Calif.
March, 1986

Roster of the AVG

NOTE: Approximately 300 people were signed up originally for duty with the American Volunteer Group. Of this number, about 100 were pilots and the rest maintenance, administrative, and other ground support personnel, about one-fourth as many as would be found in a comparable pursuit group in the U.S. Air Corps at the time.

Nineteen pilots and forty-four of the ground personnel who were original members of the AVG either resigned or were discharged prior to completing their commitment. Some fifteen or twenty additional ground personnel were later hired in China, many of them Chinese. Seven intructors-pilots came over to the AVG in the spring of 1942, helping to offset the loss of those who had been killed in line of duty. It is probable that there were never more than 75 pilots available at any given time, and often less than that number.

The roster below, in alphabetical order, lists only those Flying Tigers who fulfilled their commitment and received honorable discharges when the AVG was disbanded in July, 1942.

Adair, C.B. "Skip"
Adkins, Frank W.
Allard, James L.
Alsop, Jos. W., Jr.
Anderson, Frank A.
Armstrong, John D.
Atkinson, Peter W.
Bailey, George R.
Baisden, Charles N.
Bartling, Wm. E.
Baugh, Marion F.
Baughman,
   Edmund C.
Beaupre, Leo A.
Bell, Donald
Bent, Morton W.
Bishop, Lewis S.
Blackburn, John E.
Blackewell, Harold
Bolster, Harry R.
Bond, Charles R.
Bonham, Ernest O.
Brady, Jame E.
Breeden, Kenneth V.
Brice, George
Bright, John G.
Brouk, Robert R.
Brown, Carl K.
Bruce, Everett W.
Bugler, Carl F.
Burgard, George T.
Callan, Michael R.
Carney, Boatner R.

Carter, John B.
Cavanah, Herbert R.
Ceder, Melvin E.
Chaney, Charles
Chennault, Claire L.
Christensen, Keith J.
Christman, Allen Bert
Clouthier, Leo P.
Cole, Thomas J.
Colquette, Leon P.
Conant, Edwin S.
Cornelius, Jack
Cribbs, Charles D.
Croft, John S.
Crookshanks, Jesse R.
Cross, Harvey G.
Cross, James D.
Curran, George F.
Cushing, Albert D.
Daube, Otto W.
Davis, Doreen
Davis, William H.S.
Dean, John J.
Dolan, Walter, J.
Donovan, John T.
Doran, Francis R.
Dorris, Carl E.
Dupouy, Parker S.
Durall, Eugene C.
Engle, Charles R.
Engler, John R.
Ernst. Richard J.
Farrell, John W.

Fauth, John Edward
Fish, William H.
Fobes, Edwin L.
Foshee, Ben C.
Foster, Emma Jane
Fox, Henry E.
Francisco, Charles H.
Frillmann, Paul W.
Fritzke, Allen W.
Gallagher, Edward F.
Gallagher, Robert
Gasdick, Joseph
Gee, Chun Yuen
Gentry, Thomas C.
Geselbracht, Henry M.
Gilbert, Henry G.
Gorham, Lloyd L.
Gove, Irving P.
Goyette, Edgar T.
Greene, Paul J.
Greenlaw, Harvey K.
Greenlaw, Olga S.
Groh, Clifford G.
Hall, Lester J.
Hammer, Maax C.
Harrington, Jasper J.
Harris, David H.
Haywood, Thomas C.
Hedman, Robert P.
Hennessy, John J.
Henson, Thomas M.
Hill, David L.
Hodges, Fred S.

Hoffman, Louis
Hoffman, Roy G.
Hooker. Burton L.
Howard, James H.
Hubler, Marlin R.
Hurst, Lynn A.
Jacobson, Frank A.
Janski, Edwin A.
Jernstedt, Kenneth A.
Jones, Thomas A.
Jordan, Joe T.
Jourdan, Walter C.
Kaelin, Albert V.
Keeton, Robert B.
Keller, Daniel W.
Kelly, Thomas D.
Kemph, Merlin D.
Kenner, Charles D.
Kepka, George B.
Kiner, Melvin W.
King, Robert J.
Kustay, Stephen
Kuykendall,
  Matthew W.
Kwong, Lawrence C.
Laughlin, C. H.
Lawlor, Frank L.
Layher, Robert F.
Leaghty, Charles C.
Lee, Joseph S.
Lee, Pak On
Leibolt, Edward J.
Lindstedt, Robert K.
Linton, Jack R.
Little, Robert L.
Loane, Ernest W.
Locke, Robert
Loomis, Elton V.
Losonsky, Frank S.
Lum, George L.
Lussier, Joseph E.
McAllister, Gale E.
McClure, Edgar B.
McGarry, William D.
McHenry, Sharon L.
McKinney, Eugene R.
McMillan, George B.
Mangleburg, Lacy F.
Martin, Neil G.
Merritt, Kenneth T.
Mickelson, Einar I.
Mihalko, Alex
Miller, Arvold A.

Misenheimer,
  Charles V.
Moss, Kenneth R.
Moss, Robert C.
Mott, Charles D.
Musgrove, Willard L.
Musick, James H.
Neal, Robert J.
Neale, Robert H.
Neumann, Gerhard
Newkirk,
  John Van Kuren
Older,
  Charles Herman
Olson, Arvid E.
Olson, Henry L.
Osborne, Harold L.
Overend, Edmund F.
Overley, John L.
Paull, Preston B.
Paxton, George L.
Peeden, Joseph N.
Peret, Richard C.
Perry, Paul J.
Petach, John E.
Pietsker, Joseph H.
Pistole, Herbert
Pon, Kee Jeung
Poshefko, Joseph A.
Prescott, Robert W.
Prevo, Samuel B.
Probst, Albert E.
Quick, Carl
Raine, Robert J.
Rasmussen, Robert P.
Rector, Edward F.
Reed, William N.
Regis, James E.
Regis, Stanley J.
Richards Lewis J.
Richardson, Roland L.
Ricketts, Freeman I.
Ricks, Wayne W.
Riffer, Clarence W.
Roberts, Carson M.
Rodewald, Donald L.
Rogers, Robert W.
Rosbert, Camille J.
Rossi, John R.
Rumen, John N.
Sandell, Robert J.
Sasser, Ralph W.
Sawyer, Charles W.

Schaper, Wilfred E.
Schiel, Frank
Schiller, Ralph F.
Schramm, Leo J.
Seamster, Loy F.
Seavey, Edward H.
Seiple, Wilfred R.
Shamblin, Arnold W.
Shapard, Van
Shaw, John E.
Shee, George Wing
Shields, Milan R.
Shilling, Eriksen E.
Shreffler, Roger
Smith, Curtis E.
Smith, Robert A.
Smith, Robert H.
Smith, Robert M.
Smith. Robert T.
Stewart, Jo B.
Stiles, Edward L.
Stolet, Irving J.
Sutherland, William L.
Swartz, Frank W.
Sweeney, Joseph H.
Sykes, Willam A.
Terry, Julian E.
Towery, William H.
Trumble, Thomas C.
Tuley, Chester A.
Tyrrell, George
Uebele, John J.
Van Timmeran,
  Frank E.
Vaux, Morgan H.
Viverette, Hugh J.
Wagner, Earl F.
Wakefield, Manning
Walters, George F.
Whelpley, Donald A.
Whitwer, Eloise
Williams, John M.
Wilson, Clifford H.
Wirta, Harvey C.
Wolf, Fritz E.
Woodward, Melvin
Wright, Allen M.
Wright, Peter
Wu, Lem Fong
Wyatt, Louis G.
Wylie, Harold G.
Yee, Francis T.F.
Young, John P.

ACKNOWLEDGMENTS

Too many people have contributed in one way or another to this effort to name each of them individually. However, I am most grateful to the following for the use of certain photographs and for their encouragement: Chuck Baisden, Charley Bond, Keith Christensen, Jim Cross, Parker Dupouy, J.J. Harrington, Mel Kemph, Larry Pistole, Robert M. Smith, and the U.S. Air Force

Bob Lunday, of Spy-V-Graf Productions in Buena Park, Calif., was most helpful in the design and execution of the dust-jacket and maps.

And finally, my special thanks to Bob Andrade, a long-time friend and supporter of the Flying Tigers, who is the instructor for the Graphic Arts class of the Palm Springs High School and Riverside ROP. Bob and some of his students made a valuable contribution in typesetting and proofreading, a part-time classroom project in which his students learned at first hand what goes into the making of a book.

To one and all, my sincere thanks.

R.T. Smith

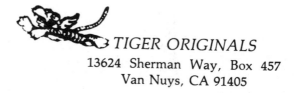

TIGER ORIGINALS
13624 Sherman Way, Box 457
Van Nuys, CA 91405